HEIDEGGER
AND THE
PATH OF THINKING

HEIDEGGER
AND THE
PATH OF THINKING

Edited with an Introduction

by

JOHN SALLIS

DUQUESNE UNIVERSITY PRESS, *Pittsburgh, Pa.*
Editions E. Nauwelaerts, Louvain

Copyright © 1970 by
Duquesne University Press
Library of Congress Catalog Number: 79-107355
Printed in the United States of America
Standard Book Number: 8207-0128-9

In Honor of the Occasion of
Martin Heidegger's Eightieth Birthday
September 26, 1969

Contents

Abbreviations of the Titles of
Heidegger's Works

ED   *Aus der Erfahrung des Denkens.* Pfullingen: Verlag Günther Neske, 1954.

EM   *Einführung in die Metaphysik.* Tübingen: Max Niemeyer Verlag, 1953.

FD   *Die Frage nach dem Ding. Zu Kants Lehre von den Transzendentalen Grundsätzen.* Tübingen: Max Niemeyer Verlag, 1962.

FP   "La fin de la philosophie et la tâche de la pensée," in *Kierkegaard vivant.* Paris: Gallimard, 1966.

FW   *Der Feldweg.* Frankfurt a.M.: Vittorio Klostermann, 1953.

G   *Gelassenheit.* Pfullingen: Verlag Günther Neske, 1959.

HD   *Erläuterungen zu Hölderlins Dichtung.* Frankfurt a.M.: Vittorio Klostermann, 1944 (Citations refer to the third edition, 1963)

HW   *Holzwege.* Frankfurt a.M.: Vittorio Klostermann, 1950.

ID   *Identität und Differenz.* Pfullingen: Verlag Günther Neske, 1957.

KM   *Kant und das Problem der Metaphysik.* Bonn: Cohen, 1929 (Citations refer to the second edition, Frankfurt a.M.: Vittorio Klostermann, 1951).

KT   *Kants These über das Sein.* Frankfurt a.M.: Vittorio Klostermann, 1963.

N   *Nietzsche.* 2 vols. Pfullingen: Verlag Günther Neske, 1961.

PW   *Platons Lehre von der Wahrheit. Mit einem Brief über den "Humanismus."* Bern: Francke Verlag, 1947.

SF   *Zur Seinsfrage.* Frankfurt a.M.: Vittorio Klostermann, 1956.

SG   *Der Satz vom Grund.* Pfullingen: Verlag Günther Neske, 1957.

SZ   *Sein und Zeit* in *Jahrbuch für Philosophie und phänomenologische Forschung,* VIII (1927) (Citations refer to the eighth edition, Tübingen: Max Niemeyer Verlag, 1957).

TK   *Die Technik und die Kehre.* Pfullingen: Verlag Günther Neske, 1962.

US   *Unterwegs zur Sprache.* Pfullingen: Verlag Günther Neske, 1959.

VA   *Vorträge und Aufsätze.* Pfullingen: Verlag Günther Neske, 1954.

W   *Wegmarken.* Frankfurt a.M.: Vittorio Klostermann, 1967.

WD   *Was heisst Denken?* Tübingen: Max Niemeyer Verlag, 1954.

WG   *Vom Wesen des Grundes.* Halle: Max Niemeyer Verlag, 1929 (Citations refer to the fourth edition, Frankfurt a.M.: Vittorio Klostermann, 1955).

WM   *Was ist Metaphysik?* Bonn: Cohen, 1930 (Nachwort added to the fourth edition, 1943; Einleitung added to the fifth edition, 1949; citations refer to the eighth edition, Frankfurt a.M.: Vittorio Klostermann, 1960).

WW   *Vom Wesen der Wahrheit.* Frankfurt a.M.: Vittorio Klostermann, 1943 (Citations refer to the fourth edition, 1961).

ZS   "Zeit und Sein,' in *L' Endurance de la pensée. Pour saluer Jean Beaufret.* Edited by René Char. Paris: Éditions Plon, 1968.

Introduction

John Sallis

The title of this collection of essays designates, first of all, an essential feature of what Heidegger's work has given us to meditate. Heidegger's thinking is a thinking along a path in such an essential fashion that every meditation on Heidegger's work must enter into relation with this feature if it is even to understand its own character as a meditation. At the same time, the title is intended to indicate the character of this collection of essays inasmuch as each seeks in its own way to come upon the path of thinking by way of an appropriation of Heidegger's work.

Heidegger's thinking is a thinking along a path, a path to which "the steps of thinking remain as close as do the steps of the farmer who sets out harvesting in the early morning" (FW, 2). Heidegger's thinking is a thinking that remains always underway. Its remaining underway is not to be construed as simply a failure to provide answers to certain questions proposed at the beginning of Heidegger's way — as though the path were only a bridge spanning the chasm between question and answer, as though it were not necessary entirely to re-think on the path of thinking our usual unquestioning manner of understanding the connection between question and answer. On the contrary, the fact that Heidegger's thinking remains underway, that it stays always on the path of thinking, is sustained by an essential correspondence to what has come to light precisely upon the path of thinking. That thinking remains always on a path has its roots in the essence of thinking as such, which, in turn, we discover only in taking up the path of thinking (WD, 1).

In his work *Aus der Erfahrung des Denkens,* a work whose character as a work of thinking still remains obscure, Heidegger writes, "We never come to thoughts; they come to us" (ED, 11). The path of thinking is not first constructed as a path by thinking but is rather a way which already lies before thinking as that which calls upon us to think. Thinking is a response to that which is handed over to it as to-be-thought — to that which is thought-provoking and thought-evoking. Thinking is sustained only in the medium of that correspondence in which it responds to what calls it forth: "We respond to the way only by remaining underway" (WD, 164).

It is essential to thinking that it enter upon a path which is no mere bridge to be left behind. Thinking requires that we let ourselves get involved in questioning. The peculiar character of questioning is such that it is especially inclined to move within the sphere of response. What is questioned needs already in some fashion to have shown itself to us in order to become questionable, and our questioning responds to what has thus shown itself as questionable. In questioning we need already to have turned towards what is to be questioned and to have allowed it to become manifest as questionable. Furthermore, in contrast to assertion, questioning remains directed towards what is in question and towards letting it have its say, letting it, in turn, respond. Plato knew to what extent questioning is inherently resistant to being inscribed in assertions so as to be passed along in "mere words."

Questioning is what is most difficult for contemporary man despite the fact that, with his liberation from the bonds of authority, he poses questions as never before. He poses questions as never before, yet questioning remains alien to him. The posing of questions, far from certifying that one is capable of questioning, on the contrary devolves into a way of not questioning to the extent that in the posing of questions we remain blind to what poses the questions to us and thus remain aloof from a genuine involvement in questioning. A way of posing questions is something handed over, not something invented with each new question, and, hence, any posing of questions moves already at its inception within a prior understanding of questioning as such. In the case of contemporary man the posing of questions occurs from out of a metaphysical understanding of questioning. But what if this prior understanding is precisely such as to conceal the genuinely questioning character of thought? Is this not the case insofar as metaphysics, since Descartes, has decided that what is to be questioned can manifest itself only within an already established ground-plan which in advance determines not only that which is to be questioned but also the character of the questioning itself and of the response which the thing questioned can make to the questioning (cf. FD, 49ff)? Today man stands in the highest danger of forgetting how to question, and this danger is manifest precisely in his ceaseless posing of questions. Yet the latter, while holding him apart from questioning, nevertheless is able to do so only by sustaining a hidden connection between man and questioning, a connection which promises to come to light just to the extent that the ceaseless posing of questions can finally become questionable. Heidegger quotes the words of Hölderlin: "Where, however, danger resides, there springs deliverance as well" (VA, 36; TK, 41).

Heidegger's thinking remains throughout its entire course a retrieve of questioning. It is, thus, a thinking which must overcome (*überwinden*) metaphysics not by opposing it but rather by returning to its roots in such a way as to liberate genuine questioning from its concealment and to make it possible to recover from (*verwinden*) metaphysics. The recovery from metaphysics is a releasement (*Gelassenheit*) into questioning.

What is imperative is that the thinker stay with the questioning rather than simply abandoning the question for the sake of an answer. *Sein und Zeit* begins quite deliberately and explicitly with an interrogation of the question to be taken up and even of questioning as such, and the published portion never extricates itself from its engagement in the questioning in that it is devoted throughout to an inquiry regarding that being that is able to *ask* the question regarding the meaning of Being. Nearly forty years later Heidegger stills asks, "Has the question about the 'meaning of Being' (as Being) — posed in 'Being and Time' — been at all treated as a question? If so, in what way and in reference to what has this question been discussed?"[1] Rather than leaving the question behind as self-evident in its character as a question, it is necessary to stay with the questioning in such a way that its presumed self-evidence is dissipated. To stay with the question does not, however, mean

---

[1] See the letter from Heidegger contained in this volume.

that we are somehow to take up a "standpoint" outside of that questioning in which the question is posed so as to be able to evaluate the question taken alone, perhaps through some kind of formal criteria. The character of such a "standpoint," the way by which it would be possible for us occupy it, and the criteria with which we would claim to evaluate the question — all this would remain questionable in such a fashion as to require us, in the end, to bring these issues back into relation with the questioning itself. It would not suffice, even if it were possible, to avoid completely all entering into the movement from question to answer. What is needed is rather that the thinker stay with the questioning and let it recoil upon itself in such wise as to reveal in the questioning what is at issue in questioning as such. To stay with the question is to take up the question so as to discover the answer that is already in the question and hence to enter into the movement between question and answer percisely in the course of letting this movement become manifest in its circularity.

Heidegger's question is the question of the meaning of Being: What is the meaning of Being? We try to hear Heidegger's question. But immediately we want to know: What is Being? What is that of which Heidegger is asking for the meaning? We want some glimpse of what is being asked about in order that we might know how to ask about it. We try to hear Heidegger's question, yet betray that we have not heard it by the fact that we respond to it only by saying it over again. But let us stay with our mere repeating of the question and try to discover whether it is merely a misunderstanding or whether, on the contrary, it might afford some genuine access to the questioning.

So: What is Being? Heidegger answers this blunt question. He writes: "Yet Being — what is Being? It is itself (*Es ist Es selbst*). This must future thinking learn to experience and to say" (PW, 76). Heidegger's answer, it seems, tells us nothing. Therefore, he urges us to seek to learn to experience and to say this answer. But in what sense is this an answer? Is it an answer at all? To learn to experience and to say it requires that we understand that, in fact, it is the only answer that could be given. Why?

Whenever we say of something that it is itself — that A is A — we apply the principle of identity. What has thus to be experienced in what Heidegger says — when he says of Being that it is itself — is the connection between Being and identity. We say of every being that it is identical with itself — Plato said this already in the *Sophist*. The principle of identity, therefore, says something about the Being of beings. It says of every being that, in its Being, it is identical with itself: "The unity of identity forms a ground-feature in the Being of beings" (ID, 17).

However, Heidegger's statement regarding Being — that it is itself — says something totally different from what is expressed in the principle of identity, for the identity which Heidegger puts at issue is not an identity of beings with themselves but of Being with itself. Heidegger's statement says, not that the principle of identity is something that is demanded by Being, not that it is something which holds for every being in its Being, but rather that Being is itself *in* an identity, a sameness with itself. What is required if we are to learn to experience and to say what Heidegger says is an experience and a saying of how Being itself belongs in an identity.

Identity, sameness we tend to regard as mere empty identity, mere indifferent oneness of something with itself. The statement "A is A" says nothing, or rather it simply says the same thing (to auto) over again, i.e., it is a mere tautology. But is this an appropriate, much less a fruitful, way of regarding identity? Does not this conception betray rather just that failure really to think through identity which was finally overcome by German Idealism? Has not the latter shown, once and for all, that identity with self is precisely a mediation between something and itself, a mediation between the self and the self in its otherness — or, as Heidegger wants to say, a belonging-together of something with itself?[2] But if identity is to be thought in this fashion, how are we to let Being come into connection with it? How does Being belong in an identity understood as a belonging-together?

Heidegger's response is a retrieve of a famous statement by Parmenides: *To gar auto noein estin te kai einai*. Heideggers retrieve commences with a translation: "Being belongs — with thinking — in the same."[3] How then does Being belong in an

[2] ID, 15-16. For example, Hegel writes: "This self-identical nature stands, therefore, in relation only to itself; *to itself*, hence this is an other, to which the relation points, and relation to itself is, more strictly, breaking asunder; in other words, that very self-identity is internal distinction. . . . That the *self-identical breaks asunder* means, therefore, just as truly, that it sublates itself as already broken asunder, that it sublates itself as other." *Phänomenologie des Geistes* (Hamburg: Felix Meiner, 1952), pp. 125-126.

[3] " Sein gehört — mit dem Denken — in das Selbe" (ID, 19).

identity? It belongs in an identity in that it *belongs-together* with thinking, i.e., in that Being and man *belong-together*. Being is itself, is able to come forth as the Being of beings in that Being belongs-together with man. This is why "man is the shepherd of Being" (PW, 90).

Does this bring us closer to experiencing and saying Heidegger's answer to the question "What is Being"? We have allowed Heidegger's answer — that it is itself — to unfold in such a way as to show that to experience it as an answer means nothing less than to experience the belonging-together of Being and man. Does this insight afford any access to its character as an answer?

When we question, and most of all when we question philosophically, our question is constrained to assume the form "What is . . .?" We ask: "What is a thing?"; "What is the soul?"; "What is man?" — and finally "What is Being?" How are we able to ask such questions? What must already be granted in the asking? We ask about the "*what*" in order to learn what something *is*. But what about the "what" and the "is"? We do not first decide out of our own resources what the "what" and the "is" are to mean and only then pose questions in which these words occur. In fact, we could seek to determine these meanings out of our resources — that is, answer the question regarding *what* the "*what*" means — *only* from out of a prior understanding of the "what." The meaning of the "what" and the "is" is not something which we first establish but rather something handed over to us in such fashion that we are always already caught up in it. We do not first create our understanding of the "what" and the "is"; rather this understanding is one in which we always find ourselves already, one in which we find ourselves thrown. We are always already cast into an understanding of Being (cf. especially PW, 71).

Thus, in asking the question "What is Being?" we do not simply address ourselves to something, as it were, over against us in order to discover what it is. On the contrary, the asking is already *caught up* in what we are asking about. We are able to address Being, to ask our question about it, only if we are already addressed by Being; in other words, we can ask the question only insofar as we already *belong-together* with Being. At the same time, we ask the question in the sense that we take up a questioning stance only insofar as in our belonging-together with Being, Being conceals itself, withdraws.

To ask the question is not to interrogate something over against us so as to find an answer to what it is. The asking of the question is not something simply to be followed and left behind by an answering. Rather, the asking of the question is nothing less than an experiencing and a saying of man's belonging-together with Being — and, specifically, of this belongingness to Being as a belonging to the truth of Being, to the revealing-concealing advent of Being (cf. WW, 26). What the question calls for, if we succeed in genuinely hearing it, is not an answer in any usual sense; what the question calls for is rather that we experience, get involved in, the question so as to understand, to be able to hear, what is said in the question, i.e., that and how man belongs-together with Being. Heidegger's answer — that it is itself — is no answer in the usual sense but rather an answer which takes the form of a directive which indicates to us that mode of comportment on our part which is appropriate in the face of this question, which genuinely encounters this question. Heidegger answers the question by directing us into an involvement with the question, into an experiencing of it in what it says as a question.

Our questioning cannot sustain the question but is directed back into it in order to experience what sustains our questioning thought — in order to experience what calls upon us to think. Thinking as questioning is not its own ground. Questioning is such that its ground continually withdraws. The ground of our questioning elicits our questioning yet withdraws from it, and it was just this eliciting-withdrawing which remained unthought in metaphysics, which was not granted as that which grants thought to us, as that which calls upon us to think. What remained concealed in metaphysics was that "What withdraws from us thereby draws us along" (WD, 5).

Heidegger's thinking is a waiting to be drawn along in the withdrawal as that which calls forth thinking. The path of Heidegger's thinking is the path of this withdrawal. Heidegger's work is an invitation to allow ourselves to be drawn along onto this path of thinking.

Each of the papers in this collection seeks in its own way to take up the path of thinking, some by retracing Heidegger's own way of being drawn along this path, some by taking up a path to which Heidegger's work has only pointed, while others seek, in following up the course of Heidegger's thinking, to come upon the path of thinking in a different fashion. Several of the papers were originally presented at a symposium on the philosophy of Heidegger held at Duquesne University on October 15–16, 1966. The letter from Heidegger was addressed to this symposium. It is hoped that both the symposium and this collection of papers have remained equal to the task of genuinely entering upon the path of thinking.

A Letter From Martin Heidegger

Freiburg i. Br.
20. Sept. 1966

Sehr geehrter Herr Kollege Schrynemakers,*

Ich freue mich, Sie und die Teilnehmer an dem von Ihnen geleiteten Symposion auf diesem Wege begrüssen zu können. Die von Ihnen genannten Redner werden vermutlich weit besser über den "Einfluss" meines Denkens unterrichtet sein als ich selbst.

Als kleinen Beitrag zum Symposion möchte ich die folgenden Fragen zu bedenken geben:

Ist überhaupt die in "Sein und Zeit" gestellte Frage nach dem "Sinn von Sein" (als Sein) als Frage aufgenommen? Wenn ja, in welcher Weise wurde die Frage und nach welchen Hinsichten erörtert? Hat die Kritik jemals gefragt, ob die gestellte Frage möglich oder unmöglich ist? Was ergibt sich aus der Beantwortung der jetzt genannten Fragen für die Kennzeichnung des Verhältnisses, in dem H.s Denken zur Überlieferung der abendländischen Philosophie steht?

Wo liegen die Grenzen der Fragestellung in "Sein und Zeit"? Was leistet die Erörterung der Seinsfrage und der Epochen des Seinsgeschickes für die Auslegung des gegenwärtigen Zeitalters der Technik?

In welchem Verhältnis steht das Denken der Seinsfrage zur

---

*This letter was addressed to Professor Arthur H. Schrynemakers in his capacity as chairman of the symposium on the philosophy of Heidegger held at Duquesne University on October 15-16, 1966.

9

modernen Wissenschaft, die durch den absoluten Vorrang der Methode gegenüber ihren möglichen Gegenständen ausgezeichnet ist?

Heute ist wohl kaum mehr nötig, ausdrücklich zu vermerken, dass es sich in meinem Denken weder um Existenzialismus noch um Existenz-philosophie handelt.

Ich möchte wunschen, dass das Symposion mit der Ausarbeitung *einer* dieser Fragen endet.

Ich danke allen Teilnehmern für das Interesse, das sie meinen Bemühungen auf dem gefahrreichen Felde des Denkens entgegenbringen.

Mit freundlichen Grüssen
Martin Heidegger

Freiburg i. Br.
September 20, 1966

Dear Professor Schrynemakers:

I am pleased to be able in this way to send my greetings to you and to the participants in the symposium directed by you. The speakers whom you mentioned are probably far better informed than I am myself about the "influence" of my thinking.

As a small contribution to the symposium I would like to submit the following questions to be considered:

Has the question posed in *Sein und Zeit* regarding the "meaning of Being" (as Being) been at all taken up as a question? If so, in what way and according to what respects has the question been discussed? Have the critics ever asked whether the question posed is possible or impossible? What do the answers to the above questions contribute to the characterization of the relation in which Heidegger's thinking stands to the tradition of Western philosophy?

Where do the limits of the questioning in *Sein und Zeit* lie? What does the discussion of the question of Being and of the epochs of the mittence of Being accomplish as regards the interpretation of the present age of technology?

In what relation does the thinking of the question of Being stand to modern science, which is distinguished by the absolute priority of method over against its possible objects?

Today it is indeed hardly necessary anymore to remark explicitly that my thinking is a matter neither of Existentialism nor of Existenz-philosophy.

I would wish that the symposium conclude with the working out of *one* of these questions.

I thank all participants for the interest which they show in my efforts in the dangerous field of thinking.

With friendly greetings,
Martin Heidegger

On The Way To Being
Reflecting on
Conversations with Martin Heidegger

Zygmunt Adamczewski

The above title covers an ambiguity. At the kind invitation of the editor of the present volume, I wish to offer the following pages in pursuit of a twofold aim. On one hand, I hope they will say something "about" man's way to be, which I have previously characterized as way to being.[1] On the other hand, I should like to relate how thought shapes itself "while" moving along this way on which it stays revolving, so to say, within the orbit of being: not speeding ahead as if drawn by a far removed and unmoved light, but displaying reflections of the clearing which is close around. Such is the thought of Martin Heidegger.

Guided this way, I therefore hope to contribute a little of some historical interest: presenting a few varying threads from conversations with him during my last three-day visit, at Todtnauberg and Freiburg, in October 1968. I shall put the oral quotations of his words, as noted at the time, in bold-face letters; and I trust it is not vain to hope that they may provide, not only for me, some philosophical or hermeneutic clarification. In this fashion I can perhaps also embody my gratitude to Martin Heidegger for the many hours graciously offered me. As I write now, I try to put myself again into the mood surrounding in his work-laden, book-filled study, and look again at the mountains and fields around, the woods and the cleared

[1] Vide *The Tragic Protest* (The Hague: Nijhoff, 1963), pp. 260-75.

12

paths, and be again within the home circle of his thought. "... we have to move around the circle. But ... to enter this circular road is the strength of thought, to remain on it is a festive occasion ..." (HW, 8).

One of the questions that can occasion hermeneutic or explanatory difficulty concerns the proper understanding of that most Heideggerian primary notion about the human being: "Dasein." Throughout the pages of *Sein und Zeit* there is plentiful usage of it with reference to a being (*ein Seiendes*), beginning with page 7. Such usage agrees with the common idiom in denoting a man, the rational animal of traditional thinking. With this must always be appreciated that Heidegger's notion of the human being (Dasein) bears a radically different connotation: not to be conceived in relation to any other animal or to any being objectively given (*Vorhandensein*), but only in the unique openness to being. Misunderstanding that would prevent any initial grasp of the intent of that work.

This is the first step: to understand properly Dasein as a being. But further, there are textual indications, rather less direct, that this notion also covers a mode or kind or form of being (*Seinsart*) which is quite unlike that of other entities, e.g., page 54 (*Seiendes von nicht daseinsmässiger Seinsart*). In other words, "Dasein" refers to you and him and me but also to the way we all are and can be. The emphasis on possibilities should make entirely clear the fact that Heidegger does not restrict himself to describing the actuality of any singled out subjects. I have, incidentally, confirmed my conviction about the absurdity of such objections as: plenty of people never experience anxiety as Heidegger describes it, so his analysis must be wrong or concern only some men. Asking him, of course not in naive self-reference how anxious I must be in order to be myself, but how significant anxiety is, compared to conscience, with regard to authenticity, I was told: **It is understood as extreme possibility (*äusserste Möglichkeit*) and as such cannot be necessary (nicht notwendig).**

To resume the main thread: it appears to me that the dual application of "Dasein" corresponds to an ambiguity which is irreducible, although it yields a logical difficulty which I shall indicate in connection with the word: "*Wesen*." But the ambiguity concerns how to think of the human being — which is the reason for my so translating "Dasein." The ambiguity is not a linguistic peculiarity of English; I pointed it out in other languages, in the text referred to above. Briefly: I call you a human being, quite idiomatically, but I can also consider the human being "in" you, available to you but not limited to you. In the latter sense I do not mean any uniform essence definable for all men, because in such indifference you as you are would be an accidental irrelevance. Nor do I mean an abstract ideal, because the whole point of so considering you is what and how you can realize. And I do not mean a moral perfection or even improvement, because your human being may come to the fore in a weakness or failure. But I do mean that you and I and all men move through life pursuing the directions of human being which can have a different appeal for every one of us but which no one can claim as exclusively his. This ambiguous relation is not reducible to that of particular to universal.

Heidegger has his own grounds, partly resting in his native language, for choosing the word "Dasein." Still, I believe that the above ambiguity is not intransferable from that word into the notion of the human being, in other languages. Consider e.g. this elaboration of his saying that Dasein is ever respectively mine, which "signifies: the human being is projected toward me in order that myself be human being . . . . Human being is 'ever respectively mine'; this means neither: established by me, nor: particular to an isolated ego" (EM, 22). And a word of caution: it would be hazardous to let the dual sense in "human being (Dasein)" coincide with the polarity of authenticity and inauthenticity; because Heidegger's notion of human being as ever mine or projected toward me holds true whether or not my self is authentic. The ambiguity, once more, concerns the sense in which "the human being" ever extends beyond what pertains to any single human subject.

This yields further reflection in respect to Heidegger's own thought on the word "*Wesen.*" To begin with, the famous statement: "*Das 'Wesen' des Daseins liegt in seiner Existenz*" (SZ, 42), usually rendered as: "The 'essence' of Dasein lies in its existence." The usual reading of it became existentialism; although on the same page, as elsewhere, the text denies the equivalence of "existence" with "*existentia*" of traditional terminology. But why the quotation marks around "*Wesen*"? Again, on this page and already in the introductory remarks on Dasein (SZ, 12) it is denied that "*Wesen*" should be here understood traditionally as equivalent to "*essentia*" or "real whatness (*sachhaltiges Was*)"; unfortunately, not many of Heidegger's interpreters and translators have paid attention to this. Yet the study of his later works makes abundantly clear that this early indication by quotation marks becomes a determinate line of his thought: "*Wesen*," often used verbally, is not essence. I have suggested in another essay why I tend to translate it as "way to be."[2]

To accord with his later usage, omitting the quotation marks and altering the spelling, Heidegger's principle reads: the way to be of the human being lies in its ek-sistence. While commenting on it in 1949, he says: "The name 'existence' is used in *Sein und Zeit* exclusively to characterize the being of man . . . . What does 'existence' mean in *Sein und Zeit*? The word names a mode of being (*eine Weise des Seins*)" (W, 203). I trust no further elaboration is required to correlate the German terms and say plausibly that ek-sistence is for man his way to be (*Wesen*), or perhaps his mode of being (*Seinsart, Seinsweise*); and this is not to be conceived in terms of man's essential qualities or relations to other beings.

The logical difficulty arises if these statements are contrasted with the following: " '*Das Dasein im Menschen' ist das Wesen* . . . ." — " 'The human being in man' is the way to be . . . ." (N,II, 358). It is a difficulty of type or level and concerns the ambiguity discussed. Because in the former quotations "Dasein" appears to denote a being, man, whose way to be is ek-sistence; and in the latter quote "Dasein" denotes the way to be. Consequently, ek-sistence here would mean something like the way to be of the way to be (*Wesen des Wesens*).

Without pressing it, I put the question in just this manner to Martin Heidegger and I was for a while put off, because his attitude was not sympathetic to it. He considered it as a rather formal problem emerging in traditional metaphysics — it certainly affects "*Wesen*" read as *essentia* in relation to *existentia* — but not as genuinely involving his thought. Nevertheless, I believe that I have obtained a proper if indirect answer which I can quote, in the course of subsequent discussion.

It turned to a further consideration of the significance of the way to be (*Wesen*) in the general framework of Heidegger's thought of being. His notion of "*Wesen*" is, of course, applicable not only to

[2] Vide "Martin Heidegger and Man's Way to be," *Man and World*, I (1968), pp. 375 ff.

man. It is a most fruitful and rich post-metaphysical idea — if meta-physics stretches from Plato to Nietzsche; but as such it is also novel and elusive, particularly in a medium other than the German language. There it is easily if not colloquially drawn from a verb; and Heidegger's preference for this induces, as verbs suggest, thinking of what develops, goes on, comes forth, involves growing, behaving, moving. It is temporal; hence its contrast with any essence vested statically in a non-temporal definition. If it is to be conceived as a universal, then rather in the sense of *"in re"* than *"ante rem"* or *"post rem"*; but I mention this only as a reference back to the history of metaphysics. Because, again unlike essence, it is never intended for abstraction from beings but for penetrating and concretizing grasp of them. The way to be of anything is for human thought the possible hold on what something yields turning in time, also turning toward or away from awareness (*An- und Abwesen*).

Here is a correlation with the already posed ambiguity of the human being. Thinking about the way to be of anything must avoid the classical Scylla and Charybdis of universal and particular. This may be disagreeable to logic but it agrees with the roots of speech as nominative. What I wish to speak about are nouns. Nouns may be preceded by articles but not always, sometimes arbitrarily, and many languages have no articles. I can say "sea" without particular-izing into "a" or "this" sea, and without invoking an abstract univer-sal in "the" sea. Unless I am badly addicted to norms and habits, the single word "sea" lets me think something. And what I then think will have both individual and more than individual aspects. The being of any sea is surely not contained either in a definition stating wherein all seas must be absolutely alike or in the ineffability of one sea uniquely unlike any other. There is a way between such extremes. And I suggest that actually for most men thinking goes on along this way, regardless of the bifurcation of universal versus particular — which can certainly serve but need not strangle thought. It is possible for me to think about the way to be of various seas. When I so think with reference to that which I swam in last summer or that which I wish to sail on or that sung by Debussy, my thought naturally embraces but does not confine itself within the concrete individuality of any sea there has been or can be in time. This example is easy but what it illustrates is by no means trivial. It may be called an ambiguity, though hardly as a fault; it is a liberat-ing adaptability for thinking about the way everything is.

I trust that my reflections here do correspond to the way Heidegger intends his use of the word: "*Wesen*." But now I come to a question meant to amplify and clarify this. I touched on it in the above mentioned essay, and conversing with Martin Heidegger I raised it in the following context.

There can be no doubt that in various texts he uses "way to be (*Wesen*)," in the sense outlined, plurally, i.e., about a manifold of beings and ways to be: of man, of tree, of ground, of metaphysics, of nihilism, etc. Although in some cases he leads into the way to be through an explication of essence or whatness, he is ever moving beyond those significations of "*Wesen*". But this is not the only displacement for thought. There are others, especially those with an intended turn: the way to be of truth, or of speech — truth, or speech, of the way to be (*die Wahrheit, die Sprache, des Wesens*). And in those situations, for the latter phrases in the turn, "the way to be" is meant singularly not plurally, as unique and incomparable, as alluding to — yet not quite a synonym of — being. How then is this plurality versus singularity to be understood?

This was the answer: **It is always the question of going over (immer ein Übergang) from the way to be of what is thought to the way to be of being (zum Wesen des Seins), to show how it yields itself in that way (wie es darin west).**

To me, this is an illuminating statement. First of all, against various misconceptions, it confirms the undeviating dedication of Heidegger's earlier and later thought to being — as expressed in this phrase: "The Same and One that yields the way to be: being (*das Selbe und Eine Wesende: das Sein*)" (N, II, 389). Further, it shows again the inadequacy of reading "*Wesen*" as a traditionally static eternal essence, since in thinking we always have to go over beyond it or bring it into motion. It points out that our thought about any way to be must itself be on the way: to being. And thinking of "*Wesen*" in English as "way to be" appears in this light as legitimate as in accord with this almost literal word connection: " '*Wesen*', when it is thought thus, names that which goes on, which is for us ever at stake, because for everything it provides the way (*Das Wesen so gedacht, nennt das Während, uns in allem Angehende, weil alles Bewëgende*)" (US, 201). It hardly needs saying that only being can accommodate thought approaching that which provides the way for everything.

From this point of vantage, let me return to the ambiguity I mentioned. With regard to the way to be of something like sea, Heidegger's statement clarifies this: if by "sea," as I suggested, we think of what a sea is individually but also more than that, then it is the movement proper to our thought between what the sea is as a being and how being yields itself therein, in this entity though not for its ineffable isolation. In other words, however, vaguely, casually, primitively, we think here across the ontological difference, if to think is to be human, and that is to ek-sist with an understanding of being (*Seinsverständnis*).

But it is on the ground of the human being in us that this ambiguous or adaptable movement of thought takes place. Beings are not statically closed in relation to our temporal way to be, as well as to think. Therefore, the ambiguity with regard to "Dasein" must be treated somewhat differently. The earlier cited reference goes on: " 'The human being in man' is the way to be which belongs to being itself . . . . Man develops his way to be (*wird wesentlich*) in entering it as proper to him (*indem er eigens in sein Wesen eingeht*)" (N, II, 358). The entry — in German literally "going in" — to the way to be is a prospect of human locomotion, because for all mobility the human being bears the locus of light (*Da*) and brings it to bear on other beings which are without such motion. Man's way to be belongs to being; and "to belong" means originally to go along, to traverse the length. But since being cannot be properly characterized in any terms of an external remote goal, any length is not determinate for man, only the going is. I am well reminded here of John Wild's suggestion with possibly other intents, to translate "Dasein" as transience. The going along man's way to be is ever transient. And so there are no formal levels or types of human essence — this is what Heidegger was reluctant to discuss with me. Still, for me, for you, for any man, perhaps on the way to belong some phases or directions of transience can be brought into light. Such may be Dasein, ek-sistence, aletheia, care, ek-stasis, temporality, bearing (*Ereignis*). Saying these words hardly amounts to an empty litany of likeness. And yet they all belong to the way along for the human being, they belong to the same and amount to the same in that which yields the way to be: being.

To take up a somewhat different thread: How is it with your present stand toward phenomenology — should it be said that you have discarded it? **Only as a philosophical movement (Rich-tung).**

After this came up in conversation, I was given to read, during a post-prandial rest period, a privately printed brochure of the "Niemeyer Festgabe" dated 1963. In it Martin Heidegger appreciates the publisher's services in the younger days of phenomenology and of his own creative work. It offers much of interest in reminiscences about his youthful formative reading, his interest in Edmund Husserl, his earlier writing, describing e.g. how *Sein und Zeit* came to be published incomplete at a dean's request. I copied for myself the last paragraph of this essay, which elucidates the above quoted words:

"And today? The time of phenomenological philosophy seems to be over. It appears already as something passed, still to be listed only historically among other movements of philosophy. Yet phenomenology in its inmost property (*in ihrem Eigensten*) is no movement. It is the temporally turning and only thereby remaining possibility of thought, to respond to the appeal of what is to be thought (*Anspruch des zu-Denkenden*). If phenomenology is thus experienced and retained, then it can disappear as a label (*Titel*) in favor of the cause of thought (*Sache des Denkens*), the openness of which remains a mystery."[3]

This statement can only be appreciated properly when read in correlation with that of 1927 (SZ, 38), where Heidegger, initiating his explicitly phenomenological *opus magnum,* already "discards" phenomenology as a movement, while stressing its high significance as possibility. I am naturally aware of drastic objections against those as against these words of his, forthcoming from those pursuing strict phenomenological research satisfying Husserl's criteria. They are likely to say that Heidegger's view of phenomenology, certainly unorthodox, is or has been too narrow and now appears out of date. Without hoping to assuage them here or anywhere, I should only like to ask whether it is phenomenology as a movement that needs defense against his depreciation of it, or whether that can be philosophically crucial. If not, then his view is hardly narrow. In relation to the elaborate argument of Richardson, which is also dated 1963, that Heidegger changed "from phenomenology to thought," it can be pointed out that according to the statement I

---

[3] Quoted by special permission of the author.

quoted, such a change is but of label or title, while in the heart of the matter phenomenology remains as the possibility of responsive thought. Retaining it in such equivalence, it occurs to me, makes any wider view of it scarcely imaginable. Nor is it very likely that thought so highly responsive to temporal turns need ever be out of date — although it can appear as "untimely" as Nietzsche's.

Perhaps just this point provides the best look out at the distance between Heidegger and Husserlian developments; also, for what it is worth, the reason for my own reservations about the latter. Heidegger's thought in almost half a century is bound to time; and his respect for history, while not invulnerable to much conflicting criticism, is undeniable. Husserl himself could never equal that respect; and his attention turned to temporal and historical questions mainly after 1927. His great ambition to build phenomenology as *"strenge Wissenschaft"* led him toward standards of validity no less rigorous than those of logic and mathematics. His *"Wesenschau"* relates to essences and has no bearing on Heidegger's *"Wesen."* The developments have been appropriate. I have listened to Husserlians failing to agree on such central concepts as transcendental reduction, pure ego, natural vs. life world. The privilege of disagreements and variable interpretations belongs to them, of course, as much as to any philosophers; but the validity of results is rather dubious when emulating logico-mathematical ones. That they do, is underlined by their claims continuing today, to atemporal or time-suspended truths. It is thus entirely rational — the "science of essences", precisely as movement, discipline or school, may be listed only within the long series of footnotes to Plato. Heidegger's possibility of thought, whether or not it coincides with philosophy, transcends that series.

That Heidegger has been with time changing his own labels or terms, need not be argued; even more drastic than with "phenomenology" is his gradual recession from the word "ontology." Partly in view of the alleged contrast between the early and the later, I was curious to know how he now regards some of his passed terms. What he said hardly indicates any antipathy toward the phenomenological undertaking, particularly as amounting to hermeneutic explication (*Auslegung*: SZ, 37).

I had in mind a hermeneutic or paedagogical difficulty of my own experience, viz. how to pose the relation of phenomena to concepts when discussing *Sein und Zeit.* In particular, I was concerned with the way anxiety is shown as a clue to care; this is easily misunderstood, not only by students, as though the two had an equal status. Thus I have tended to emphasize anxiety as a passing phenomenon which may and may not show itself individually, in contrast to care enfolding the human being, in a complex structural whole explicated in a definition (SZ, 192), which can be, therefore, called a concept — for this there is textual authority (SZ, 200). And yet, when I put this forward as an example of the relation of phenomena and concepts, Heidegger was hesitant as to whether care had better be called concept. In subsequent conversation, he showed no reluctance at all in speaking further about "phenomena" in *Sein und Zeit*, while he expressed himself sceptically about the use of the word "concepts." Bearing in mind the contemporary acceptance of concepts as instruments or elements of thought, the conclusion is interesting: that "phenomonology" is still closer to him than "thought," in one popular sense of it.

He made the following points. **Concepts taken in the modern sense are too objective (*gegenständlich*).** This, of course, is to be understood not as favoring any subjectivism but on the contrary as criticizing the significance of concepts in the subject-object relation. Supplementary to this observation was that **ancient categories of Aristotle were not concepts so intended (*nicht so gemeint*).** I trust it is clear that he was speaking of the modern dominance of subjectivity introduced by the Cartesian "cogito" (compare N, II, 71 ff., 153 ff.). The objectivity of concepts in modern philosophy sets up their immanence for subjects' representations, wherein they become defined, fixed and even formalized logically. This trend is traceable from Descartes through Leibniz, Kant, Hegel, to its break-up in Nietzsche; whether the essential formulations tied to some ego in Husserl are different, may be wondered. The formal and scientific virtues of such objectivity establish its achievements today, when thinking becomes learning and computing of data. This has been circumscribed by Heidegger as a spread of "information trade." Contraposed to this must be his statement: *Sein und Zeit does not pass out any information.* It is not surprising, since the Introduction text warns against expectations of any "isolated and blind statement, communicable in repetition" (SZ, 19), and explicitly mentions phenomenological statements as so vulnerable when "vacuously passed on" (SZ, 36). At that early time Heidegger had no intention of producing a fixed doc-

trine or body of "information," and it is worth noting that then
as now he has understood phenomenological approach to phenomena as a method of moving spontaneity unlike the more formal and
computable procedure with concepts. I might mention here that
in another context, while using an expression very important for
him, "ontological difference," he said he found the second word
too static.

One other point belongs here. In this discussion of concepts,
Martin Heidegger also told me that already in his early lectures,
phenomenological or not, he used to reiterate that proper **conception is always co-attainment** *(immer Mit-vollziehen)*, viz. in
the course of study (compare EM, 16). This means the reading of
a philosopher has always been for Heidegger philosophizing with or
even against him but never away from him. Reviving the original
metaphor in philosophical "conception," it means partaking grasp,
gathering novelty, bringing to bear within one's own thought; and
all these phrases connote activity. The present scope permits me
no more than mentioning the question not without weight, what
differences, levels or roles may be proper within the field homo-
genized in the word "concepts." But to relate it still another way,
for Heidegger conceiving pertains not to accumulation of dead inter-
changeable data but to reflection enlivening sense *(Besinnung)*.

What do these brief observations amount to? Phenomenology as
an open possibility of thought; its description of phenomena as unfolding explication; concepts not appropriate when statically objective; and reaching them for everyone actively taking part. I hope
that points in this thread, while explicitly different from the previous
one, point in the same direction. They characterize Heidegger's approach to the way to be of thought *(Wesen des Denkens)* as remaining on the way *(unterwegs)*. Whether or not it be entitled
phenomenological, the cause of thought is no cause if it does not
move the thinker on. Thought philosophically fruitful he understands as reflection *(Besinnung)* which "places us on the way" to
"where we stay long" already (VA, 68). Thus it is not a way into
alien distances; the cause is one of staying on the move, which is
also our homecoming. The way is old, not new; Heidegger so alludes
to it in the foreword to his latest collected volume *Wegmarken,*
written in 1967, with significance he stressed to me: "The way
(Weg) to determine the cause of thought ... staying in the same-

ness of the same ... to lay out (finding its proper location) what
the word 'to be' has once disclosed as to be thought . . . ."

I have said a few things about man's way to be which also dis-
poses his way to think. The cause of thought is the cause of being
human, not in the sense of a causality but of a ground; thus it is
also the "cause" asked for in the question Heidegger often returns
to: why is there anything rather than nothing? For this cause man
moves along, locating what is cleared for him with the word "to be";
and this way I have referred to as the way to being. But the sense of
this expression is not sufficiently clarified by saying that the way
does not lead on to any distant goal but that man finds himself on
it coming home. Taking up a different thread now, I shall try to provide another bearing.

In my textual understanding I have had difficulties with adequately distinguishing the exposition of temporality in *Sein und Zeit*
from that of historicity. Both are provisionally introduced in paragraphs 5 and 6, with the former underlying the latter (SZ, 19),
which is then circumscribed by its etymological kinship in German
with "happening" (*Geschehen*). The historicity of the human being
means there that it is as "it has been already" and, more strikingly,
it is "from the future" that being "happens" in the human way (SZ,
20). These remarks are anticipatory. But in the latter part of the
work extant, after the existential analyses of being toward death
and of conscience-heeding authenticity, temporality is explicated
as unifying sense of care, i.e., of the human being (Dasein) on its
ecstatic grounds; and an italicized sentence reads: "The primary
phenomenon of original and authentic temporality is the future"
(SZ, 329). This question then appears legitimate: how different is
ecstatic temporality, finite in death and "temporalized primarily"
from the future, from the human being's historicity, again finite and
ecstatically one, which "happens" from the future? There is, of
course, a subsequent chapter entitled "Temporality and Historicity,"
but I have not quite experienced their differential weight — except
for one notion. That is introduced (SZ, 384 ff.) by means of two intertwined words: "*Schicksal*" and "*Geschick*"; the English explanation will follow, but it must be noted that the translation "fate" does
clash with the explicit context. In German, though, the old ties are
fixed here: "*Geschick*" with "*Geschichte*" (history) and "*Geschehen*"

(happening). Still, the use of *"Geschick"* is rather sparing as compared with *"Schicksal";* one point in their relation is that the latter
pertains more to human individuals and the former to their plurality
in coexistence (*Mitsein*). Yet since the very notion of "Dasein" is
always understood as being in the world shared with coexisting
others, this point is not as significant as it would be for a subjectivism of isolated egos. I think it can therefore be said that the sense
of *"Geschick"* is not fully developed in *Sein und Zeit.*

I put my difficulty frankly to Martin Heidegger, saying that
historicity had tended to merge for me with temporality until I
came to appreciate the sense of *"Geschick"* explicated in his later
works. And he granted this, viz. that a fuller understanding of
"Geschick" is necessary for a proper look back at the intentions of
Sein und Zeit.

How then in this notion to be understood? In the aforementioned
essay I cited reasons for translating it as "becoming"; I still incline
this way, but any rigid translation of Heidegger is self-defeating,
and I shall try to amplify. First, let me point out that after *Sein und
Zeit* Heidegger almost refrains from using the word *"Schicksal."*
Why? That word probably should be rendered as "destiny" for the
human being, but as it emerges in authentic resolve, it must have no
fatalist flavor whatever. Still, it belongs within human ek-sistence,
of which Heidegger speaks later less directly; hence its gradual
disappearance, though not obsoleteness. But the word *"Geschick"*
grows in import, ever with regard to being. What is involved? To
say: "the becoming of being" can certainly confuse, when the two
notions are metaphysically opposed, especially with "being" immutable and "becoming" mutable. I need not reiterate that for Heidegger being is hardly immutable; nor is becoming intended here as
equivalent to indifferent mutability in time — although the temporal
aspect does play a role. The clear intention, however, is to speak of
how being becomes man temporally, i.e., befalls, befits, properly
yields to, endows, illuminates, addresses or directs itself to — the
direction quite strictly coming from being toward the human being,
not vice versa. And therein lies human destiny (*Schicksal*): in
ecstatic ek-sistence resolutely embracing the way being becomes
it, comes to be available, renders the proper bearing. This is why I
have said that historicity in *Sein und Zeit* hinges on one notion in
two intertwined words; with regard to the human being this notion
can be expressed as "becoming destiny."

Within the scope of analysing ek-sistence in *Sein und Zeit* Heidegger only paves the way for his further thought on the becoming of being through time. The following statements from *"Zeit und Sein"* of 1962 help to make this clear. *"Das Geschick, darin es Sein gibt, beruht im Reichen der Zeit"* — "The becoming in which being obtains, rests within the reach of time" (ZS, 52). That is the temporal aspect I mentioned, not at all receding 35 years after *Sein und Zeit*. On the other hand, there is no question of "becoming" as indifferent change: "The historical ... determines itself through that which becomes (*aus dem Geschickhaften*) ... not through an indeterminately meant happening (*Geschehen*)" (ZS, 30). This is the divergence from the usual already anticipated in 1927: for the human understanding of being there is properly (*eigentlich*) in time no "becoming" (*Werden*) in the sense of a neutral sequence of now to measure changes, nor "happening" in the sense of a succession of occurrences (*Geschehen*). In the last chapter of my *Tragic Protest* I have tried to relate human hap-pening to its source in hap or mis-hap, thought of as destiny that may be mis-becoming.

To return once more to the question of historicity as presented in *Sein und Zeit* and its limitation in the text: the preceding quotation stresses that the triad *"Geschehen-Geschichte-Geschick"* should not have an equal status. Heidegger acknowledges the difficulty: "Because the becoming of being (*Seins-Geschick*) is everywhere represented only as history (*Geschichte*) and this only as happening (*Geschehen*), it is a vain endeavor to interpret such happening through what is said in *Sein und Zeit* about the historicity of the human being (Dasein) — not of being" (ZS, 32). In other words, the reading of the early text can fail, as mine did, to appreciate what is distinct in human historicity in relation to temporality, when the thought of its "happening" is not adequately grounded in "becoming destiny" of man. But to pursue that thought it is required to exceed the bounds of anything human and to turn to being. Temporally ecstatic ek-sistence is the locus (*Da*) on which being bears with the clearing (*Lichtung*) of truth; only this properly becomes an open destiny for the human being — to see what "to be" signifies for it.

And still, the "it" standing for the human being must also, as observed earlier, pertain to me and you and him, since Dasein is "ever respectively mine." The human hold on being is not like the mind's impersonal relation toward *universalia*. I have therefore tried to connect the thought of becoming destiny with that rather singular statement on p. 38 of *Sein und Zeit* where in contrast to any "universality" of genus Heidegger ascribes to being as open to man "the possibility and necessity of the most radical individuation." When I first referred to it, he immediately stressed that **this is said about the being of Dasein only.** It is indeed easy to overlook, because the six surrounding sentences in the paragraph speak of being as such. And the point remains: so "individualizable" is the human being (Dasein) which is determinable only in its open relation to being.

I, therefore, felt free to pursue the connection and ask whether such individuation is later to be thought in the turning and variable way being becomes every man. The answer to this was: **Yes, this is so; the becoming of being (*Seins-Geschick*) is meant always for the historical human being (*immer für geschichtliches Dasein*).** But then Heidegger went on: **That is, for the Hellenic, the Christian, and so on.**

The addition, I confess, rather put me off. These words of Heidegger agree, of course, with the statement in *Sein und Zeit* (p. 384-85) where the word "*Geschick*" is referred to the community, the people, the generation and the chosen recapture of the past through tradition; and again, they establish a distance from modern egocentrism. Nevertheless, an exclusively plural scope would make Dasein only "ours" rather than "mine" — whereas both are needed in human worldly coexistence (*Mitsein*); and my question about individuation had to concern individuals as well. So I persisted: but how is it being becomes individual human beings such as e.g. great poets with a new vision which is properly their own? To that, the answer was at first unexpected: **There we should speak of how they yield their individuality (*Individualität preisgeben*)** — but the continuation provided a clearing: **I do not mean dissolving (*Auflösen*) individuality but dis-closing and offering themselves to being (*sich dem Sein erschliessen und opfern*).** I hyphenate "dis-closing" here to emphasize its contrast in German to "closing" (*schliessen*).

Heidegger's statement deserves, I think, reflection and elaboration at length I can not project here. But a few comments I have to submit. The individuation of being as it may become any man must not be taken for granted universally: it is granted but to the human being as such, for which individuality is possible and as necessary as a proper way to be. The statement quoted steers a course between, on the one hand, a mystic renunciation aimed at dissolving human individuality and, on the other hand, an assertion of subjectivity which would be self-closing. The latter appears to me in the inevitable prospect of insistence. The text *"Vom Wesen der Wahrheit"* refers to it thus: "Man . . . taking himself exclusively as subject to measure all there is . . . sticks to securing his self. . . . As insistent, man is turned ever to the closest manipulability of entities. But he insists only as already ek-sistent. . . . He goes astray" (W, 91-92). Straying on the way is an ever human possibility; and so subjectivism is historically justified. Yet if subjective insistence on oneself and whatever is closest were the only possibility for man, his straying would be without remedy. It presents an image of individuality but not, in Heidegger's thought, the proper one, because the ek-sistential entry onto the way to be, while open, is forgotten. The other individuality of which Heidegger spoke, where the self means the task called for in conscience, is a man's becoming destiny, not established nor secured by him. Therefore, in question here is not sticking to but offering, not closing but dis-closing, a man's way to be proper to him (*eigentlich*), though without a guarantee against straying. As for the great poets so for you or me, this can be granted but not taken for granted.

How being becomes or properly fits and enlightens any man, individuating him in his destiny, this is again a way of transience, of temporally going along. But it hap-pens from the future; this word (*Zukunft*) Heidegger ties in his language to "coming toward" (*Auf-sich-Zukommen*), i.e., toward the human being. With this regard, it appears less appropriate to speak of man's way to being. While the way is the same and within the same, a turn around in direction has to be noted: if "toward" man then "from" being. Not the prepositions matter here but something does, greatly: not to think of being as a mere vacancy into which only man brings on the way his enlivening occupation. Such thinking on man's way to being would mirror self-insistence, whether it be labelled subjectivism, existentialism or even humanism. In his "Letter" on that theme Heidegger contrasts Sartre's "il y a seulement des hommes" with "il y a principalement l'Etre", also expressing himself there inaccessibly to existentialism: "It is rather man who is 'thrown' by being itself . . . to ek-sist guarding its truth" (W, 161-65). If it does not stretch the metaphor, I might visualize being not in the vacancy of space but in its power of gravity "throwing" man into that orbit which becomes his way. And the uniqueness, activity and dignity of *homo humanus,* far from any degradation, receives nowhere an affirmation stronger than in the exegesis of Sophocles (EM, 112 ff.). *Homo viator* moves on his way there as a trail blazer, a home-seeking stranger, a Nietzschean breaker-creator, a tragic hero standing out over all nature. Yet this strangest human power moves owing to and inmidst of "the overpowering." Man's powerful history is thereby determined as finite and fallible if not fruitless: the over-powering means being of which man is the fruit or issue. Of that more should be said.

Is it still legitimate to speak of man's way to be as moving him to or toward being, now that the way has been marked as not uni-directional, that its overall sway or throw originates not in man? The overpowering surrounds any circle of human steps and, as was said before, being provides for everything the way it yields. Perhaps the turn of speech, well understood, is not unlike Heidegger's own incorporation of "insistence" within "ek-sistence," and his use of that word, in the sense of man's standing and reaching forth, to al-low for the thought of the human locus within the reach of being. The human being must through such statements fill the scope of their subject — ostensibly.

To remain in the home circle of Heidegger's thought, once more to go around the way man comes into being as being overcomes man — I shall follow still another thread.

"Once in a while . . . being needs reflection. . . . This need (*Bedürfen*) knows no restlessness of a lack, it is the restfulness of abundance. . . . At some times being needs man's way to be, and yet it is never dependent on the mankind there is. . . . At such a time from the appeal of being emerges for a while the attempt to respond. . ." (N, II, 482-83). These words to open with, partly to point out the explicit ties between the "need" — which is no lack — and historical attempts to respond in thought, and partly to note the German word standing here in the place of the more frequent "*Brauch.*" The latter noun with its cognate verb can colloquially signify: need, lack, want, use, custom, requirement.

It is this expression of Heidegger's thought I wish to reflect on, again for my own instruction in the care of explicating his texts, in many of which the question can arise; I hope it will not be judged too simple and singular. When speaking about the "need" of being — which is more often not located historically "at times" — I found at least three likely sources of misunderstanding. One, that need is hard to divorce from absence, lack, even desire, and with such connotations it can be placed in texts from Descartes to Sartre; two, that need affects variably individual beings, if not personal then at any rate living and conscious; three, that to speak of need with reference to being suggests anthropomorphic thinking. I tried to discuss these difficulties with Martin Heidegger.

On the first point, the above quotation surely throws light, especially when in contrast to lack is mentioned abundance, in the spirit of Nietzsche's natural overflow; but I shall report further what Heidegger said. With the second, I have not had serious difficulty, because it is not hard to imagine correlations neither individual or conscious in e.g. what stones need, what our time needs, etc.; Aristotle discussing purposive tending also transcended such factors. Having used such references to clarify, I mentioned to Heidegger my reasoning by analogy, and within that limitation, he allowed its legitimacy. The third point, suggesting anthropomorphism, he did not find plausible at all. It is indeed scarcely a point without the first two: if to speak of need does not imply a lack, as it may — but only may — do in humans, nor does it presuppose consciousness or individuality, then the thought about the need of being can stay free of any anthropomorphic tendency.

But as the conversation went on, although in German, its main tenor for me became the question of rendering Heidegger's word "*Brauch*" in English as "need." Let me remark that another word, "*Not*" equally well means need, and also necessity, constraint, pressure, even misery; and compare the passage in *Einführung* (p. 124), where "*Not*" refers to man but "*brauchen*" to being. Similarly, in the statement I opened with the word "*bedürfen*" for which I put "need" to introduce the question, can mean "requiring" which also signifies calling for, enclosing, imposing from power rather than from any lack. However, the principal notion in this way of being for man is that of "*Brauch*."

Heidegger at first reminded me of the explication of his intent in the essay on Anaximander (HW, 338 ff.); the interpretation there concentrates on the Latin "*frui*." This can mean fruit-bearing, also enjoying and having use of (*geniessen*). But the enjoying is dissociated from any mental or bodily possession or exploitation; and the using is intended for sustenance rather than gradual evanescence — thus the proper association is with the way works of art are made use of, in contrast to utensils made to be unnoticed and worn out (cp. HW, 23 ff). The explication of *"frui"* in the text says: ". . . handing it over to its proper way to be and holding it, so present, in a guarding hand . . . grants the partaking of time (*Anteil seiner Weile*) . . . preserves and collects for itself whatever is handed out . . . finalizes *(be-endet)* what is present, handing out its term *(Grenze)* . . . is also *'to apeiron,'* the in-determinate *(ohne Grenze)."* The *"apeiron"* is further mentioned as precursor of *"Moira"* that grants the partaking, and of *"Logos"* that collects *(Versammeln); needless* to say, for Heidegger all this recalling of ancient thought pertains to being.

How, then, is such fruition to be expressed in thinking of *"Brauch"*? It appears to me that the most true, if not literally correct, rendition will be to say "issue" — with the understanding that, apart from anything else that is, being issues in the human being and that man's way to be ek-sists toward the issue of being. The essay on Anaximander stresses this unique relation just at its end. But it is important to have this in mind: the issue (*Brauch*) of being, as cited, involves the presenting or presence of what is present (*Anwesen des Anwesenden*), i.e., of any beings, and Heidegger leads up to his explication by relating this with the ontological difference of being and whatever is or any entities (*Unterschied des Seins zum Seienden*, p. 336) — it is in this difference that only the human being ek-sists. Or, to put it otherwise, no entity could be present without the clearing of aletheia, discoveredness, truth; and its locus (*Da*) establishes the human being as Dasein. The thought might now be pursued: in one sense all entities issue from being, as presented by being. But in another sense — more direct or "required" by being — only the human being (Dasein) is there as the issue and for the issue, to clear the ontological difference or issue, in the non-directed sense. Thus our questionable human stake (*das uns Angehende*) is the way "from" being, which falls or is thrown "between" being and all beings (*Wesen des Menschen — "der Zwischen-fall zu sein,"* EM, 125).

To pause for a moment: I can perhaps leave now without elaboration the question how the human way as issue corresponds to the need or requirement of being. But it seems to me properly cleared in the foregoing discussion that the "hermeneutic" difficulties I had mentioned can be eliminated, even if the word "need" be retained. Suggestions of lack or absence lose relevance as the issue comes from abundance presenting itself; and those of individuality, consciousness, or anthropomorphism reach an explicit limit of analogy: as pertinent to some beings, they can be described as ontic or on one side only of the ontological difference – into which the above discussion leads, if it is understood at all. I can now return to some further remarks Martin Heidegger made in this context.

To follow his, or anyone's thought beyond beings, at least a great effort of care is indispensable with regard to the meaning of sameness and otherness (compare in the letter *"Zur Seinsfrage"*: Man is "enclosed, not excluded" from being – W, 236–39). I inject this word of caution for what follows. After the discussion of *"frui,"* Heidegger made two statements to be quoted, the relation of which again shows an ambivalence or turning round of man's way to being. One: **The human being (*Dasein*) and the clearing of truth can only be thought in the proper way (*wesentlich nur*) within being.** This, stressing the enclosing of the issue, may revive the words, referring to *"Wesen,"* that I quoted earlier on "always going over to being." And the other statement: **Being issues in — needs? — (*braucht*) man as the human being there (*als Dasein*);** with a stress on the word "as."

The correlation may at first be taken as simple and without any novelty. First, man arrives and remains on his proper way only as clearly surrounded by being, never in contraposition (*Gegenüber*). Second, there is in being an allowance for the human light of discovery. The statements could even seem traditionally metaphysical, concerning man, an entity among others in being, but privileged as rational; such "reading" of Heidegger might refer to metaphysical subjectivism, interpreting:*"Nur solange Dasein ist, gibt es Sein"* – "Being is there only as long as man is" (SZ, 212). From there let me now take a turn. In the letter to Beaufret on humanism, Heidegger denies this statement could say – and could it without absurdity? – that actual existence of man as an ego should "create" being. What does it say? I render it otherwise: "Being obtains or yields itself only while there is its locus of (human) being." I put it thus, because the letter goes on, "This means: being bears properly (*übereignet sich*) on man only while its clearing is born (*sich ereignet*) ... the locus – the clearing (*das Da, die Lichtung*) of discovered-

ness of being.... (W, 167). My terms here depend on thinking
"*Ereignis*" as "bearing"; to this I shall return.[4] The crux of this whole
matter, perhaps the great hardship in pursuing Heidegger's thought,
is the question of sameness with unlikeness (*das Selbe − nicht das
Gleiche*), when leaving behind all entities whose identities and differences we deal with usually. I make no claim to remove this hardship; I can only cope with it in reflection.

The last phrase quoted allows no separation of the clearing and
the locus (*Da*) of being, which pertains to "Dasein"; this, I have
been saying, means the human being − how right is that? It is quite
plain, once more, that Heidegger does not speak of man as one of
many entities with given qualities and relations; nor even of his
grasp of being as "an adventitious encounter" (*ein Bisweilen zukom-
mendes Gegenüber* − W, 239): Dasein is no subject against the
object of being. But then, how "human" is Dasein? Its way to be,
strangely, is the "same" with being; this is surely the thought in the
first of the above two statements Heidegger made to me. This
thought must be pursued deeper, and confirmed: "Being endows
itself ... with the locality (*Ortschaft*) it comes to .... This Where as
staying locus (*Da*) belongs to being itself, 'is' being itself, and is
therefore called: Da-sein" (N, II, 358). Dasein "is" being, not just
"in" being; the quotation marks cannot break the sameness, yet can
hint at unlikeness. I cited earlier a phrase about "historicity of Dasein − not of being," presumably not alike. The present statement
stresses the over-coming power of being with its "endowment"
which is another verbal reference to its becoming (*Geben-Geschick*,
cp. ZS, 30 ff.) and can also be linked with its presenting (*Anwesen*).
But an even stranger correlation must be faced: "... a suggestion
(*Zumutung*) of being .. to man in his way to be (*Wesen*) .... This
way to be is nothing human. It is the placement (*Unterkunft*) where
being comes, with which placement being endows itself and to
which it sets out on the way (*sich in sie begibt*), so that 'it' − accordingly and only thus − yields being" or "thereby being obtains
(*Es gibt das Sein*)" (N, II, 377).

What may strike the eye first is that man's way to be, which also
means Dasein, is "nothing human" − just that which I have been
calling "the human being." I do not wish to insist on a rigid translation; yet once more, it is hardly the correctness of words that matters. And the truth of the thought seems to allow this: ek-sistence,

[4] Vide "Martin Heidegger and Man's Way to be," p. 369.

locus of being, way to be — none of this "is" human, but rather "is" being. On the other hand, speech with these phrases intends to characterize that which lets man — the entity, the animal, the possible self — become properly human. Taken widely, this may be parallel: the world is that which lets the seas and hills and roads come into their own. Heidegger thus speaks of presenting, granting, becoming.

More strange in the above passage is the impression that through man's way being yields or obtains. And I do not mean another subjectivist mis-interpretation of man as master or creator of being. The strangeness concerns the placement of man in the "it" (*Es*), particularly in view of the hint in *"Zeit und Sein"* (p. 56) that the "it" identifies the bearing (*Ereignis*); although the hint is retracted as identification would involve what is present (*Anwesend*) which the bearing is not. Heidegger's notion of *"Ereignis"* covers his most mysterious allusions to sameness, even with the history of being, where "nothing happens, the bearing bears" (*das Ereignis er-eignet*, N, II, 485). Yet the epitomy of sameness does embrace unlikeness: the bearing yields and withholds (*Sichentziehen*), presents and absents, perhaps in the sense that bearing offers the born but not itself. Thus it even seems to bind the sameness and unlikeness of being and nothing; I can only so understand the mystifying phrase: "Being vanishes in the bearing" (ZS, 62). At any rate, Heidegger's intent is definitely to say — refusing any "logical subordination" between being and bearing — that being is ever born with time. Born, presenting, yielding itself, being becomes — man; in the same text "man belongs to the bearing" (ZS, 64). Still, the impression above could have been stronger: "it" — the bearing? — as man's way to be yields being. "Da-sein" might equal *"Ereignis"*? But it must be noted that the questioned phrase is subject to the interjection: "accordingly *(demzufolge)."* The way of being with man obtains in accord with the self-endowment of being, following it or going along properly means the issue. Being as bearing-born, being with the time endowment of presenting "requires" issue.

In this roundabout manner I return to the statements quoted from my conversation about *"Brauch."* It may have been noted that the first one does not contain that word; its tie to the context may be clearer now. The "local" clearing of truth for man is not to be transposed in thought "from" somewhere else "to" being: it must be thought "there" to begin with. The human issue is no counter-

part to being, it does not de-part from its home. And it is interesting
that in the light of the preceding considerations the second statement (***Das Sein braucht den Menschen als Dasein***) can also be
expressed; **being — as (human) being there — issues in man.**
My reason for the bracketing is transparent.

The word "issue," from the Latin *"ire (exire)"* which means to
go (out) must in its sense compose an umbilical cord of sameness
though not likeness between that which issues, the issuing, and that
which it issues from. But the sameness signifies belonging together,
no equality or interchangeability (EM, 106). It is, therefore, possible to speak of being as issue (*Brauch*) in which man belongs to
being, not vice versa. He can so belong "there" to the clearing for
the sake of presenting the endowment, of time bearing.

Bearing as the giving of birth is not to be dissociated from
fruition. Again, the fruit, while of course conceivable in a separate
entity, as fruit of fruition must be at one and the same with it. Wine
grapes belong to the vineyard plants, the soil, the hill slope, the sun
and rain; without all this they can not become themselves in culture
and enjoyment. Keeping this in mind, let me come round once
more to Heidegger's explication of Anaximander, to introduce his
last words on it. Being as issue of fruition (*Brauch*) "preserves and
collects for itself" all that is, but finalizing for anything its term and
its time; in my image of fruits any of them owe their finite spatio-
temporal terms to how they are born. Yet while so determining,
being which bears is also called in the text "the indeterminate —
apeiron", at least as early an expression for it as "physis" or
"logos." Then, from the pre-Socratic thought of Anaximander, the
historical line moves traditionally through Plato, Aristotle, Aquinas,
Descartes, Spinoza, Kant, Hegel: the line from the *apeiron* to the
absolute. That the determinate is finite, need not be argued; but
the indeterminate, through the thinkers who followed, surely becomes the infinite, under varying names: God, Substance, Absolute, etc. The question arises: recalling his early thought on temporality in *Sein und Zeit*, how does Heidegger see this line from a
"later" aspect?

This is what he said: **I make use of this word 'Brauch' also
to express my thesis (*These*) about the finiteness (*Endlichkeit*) of being, to say that being is no absolute.** This thesis,
while in implicit accord, has not received much explicit elaboration
in his published work. Considering the text of *"Zeit und Sein"* as

well as *Sein und Zeit,* it is proper to say that the finiteness of being means neither more nor less than the finiteness of time. It would be also possible to include space as viewed in contemporary cosmology, of which he has been aware for decades; although space could never equal the ontological significance of time in his thought. Yet I doubt that was in his mind as he spoke, especially closing in the contrast with the absolute. The absolute of Hegel, as its philosophical predecessors, raises problems of the relation infinite-finite, and also of the relevance of its abstraction. For Heidegger being, the antithesis of abstraction, is finite and no absolute; and he says this while weighing his word *"Brauch."* Its significance, then?

Without discarding my preceding explications, I wonder if I could not add to their weight by returning to the sense of "need"; certainly without the connotations of privation, conscious lack or misery, without any intent of evaluation. But need might correlate with finiteness. Plato's realm of Ideas is, if anything, distorted in becoming; Spinoza's God is eternally perfect and transient temporality beneath him is but illusion; the Absolute could be absolved from anything. In such thoughts no need can emerge, and perhaps therein lies their abstraction. But being, in Heidegger's thought, is concrescence — and finite. Being yields itself in the dis-coveredness (*a-letheia*), implying cover; presenting, turns toward the clearing which is "there" (*Da*), but not everywhere; bearing on man, issues the appeal (*Anspruch*) to echo with his responses (*Entsprechen*) and thus speech (*Sprache*), not man-made, becomes the human being. Throughout history, the need of responsiveness corresponds to the finite issue of being: such is the concrete "cause" of thought.

An earlier quotation referred to man's way to be as the placement or housing (*Unterkunft*) to which being "sets out on the way." In the foregoing reflections I have tried to bring into light such motion in being, which does not leave man unmoved in irrelevance or indifference. The human issue is primarily the way founded on and "from" being. At the same time, the way turns round to become — as is needed — the human way to being. This is the search of the ground to be at home, the orientation in the manifold of ek-sistence in the world, the ongoing reflection (*Besinnung*) to disclose sense (*Sinn*) which can only obtain with being.[5]

[5] Vide "Being and Sense," *Journal of Existentialism,* VII — 25 (1966), p. 33ff.

The autumn days were closing in the horizon: from the height of the hut the vast view of the Alps was covered, and Freiburg was dark with rain. The long way home occurred to me, occasionally. I asked Martin Heidegger, not for the first time, whether he would not care to come and see the lands across the ocean. He said he was not moved by that need in this, his eightieth year. Yes, I thought, he is and always has stayed not far from home.

The home of his thought, though, is on the way: "The way lets us arrive where we stay already. . . . Then, why still a way ahead? . . . because we are there without properly reaching that which concerns our way to be" (US, 199). I have tried to reflect on this way, close but far-reaching, familiar and still not easy to go, full of turns yet moving us most directly. Perhaps my reflections are too sharp; but I hope they have not strayed from the way which leads on. Musing on oriental thought — I put it so because he disclaimed to me any authoritative acquaintance with it — Heidegger says of Tao: "It could be the way . . . such that only on it we can think what reason, spirit, sense, logos properly say. . . . The way is all. (*Alles ist Weg*)" (US, 198).

The question is not how well Heidegger knows it, how properly anyone says it. Is there a way which is all, for man? That is his way to being.

Heidegger's View and Evaluation of Nature and Natural Science[1]

Edward G. Ballard

There is no doubt but that Heidegger questions the profit-ableness and legitimacy of many of the favorite beliefs, standards, and aspirations which are most characteristic of modern Western culture. Thus to be the critic of this culture, he must take up a position in some sense outside it; he must discover or construct a vantage point from which it may be understood and then judged. This critical motive is surely not the only one which prompts Heidegger to seek to enlarge his horizon, but it is the one most relevant for grasping his understanding and evaluation of the objective and technological world within which we find ourselves today.

In proclaiming his criticisms of modern culture, Heidegger inevitably arouses the hostility both of those who are passionately attached to it and of those who are intellectually committed to it. This attitude as well as other motives have elicited many negative reactions to his philosophy. The general drift of the criticisms with which this study will be concerned tends to the point that his philosophy is anti-scientific, "subjectivistic," and even, perhaps, irrational. Karl Löwith summarizes one important aspect of this sort of criticism by concluding that Heidegger offers a doctrine of man without

[1] Substantial portions of this article are to be included in Chapter 8 of my forthcoming book, *Philosophy at the Crossroads*.

a natural world.[2] In seeking to explicate Heidegger's view of objectivity within its context, I shall at the same time be concerned to respond to this criticism.

There are other closely related criticisms with which I shall be concerned in passing. For instance, there is the not infrequent accusation of anti-scientific emotionalism.[3] To another critic, Heidegger appears to desire a violent return to an irrationalism or to a kind of mysticism.[4] Still another concludes that his philosophy attacks conceptual thinking and culminates in a sort of subjective idealism.[5]

No doubt a careful exposition and interpretation of Heidegger's views on the natural world and its sciences provides the constructive way to place these criticisms in their appropriate and most profitable light. Upon this tactic I shall mainly rely.

It will not be amiss to anticipate the answer which this study will develop to criticisms such as those cited by observing that Heidegger does indeed take issue with the intellectualist version of the rational ideal. This version of the ideal identifies all being with being as evident to the mathematical and scientific intellect. Heidegger would replace this ideal with one which embodies respect for a being conceived more concretely. However, in the development of this new ideal and its rationale, most commentators discover elements which are difficult to assess. But to assume at the outset that these elements are merely emotionalistic, irrational, or "mystical" would be captious.

After remarking upon some of Heidegger's terminology, I shall

[2] Cf. his *Nature, History, and Existentialism*, tr. A. Levinson (Evanston: Northwestern University Press, 1966), p. 103; also his *Heidegger: Denker in dürftiger Zeit* (Frankfurt, 1953), p. 16f. Löwith is undoubtedly Heidegger's most learned and most careful negative critic.

[3] Cf. A. Stern, *Sartre, His Philosophy and Existential Psychoanalysis* (New York: 2nd ed., 1967). Though this book is primarily about Sartre, the author introduces a great deal of discussion about Heidegger. For example, he translates *Sorge* as "sorrow" (p. 29), then berates Heidegger for emotionalism and irrationalism.

[4] Cf. Walter Kaufmann, *From Shakespeare to Existentialism* (New York: Doubleday and Co., 1960, first ed. Boston: Beacon Press, 1959), chap. 17. Kaufmann's screed of grievances against Heidegger adds up more or less to the accusation of unreason: cf. "The lack of clarity and contempt of grammar . . . borders on obscurantism in Heidegger's philosophy of Being" (*ibid.*, p. 366). Another, F. H. Heinemann, finds that he uses an "unbearable jargon" to transform Hegel into an "ontological mysticism," cf. *Existentialism and the Modern Predicament* (New York: Harper and Bros., 2nd ed., 1954), chap. VI.

[5] Hazel E. Barnes, *An Existentialist Ethics* (New York: Alfred A. Knopf, 1967), chap. XII.

proceed through a consideration of the problem which the sciences offer and of the nature within which they exist to a consideration of the relevant ontological structures of human Being or Dasein, and of the authentic mode of existing. By this route it will be possible to come to an understanding of Heidegger's view of the alienation in modern times of man from the world and to understand his evaluation of the modern scientific enterprise. The questions concerning his supposed rejection of nature, his antipathy to natural science and rationality, and his idealism will thus be placed in a context where they may be answered or appropriately judged.

Part One — Some Heideggerian Terms

In order to begin an intelligent study of Heidegger, an initial grasp of certain terms must already have been reached. These are terms which, for the most part, are defined in his writings only in context. I begin with a brief sketch of a few of these.

For Heidegger, the *archē* of philosophy is not conscious being nor the being of consciousness; rather it is Being itself. But to specify the beginning by this term is ironical, for in Heidegger's opinion the basic function of philosophy is to inquire into the meaning of Being. An initial meaning, indicating Being as that which is responsible for the emergence and persistence of beings, is most difficult to describe. "That which gives possibilities" is not Heidegger's phrase, but it is not an un-Heideggerian description. One of his expressions, "the power of world-making" will become more intelligible later. He believes that the Greek term, *physis*, related to *phyein*, "to give birth to," preserves much of this meaning in both the verbal and nominative senses; it meant both an active originating and a remaining self-identically present. But then the verbal and more ontological sense was forgotten in the Classic tradition. Here we shall have to hope it will be to some degree recaptured in context. In order to avoid reifying the notion, it may be helpful to think of Being as light, of which one is not ordinarily conscious unless something interferes with it. At least Being in the ontological sense will always be distinguished from particular things or beings which belong to the "ontic" order: thus, Being is "no-thing," the shadow of beings. Also it will be distinguished from beingness, the abstract quality possessed by all beings and all kinds of beings.

Many of the difficulties in understanding Heidegger cluster

around the term, *Dasein*. For the most part, this term is inade-
quately translated by "human being" in the usual sense of this
phrase, or by "human nature." Dasein is an ontological term. Literally it means "there-being," but this "there" *(Da)* must be understood as the "place" or the situation in which Being, *Sein*, becomes
apparent in and as beings or becomes phenomenally evident. Just
as Kant produced an ethic valid not for man only but for all rational beings, so Heidegger proposes to elaborate a fundamental
ontology valid for any being which exists disclosively or as the
"there" of Being.[6]

Heidegger also uses 'world' as a more inclusive term to indicate
this place where Being emerges into persisting presence. World in
his sense is not the collection of objects, nor is it "all that is the case,"
nor even is it the unity of intentions, as it was for Husserl in his
earlier writings. It is more closely approximated by the concrete
Lebenswelt of Husserl's *Crisis of European Sciences*. Essential to a
world is its being inhabited, in the pregnant sense of this term. Thus,
Dasein might be translated by the ontological-ontic phrase Being-
in-the-world. It is both "being" and "in the world" where beings
come to be. The point is that the being (Dasein) to which appearances are present is essentially linked to the place (a world) where
appearances can be present.

If, now, man is a being to whom appearances are present, then
he is indissoluably related to his world; he is nothing without a concrete and historical world. The expressions 'Dasein' and 'Being-in-
the-world' clearly embody the Husserlian notion of the ego intentionally related to the object, but at the same time Heidegger's terms
are intended to include not merely that of which one may be conscious, but all that to which a being like man can possibly be in any
way related. Heidegger's term 'world' is, therefore, a more concrete
and inclusive term than the Husserlian *Lebenswelt*.

Man is a concrete individual, and he ex-ists.[7] He is the being
whose purposes are or can be intrinsic to himself. The existence
essential to man is described as the power either to be or not to be
his authentic self. This power either to be, to live one's world as the

___

[6] The "there" is also described by such terms as "Spielraum," cf. KM, 69f.;
EM, 110, 125; FD, 71, 188f. I shall continue to use the term "Dasein" in this
discussion.

[7] SZ, 12. It is a serious, but not uncommon mistake to suppose that the
existense or prejudice of the world which the Husserlian reduction suspended
is the same existence which Heidegger affirms to be the essence of Dasein.

being which one is, or else to identify oneself as other, to disguise oneself as something or as someone one is not, express modifications of the way in which one is open to that Being which gives possibilities. The insight and decision relative to a person's own being makes an essential difference with respect to what he is as well as to the whole structure of the world which a man inhabits and even to the character and function of the sciences of it.

The study of this being which is both individual and ex-sists is called fundamental ontology, the topic of the published portion (Divisions I and II) of *Being and Time*. It is regarded by Heidegger as preparatory to the study of general ontology, which is a "thinking" or recalling of Being as such. And it is a necessary preparation, for only a man (*this* existing individual) whose relation to his own being has become relatively transparent can expect to "think" or to have a clarified access to Being itself of which he is usually only pre-ontologically aware. But unless the meaning of Being as such is grasped in some sense, e.g., pre-ontologically, its more special disclosures and closures in human life cannot be understood at all. Thus the point, essential to understanding Heidegger, is suggested: that Dasein is "between" Being itself and its particular disclosures in the (ontic) beings of the world. Dasein, or Being-in-the-world, is the opening through which beings come to appearance or enter history. And the structures which can be discerned in Being-in-the-world will be those existential-transcendental structures which determine and limit the kind of world we live in. The task of ontological phenomenology is so to describe phenomena that these structures of Being (*logoi*) become evident. Heidegger's ideal is to bring these structures, by means of his descriptions, to emerge, as it were, from the phenomena, not to impose them upon the phenomena.

The structures which Heidegger's examination discovered in Being-in-the-world point to their temporal character, a fact not surprising when one recalls that Heidegger from the outset resolved not to neglect the temporality or concreteness of the world and of human existence. He reached the conclusion that human existence is essentially historical in all its aspects. An important consequence of this recognition is his reevaluation of human powers. The essential historicity of Dasein is seen to entail its finitude. This consequence is crucial in enabling him to reach a judgment of our scientific and technological epoch.

Part Two — The Object of Science and its Ontological Basis

In the modern world Being has become evident primarily as object. We are surrounded by objects, objects which we can view clearly, analyze, measure exactly, explain, predict, control, and exploit profitably. Moreover, we often seem to ourselves to be objects such as these, and the science of human engineering is advancing apace. Is this identification justified? What sort of being, we must ask, is object-being? Is it true that we, who ask this question, are — or ought — to be counted among objects? The understanding and evaluation of the objective world of the science of objects, and of the scientist himself will depend upon the management of questions such as these. More than this, we live in a time when the sciences are commonly given a technological interpretation. Man and the world are regarded as human and natural resources. We must inquire, therefore, what it means to exist under such conditions as these.

First, let us ask, what is science? According to Heidegger, "science is the theory of reality" (VA, 46). 'Reality' is the translation for the German *Wirklichen*. Heidegger connects the German term with the word, *wirken*, meaning "to effect, to establish as present." And theory, of course, he relates to the Greek *theōrein* which has to do with contemplative seeing, in particular with an intelligent viewing of the aspect of being which comes to man through appearances. Then he interprets his definition to mean that a science of facts acquires its object by "working it over" until it can be viewed as present and "real."

This "working over" is accomplished by a change in the more common and basic practical relation to a being. It modifies certain of the relations which constitute a thing as a being in the life-world. For instance, the tool character ("involvement") of a being in the life-world and its "place" in a possible work-process become indifferent to the scientist (cf. SZ, § 69). The iron in a hammer becomes for the chemist just the metal. More importantly, the way in which the object comes to be "seen" changes over from the kind of practical estimation characteristic of the workman to a seeing which is sensitized, prior to specific experiences, to just those aspects of the object which can become data for scientific theory. For modern science, this working over has come to be understood in the Cartesian tradition and is initially effected through the operations of measurement. By means of the techniques of measurement, the object is disposed in a new way; it is reduced to a mathematical structure which may then be symbolically transformed and managed by mathematical methods.

The Cartesian procedure is to presuppose that any object (body) belongs to the mathematical and objective world and can be exhaustively known only within it. But within this context, the object can be seen to obey exact laws which are discoverable by means of experiment. And "the experiment is that experience which in its plan and execution is guided and carried along by its basic law in order to elicit the facts which verify or disconfirm that law."[8] Science is specifically modern when it has thus conceived in advance of the possibility of experiment as taking its departure from mathematically expressible laws hidden within experience or nature. When such laws are ascertained, a new relation to the object is rendered practicable. By utilizing this new relation, modern man seeks to place objects altogether according to his will in a world subject to his technology. Technology embodies this new relation; it profits from the predictable results of mathematically grasped laws in order to take the object into its control (VA, 56). The being so "worked over" becomes the object which may be possessed and disposed of by mathematical-technological methods according to man's will.

In short, the scientist works over or thematizes the object until it can pass into the standard concepts of modern scientific theory; in this way the object comes to be subjected to calculation and control. Heidegger quotes Max Planck: "Reality is what can be rendered measurable." But in making its measurements physics must leave behind much of that which the life-world presents. It must, for example, consider the Greek physis as non-anthropomorphic, a lifeless and calculable interrelated unity of separate moving bodies in empty space. Thus, physics unveils objective nature, and other sciences take their cue and their ideal from physics. At the same time physics conceals or forgets the non-physical; it forgets the life-world.

Modern research scientists, guided in their experimentation by the ideal of exactitude and objectivity, have achieved dramatic successes. Nevertheless, they have also been said to have entered into a state of crisis. Husserl had argued that the sciences have encoun-

---

[8] HW, 75. Herman Weyl's description of experiment is not dissimilar, cf. *Philosophy of Mathematics and Natural Science* (Princeton, 1949), p. 153.

tered a crisis at their basis, as evidenced by the modern failure to relate the sciences to human subjectivity and to the life-world and by their consequent absorption of man himself into the sciences as if he were merely a complex natural object. Heidegger's approach to this crisis is an effort to understand its beginning and its ontological character.

Heidegger points out that physics cannot take itself as its own object of study, for its methods cannot work the whole science over into a single item within the same science. Thus, it cannot investigate itself. In general, sciences are non-self-reflexive. This inaccessibility of physics — or of any science — as a whole, to the techniques and concepts of that science is part of its "unapparent content" (*unscheinbaren Sachverhalt*, VA, 66). In fact, no being as a whole is accessible to a science. For "working over" the object is precisely simplifying, specializing, "mathematicizing" it; this identifying of an object as a sum of parts is the very condition for rendering it an object for a science. At the same time, the non-self-reflexive character of science prevents any evaluation of the mathematicized object in comparison with the concrete phenomenon with which a science began the "working-over" process. Other senses in which the whole being is forgotten or exceeds the range of a science will be recalled later. The present point is to note that objective reality is haunted by this concealed or unapparent content which the methods of science unavoidably leave aside, and so conceal, and so fail to respect. The scientific object is radically incomplete; ideals of scientific exactitude and objectivity may dominate a field of thought but this field can be no more than a dependent state within a larger state. And that larger state cannot in principle be subject to scientific method and rendered perspicuous on the pattern of the smaller one.

The dependent status of the physical object becomes even more obvious when it is remembered that the processes of measurement by which the object-for-physics is determined are operations; they are purposeful activities, means to ends. The object-for-physics could not be attained without the scientists' operations. In respect to its dependency upon such operations, the object-world lies within the life-world of human activity. However, it is characteristic of the scientific attitude to contemplate the physical object in abstraction from the purposeful operational processes which elicited and defined it. In this abstraction lies its impersonality. Indeed, part of the objectivity of the object is just its fixed and public aspect, its independence of any particular worker's measurements or observations. The function of the operational definitions and measuring operations in eliciting the object, in rendering it accessible, thus, tend to drop out of view. Thereby they also become part of the "unapparent content." By contrast, a part of the obligation of philosophy is to retain or regain awareness of this unapparent content.

At the present epoch in history, this neglected responsibility needs to be engaged *ab ovo*. We need, therefore, to seek out that element of Dasein through which a world of a definite sort first comes into view.

Heidegger gives the name *Befindlichkeit* to the first and determining awareness of oneself in the world (SZ, § 29f.). *Befindlichkeit* is passive; it is a given sense of the way in which one is in his world. This sense is manifest in different modes of attunement to the world. I think we may understand these modes of attunement (*Stimmungen*) or moods as the psychic aura which prevails in a world and persuades or compels its inhabitants to submit to its dominant type of motivation. They are the initial ways in which intentionality is determined, and they provide the immediate foundation for more specific intentions.

Some mood or mode of *Befindlichkeit* is always present and performing this determining or orienting function. Certain moods are relatively permanent; others are derivative and transitory. Heidegger offers an obvious example of the latter: the mood of fear. For however long it may endure, fear is a response to a threat which tends to organize all one's intentions and behavior around itself. In general, one's whole way of being in the world is always polarized in a characteristic manner by some mood. Thus moods, which were discarded as non-measurable and hence as "subjective" by many philosophers, play the initiating role for Heidegger. They suggest the way in which his philosophy develops that function which in many others is discharged by a doctrine of values. But in no sense could this element of Heidegger's philosophy correctly be described as emotionalism; rather, it offers his account of the reason why a certain emotional atmosphere, why certain unquestioned evaluations, pervade a world — e.g., our technological culture — and determine its orientation or its convictions about its own development. To understand the fundamental orientation of an epoch, then, one must discover its dominating and persistent mood or attunement.

To understand the scientific and technological era we must discover the mood which leads men to the scientific laboratory and provokes nations, during an interval of "peace," to concentrate their major energies upon sending a man to the moon.

In his essay, "Die Frage nach der Technik" (VA, 15-45), Heidegger inquires into the mood-basis of modern techniques. He proceeds by contrasting ancient techniques with modern techniques. Both reveal nature as changeable by man's manipulation, but they reveal its subordination to different kinds of intentionality. Ancient techniques (e.g., Greek *technē*) rearrange the parts and energies of nature for man's use. For instance the field is plowed and planted so that natural processes can continue, only rearranged to suit man's needs. It is otherwise with modern techniques. These techniques might strip mine the field, thus destroying it as a field in order to secure ore for smelting. And smelting is changing by processes other than those which occur naturally. These are processes which work over and release hidden energies so that they may be used in turn to release other and yet other energies. If ancient techniques merely rearrange or change the place of objects and energies, then in contrast modern techniques displace, pro-voke (*herausfordern*) and transform (*umformen*) them (VA, 31). Modern techniques reveal *(entbergen)* the character of nature by ex-propriating it. It seems to me that Heidegger's terms convey the sense of mis-placing nature and natural objects; *herausfordern* suggests a calling forth of what would otherwise remain hidden. Objects in nature which are thus intended to be used up are called *Bestand*, "stock" or "supply," something awaiting an annihilating use (VA, 24). What is the mood, Heidegger asks, which would lead one to this persistent and systematic provoking and expropriation of the natural?

Heidegger finds no word in German, and there is none in English, to name this typically modern mode of attunement to the world. He therefore adopts a word which we also shall use — *Gestell* (VA, 27). One usual meaning of this word, he notes, refers to an instrumentality for placing things, suggesting not only a basic sort of framework but also something dangerous and fearful. The name is appropriate to the mode of attunement which directs us not merely to alter nature in order to satisfy our needs but to regard it as a calculable nexus of forces altogether disposable by our ingenuity. To this mood things are as they are placed by theories and provoked by techniques. Gestell is, so to speak, the skeleton or general pattern of modern technological culture. Viewed in this mood, everything may be an instrument for freeing the energy from something else.

An important aspect of mood as elaborated in *Being and Time* is its cognitive aspect (SZ, § 31). Every mood has its understanding (*Verstehen*). The understanding which is determinative of Gestell is nowhere so clearly developed as in *What is a Thing?* (FD, 69-83). There the term "the mathematical" is used to refer to that which is taken by an epoch to be axiomatically or self-evidently true and thus is known in advance about the whole world. The quantitative mathematical properties of the world are, for Gestell, presupposed in this manner. They were divined by the Greeks, but they reached clear and explicit expression with the Newtonian laws of motion. Thus these physical-mathematical laws become for Seventeenth Century and for much of later metaphysics the invisible but real skeleton on which the experienced world is constructed. The mathematical physicist alone has the discipline and the knowledge necessary for acquiring insight into the articulation of this reality. Only he can "work over" the experienced object and reveal its hidden but real structure. Only he by penetrating to the secrets of nature can come to dominate it. Thus, the most powerful and efficient instrument at our disposal is scientific knowledge.

The technological interpretation of knowledge follows quite naturally to men of Gestell, men who are possessed by the Cartesian motive to become the masters and possessors of nature. But this mood, this initial way of Being-in-the-world, comes first. Heidegger observes that mathematical and experimental science historically preceded the development of modern technology; nevertheless, they are a single growth. Neither would have been possible in a world not dominated throughout by Gestell. The "unapparent content" of modern thought and experience is all of that which is concealed by Gestell. A criticism of the modern world or an alternative to it must, therefore, be sought in the direction of that which Gestell conceals.

Heidegger affirms that a very great danger to man lies among the possibilities of Gestell. We shall want to reach an understanding of this Heideggerian diagnosis. We shall, therefore, have to elaborate the notions of world, its relation to Dasein, and to authentic Dasein. Thus a context will be elaborated for understanding the danger offered by Gestell and for evaluating the sciences.

Part Three — On the Origin of the Real Object

Science, then, is the theory of reality. Technology is a method for calling forth and transforming the stock of reality according to will. Can some way be discovered for grasping the "real" object within its world and in its concreteness? Is there a way back to the initiation or origination of the man of Gestell who is concerned to bring the object into the scientific context and finally into this own control? The way back, Heidegger holds, is through phenomenological reflection or thought about the logos (meaning) of the being manifested as ordinary phenomena.

Just as a thing can become apparent as an object with a specific atomic structure only to the specialist who is trained in atomic physics, so a something emerges in the first place as a distinct being only to someone for whom the being *can* be there in the world. That is, the scientist's training is to the scientist rather as the human ontological endowment (*Dasein*) is to the human being; it enables him to function as the being he is. We have seen that an ontological consideration of physical objects and objectivity begins with their first emergence and transition onto the human horizon. Also it must begin with the being who possesses such a horizon, and hence to whom beings can emerge or be recalled.

Consider, by way of an analogy, a transition over a physical boundary, say by means of a jump. The actual jump is a being. We shall assume that the appropriate mood, in which the intention to make such a jump is grounded, is possessed by Dasein. Also we assume that the intention to make the jump is given. Then in addition, the act is rendered actually possible by means of a rather elaborate, though habitual, process of selecting the solid ground to leap from, measuring the distance by eye, choosing the place to land, selecting and flexing the necessary muscles, engaging the preparatory breathing, and the like. Then the leap occurs. The factual world, including one's body and its whole region, are used as tools to effect the intention. All in all, one may say that the jump is born into a place prepared to receive it. A man can jump just because he can prepare the "place" into which the jump can come to pass. We take the leap to be typical. Any human act is possible just because and to the extent that its happening can be so prepared. Furthermore, the actual preparation for an act, such as that just described, consisted of other acts. They too required preparation, in order to come into being. And shall we say that those earlier acts required yet prior ones? If the man who intended the leap and made it, is not excluded by reason of some prejudice, perhaps we may find in him the meta-physical (non-ontic) possibility or the kind of being, through which the intention to jump can make the transition from its beginning, through its preparation, and into the lived world actively and in fact. Heidegger's philosophy moves toward insight into the coming to pass of beings through the conditions for their emergence into the human world.

Any being comes "there" into our world or emerges into the horizon of our awareness in virtue of an advance preparation, as suggested by the analogy just used. Making this preparation, which throws open the horizon (the *Spielraum*) for a certain kind of experience in advance of the actual experience, is one aspect of the function of Dasein. Dasein is the opening where beings can be disclosed and acquire meaning (SZ, 137f.). Dasein must, then, be structured so that this functioning is possible. And it must be "motivated" to use this structure, that is, it must care in some fashion, for Being and its manifestations. It is this power, this care (*Sorge*) rather than some specialized view of beings already geographically there, which endows us with humanity. The structure or character of this Dasein, our Being-in-the-world, can to some extent be revealed by phenomenological reflection and analysis. We have already touched upon the most pervasive element in this structure, *Befindlichkeit*, its different modes or attunements, and its *a priori* cognitive element. In particular, we have considered Gestell, the mode of attunement or the initial preparation for the modern world. In the next section other elements of this structure will be indicated.

Our analogy of the jump over a boundary bears reference also to another ontological characteristic of Dasein: its limitations. To make the decision to leap in one direction is precisely to decide not to leap elsewhere. One course of action tends to exclude others. The value of other possible jumps is, thus, lost. Opposing moods, projects, actions must wait for other times for their realization. We have already noted that the temporality of our opening upon beings is one of the ways this finitude was brought home to Heidegger. Being is accessible to man only in time. The opening prepared for the emergence of beings (and for man himself understood as a being) is historical; in different epochs, different aspects of being have become disclosed. Correlatively, other aspects have remained hidden. The reign of Gestell in the modern world, for example, would conceal as much as it reveals. Thus, all disclosing of possibilities is also a closing of them off, a concealing. All coming into being is at the same time a passing away into non-being; this insight is fundamental for Heidegger's philosophy.

Physical objects, as we now know them, did not come to pass all at once upon our horizon; the present way of "working over" beings in order to gain access to their hidden mathematical structure so that they might be controlled was itself prepared by earlier and now obscure stages of change. In leaving behind these earlier stages — pre-Homeric, Platonic-Aristotelian, Cartesian — into which earlier men were thrown, much has been lost and forgotten, even of the originally limited disclosure. To understand the origin or emergence of physical objects, we must first distinguish the earlier levels of the power of encountering things and also attempt to recover — to "recall" — as much as possible of that which has been forgotten. Heidegger's progress toward this clarifying repetition goes from Dasein, the transcendental foundation of the world of human activity and life, through the work-world, and then to its modified form, the object-world. Here we shall note only the priority of the work-world and the emergence of the object-world from it.

Part Four — World and Reality

As the jumper prepares his leap, so Dasein prepares the life-world of instruments and tasks. Heidegger analyzes the work-world of ancient techniques in terms somewhat reminiscent of Aristotle's causal doctrine and works out a view of the "significance whole" (the "worldhood of the world") through which Dasein transcends into the world of its daily occupations *(Besorgen)* and of which Dasein and its being itself form the *Worumwillen*, the for-the-sake-of-which or final end (SZ, § 15-18). Then within this sphere of praxis, the object-world comes to be defined by the expedient of disusing certain of the tool-relations, for instance the relation to an end. It is as if the tool were broken and so dropped out of the purposive movement of praxis; still the tool remains unused, looked at with regret or curiosity. Now if this curiosity becomes impersonal and persistent, then the object may become the topic of scientific inquiry. Thus a thing comes to be real (objective) in relation to an object judging subject. The real world is derived from the work-world by a kind of abstration, or by only a partial use of the work-world. Now, the man of Gestell is oriented upon or values primarily this real object-world. Furthermore, this object-world has acquired for him the significance of a tool, not for enabling Dasein to be itself, but for enabling it to satisfy just those selected desires which are necessary to maintain the technological machine in operation.

Here the point needing emphasis is that an objective being is a real object only to an object-judging subject. To think of being primarily as object, then, is also to overlook any other function than this object judging function. Thus, this view tends to conceal not only the life-world of activity but also the Dasein which gives any world its structure. As Being-in-the-world is concealed by Dasein's directing care specifically upon its work or the task to be done, so the life-world of activity and Dasein as artist are concealed by one's self-limitation to theoretical seeing. Being tends to be concealed by revealing the life-world, and the life-world is concealed by fixing attention upon the object-world.

Is there ground for supposing Heidegger to be anti-scientific in this view of the status of the world open to theory? Of course not. Rather, Heidegger has taken as his task to point to that which has been concealed but which must be rediscovered and seen to complement objective theory and the particular world which is its object. The discovery of Dasein as mediating between the ontic and the ontological is just the discovery of a means of access to an understanding of the intention of science and of its natural or objective world. Heidegger's is no irrational rejection of science, nature, and technology, but a reasoned opposition to accepting as final and basic any view whose bases and functions have been forgotten. The ideal of objectivity and precision in formulating theories of reality is a worthy ideal surely, but it is so only because the sciences and their objects are human achievements and are derived from the life-world and its intentional structure which in turn are grounded upon Being-in-the-world. Heidegger, therefore, does not offer a view of man without nature; but he does offer a theory which finds nature or the object-world to be derivative from the life-world and from Dasein.

Part Five — The Structure of Care and Man's Separation from the Object-World

Heidegger elaborates in detail the view that the object-world is derivative from the life-world of mankind's work and activity and that both of these latter are rendered possible by Dasein and the structures through which it ex-sists into the world. Human health and well-being, or even being, are functions of the ways in which this derivation is understood. What, in fact, are the ways in which this understanding is exemplified? Obviously, Heidegger's views stand in opposition to naturalistic philosophies which identify man as nothing more than an object in the object-world. Do his views offer an adequate solution to the problem following from the Cartesian separation of man from the world? Is his solution an advance over somewhat similar proposals of Kant, Schelling, or Husserl? Or if his solution is different, is it merely a species of irrationalism? We shall have to review certain elements of the ontology of man so far developed in order to open the way to a consideration of these questions.

Heidegger views man's relation to the world not as the relation of a rational animal somehow responsive to a pre-existent rationally ordered universe but as a relation which is identical with Dasein. Man as an embodiment of Dasein is the means by which meanings, whether rational or other, are given both to himself and to other beings.

According to Heidegger Dasein is not an empirical subject. It is "in" the world only as mediating between the ontic and the ontological; it is that through which the world is given its unified structure of worldhood, and consequently it may be said in this mediate sense to be the source of the meaning given to worldly beings. Since Dasein functions as the mediating source or the beginning of the meaning assigned to beings, whether to subjects or to objects, the concept of Dasein suggests a solution to the problem of man's alienation or separation from the world.

Consider an illustration of meaning-giving. We say that a house is not a home except insofar as the house is given a meaning by one's dwelling in it and caring for it. Quite possibly, though, this consequence of one's care is not recognized until the home has been destroyed or until for some reason one has left it. Similarly one's life-world is such in consequence of one's living and working in it and caring for these activities.

But one might ask, why care? Why does Dasein project a world? As the place of a tool in the work process does not become evident until the tool is broken or inoperative, so the role of world is not evident until the familiar world itself is somehow cancelled.

Heidegger in several famous passages describes the fading away of the world in the attunement of anxiety (*Angst*, cf. SZ, § 40f.). For anxiety is fear, but it is a formless fear; it comes from no specifiable source; it is of nothing. In this basic attunement one is alone, and the world loses its familiar presence. One feels *unheimlich*, uncanny, alien. Beneath the familiarity of the world is thus revealed a threatening worldlessness. One may, therefore, suspect that the everyday world usually projected is a protection against this strange worldlessness. Still it can be asked: what of worldlessness? Why desire protection against it? The answer is not far to seek: the end of one's world is death; anxiety in the face of the nothingness of death requires no apology. Furthermore, a sort of worldlessness is suffered by anyone who is masquerading or leading an inauthentic life, a life not his own (*uneigentlich*). Dasein projects a world precisely in order to be itself. It cares for the world because it cares for itself, indeed *is* this care. Thus, the phenomenon of anxiety brings the everyday empirical self face to face with the more original self which cares for self and world indivisibly. One may say, then, that the phenomenon of self-world is a primordial and unitary phenomenon.

The problem of the relation of the ontic (empirical) subject to the object is, therefore, not so much resolved as transported to the prior phenomenal plane where self and world are, at least under certain conditions, experienced as one. This experience may become the topic of analysis, an analysis which will throw light upon the ontic separation of subject from object and perhaps also upon the alienation of modern man from the technological world.

Dasein, accordingly, is said to be care, but care is not easily defined. Moreover, since care is not an object and in no way has the character of any object definable within a conventional universe of discourse, it may appear not to be definable at all. Nevertheless, care is not merely a vague notion; it can be placed within its limits and these limits can be seen to have a phenomenological basis. In this sense, care can be understood. Its limits are first expressed by the ontological terms: existence, facticity, and fallenness.

Existence used in this ontological sense refers to Dasein's initial unity with a world and to his power for living in and working in (and on) this world. But living on and working on the world tend to change it; hence, existence refers also to his tendency to turn away from this world and to destroy it. Dasein's existence is also

limited in two other closely related ways; these are indicated by the
terms facticity and fallenness. Facticity refers to the pre-determined
character of the context within which Dasein finds itself. It alludes
to the way human being is involved with and necessitated by other
beings and is dependent upon their being just as they are (SZ, 56,
135). Facticity is to Dasein as factuality is to non-Dasein-like beings. The primary instance of facticity is a man's being thrown into
his world and time without any choice on his part and without any
reason why this context rather than that. One is born into an elaborated world and into an epoch of history. The absolute contingency
of this fact simply cannot be controlled or rendered transparent (SZ,
103). Moreover, the circumstances of the given environment limit
one at every turn. The beings among which one is thrown are what
they are. Facticity is a denial of any sort of fancied power to originate or directly to control or to alter their nature. It is the representative in Heidegger's thought of the ancient fate *(anagkē)* and effectively prevents classification of his philosophy as an idealism.

The third way in which Dasein's transcendence is limited is
rather more subtle, but it is also indicated by the etymology of the
word 'existence.' Heidegger points out that existence derives from
the Greek, existasthai, which he translates to mean departure from
permanence (EM, 49) and refers it by way of a grammatical
metaphor to a declination away from the primary Being. At its extreme, this declining will end in non-being. This declination I interpret to refer to the "falling" of *Being and Time* (SZ, § 34B).

Falling, regarded as a constitutive element in care must not be
identified with inauthentic Being, although clearly there is a relation between the two. Care, whether authentic or inauthentic, is
always falling since "falling belongs to care itself" (SZ, 294). However, Heidegger so vividly describes one sort of fallenness in terms
of "unrooted" idle talk, vain curiosity, and identification with the
impersonal mass man that many interpreters tend to see in these
phenomena the whole reach of fallenness (SZ, 166 sq.). This view is
superficial. Falling may better be interpreted as the necessity of
Dasein for caring for other beings.

Acceptance of and active engagement in the world is scarcely a
matter of choice; rather, it is the consequence of throwness and of
the limited ways in which Dasein can accept and deal with the
facticity of its worldly involvements. Dasein must be involved with
other beings, it must be concerned with the beings, roles, minor and

major purposes required by the demands of daily life. These insistent tasks cloud over or conceal Dasein's vision of its own individual possibilities for Being. For instance, they conceal Dasein's function as the *Worumwillen* of the world. In consequence, Dasein is diverted or falls away from its own Being. Its vision of itself as the final end or essential for-the-sake-of-which that defines its world, is liable to a tragic distortion. This distortion is experienced as an alienation of man from his world. Today it is conceptually expressed in many ways: for example, as the Cartesian subject separated from the object world, as the Positivist man-as-object estranged from man as he knows himself subjectively, or as the technological culture by which man expected to dominate the world but by which he appears to be wholly dominated. In short, according to Heidegger's view, modern man can scarcely be said to have a very perceptive grasp upon his fate.

Fundamentally, falling is an inevitable inclination to lose sight of the truth of one's Being. It is a dimming of the understanding of oneself, of one's possibilities and limitations. This failure to grasp one's Being with transparency and clarity is a source of guilt, surely, but an ontological source, one which belongs to Dasein's finite character. For Dasein is not possessed of an infinite understanding to which the whole of Being and of beings could be simultaneously transparent. Dasein's unavoidable engagement in the life-world, which is already a falling away from its Being, places a limitation upon the possible intelligibility of its world. Obviously this doctrine is not a run-of-the-mill irrationalism; in no sense is it a surrender to unreason. Rather, it is a thoughtful reinterpretation of the phenomena presented by human life to the effect that no ontological defense can be discovered for the presupposition that being is or can become completely intelligible to man's intellect.

Heidegger's own questioning led him back by way of the experience of anxiety to the phenomenon of his own oneness with the life-world, a phenomenon whose logos is care and the structure of care. Analysis of this structure led to his interpretation of the current metaphysical and epistemological separation of subject from object in terms of a blind or inauthentic fallingness. Thus, an ontologically prior unity gives rise to a derived duality of subject and object, but this duality appears to be basic and irreducible from the point of view of a Dasein which is unaware of its own falling. That this solution of the problem elicited by Descartes' separation of man

from the world is neither a repetition of old attempts nor a recourse
to irrationalism or to idealism I take to be evident. But it does belong to the transcendental type of solution, and it does lead to a
limitation on rationalism. That this solution is in every respect complete is another matter, one to which I shall return briefly in the
last section of this study.

From the present day perspective of Gestell, the typically
modern scientific world picture could become current only under
the circumstance that a single view of man as the knowing subject
and of objects as illimitably knowable, given the correct method,
should come so to dominate the scene that no other view could offer
competition. Thus, Dasein as Being-in-the-world became lost, forgotten. The world of familiar objects ranged over against subjects
came to appear to be final, given. Likewise, all the philosophical
problems concerning the relations between these two metaphysical
ultimates, subjects and objects, became insistent, but insoluable.
The next and final step of this development arrived when it appeared possible and advantageous to some philosophers to redefine
the subject exclusively as a peculiar and complex sort of object.
Thus, human subjects could become the objects of a science.

Now, man regarded as a peculiar object which can somehow
get into sufficient touch with other objects to acquire objective
knowledge of them and to control them is the popular view. Govern-
ments support it. Just this apparent ultimacy of man's separation
from the world is presented by Heidegger as a sort of ontological
illusion which follows in part from the intrinsic limitations of men's
being, the inclination toward fallingness, and in part also from his
avoidable failure to question his being in such a way as to keep
those limitations transparently before him.

Much of Heidegger's attention is given over to the description
and analysis of the contrasting modality of Dasein's existence, the
authentic or "owned" *(eigentlich)* existence. His views on this topic
cannot be developed at length here. Suffice it to observe that one of
the elements essential to being authentic Dasein is a noetic component which Heidegger calls transparency (*Durchsichtigkeit*, SZ,
146f., 307). The term refers to a persistent awareness of the finite
character of human existence, of its involvement with facticity, of
its inclination to fall away from its world, of its indebtedness for its
own being, and of its thrownness into history and to death. Preservation of this awareness can alter the quality of the time and the

character of the world which one inhabits. One may say that this authenticity is a resolution to make one's subjectivity more thoroughly one's own. It also may be said to be a resolution to respect the whole of Being.

Heidegger has asserted that the terms authentic and inauthentic are intended to be descriptive only and not evaluative. I think it clear, though, that they are intended to provide a basis for expressing an evaluation of the modern world. We now turn to this evaluation.

Part Six — Evaluation of Science and Technology

The evaluation of the sciences and technology which follows from the philosophical standpoint here set forth emerges when three elements are related. These three are science and technology, authentic Dasein, and Dasein functioning as the for-the-sake-of-which. When these three are appropriately juxtaposed, some apprehension should develop of the nature of the danger which is said to lurk in Gestell. Then science and technology may be evaluated in terms of their relationship to man. The several sections immediately preceding have sketched the perspective within which the three elements may be appropriately juxtaposed.

First, we may eliminate the most common objection to Heidegger's philosophy. In opposition to the critics who say that Heidegger exhibits a Romantic rejection or devaluation of the natural world and its sciences, we must observe that natural science and technology are not ontologically independent beings. They are founded within the life-world, and their evaluation must be related to this dependence. Let it be emphasized that the sciences and technology could certainly be pursued by authentic Dasein. There is no reason in this philosophy for concluding that the sciences of nature and their utilization are inauthentic in their own right. To the contrary, they are beings within the life-world and are dependent upon it. The structure of world, it will be recalled again, is revealed in Dasein. And it is Dasein, not technology, which may properly be either authentic or inauthentic. Dasein, by misunderstanding its own being and misplacing itself in inauthenticity, may render the whole world inauthentic in a derivative sense. Under these conditions, but only in this derivative sense, could nature or the sciences be judged to be inauthentic. We must conclude that Heidegger's evaluation of the sciences is determined rather by what he believes contemporary man has made of them than by their independent character.

Heidegger's criticisms and warnings are addressed to contemporary man and are provoked by his recognition of the danger inherent in the modern outlook (Gestell) upon the world. The danger follows from the fact that men today are not merely preoccupied as of old with the tool-world and other workers in order to provide the basic necessities of life together with a modest supply of luxuries. They are tempted to become entirely absorbed — Heidegger's term is "fascinated" (*benommen*, SZ, 271) — by the very demanding universe of natural objects studied and manipulated by the sciences.[9] Hence, a much more compelling temptation follows to interpret the self on the model of some being other than Dasein. To interpret the self on the model of an object, however, is to forget perhaps even to lose authentic Dasein.

Gestell, understood in abstraction from Dasein, seems to offer a limitless perspective upon nature. Also, again understood in abstraction from other and latent possibilities of Dasein, Gestell seems to open the *only* reasonable perspective upon nature. Finally, the astounding successes of this view of the world seem to confirm its infinity and its unique appropriateness.[10] The threat of Gestell, in short, is the seductive promise of infinite power over the world offered upon one condition: the forgetfulness of Dasein. And modern man continually yields to this temptation. No doubt in our time we should be reminded of the machine model, the computer model, or the rat model of the human being, or the model of the impersonal organization man. In other words, modern man, tempted away from an understanding of his own distinctive being, has been persuaded to "work over" himself — and others — as the technical scientist works over the useful thing, in order to reduce it to an object and to subject it to scientific examination and then to technical control.

This interpretation of the self on the model of some non-human object and the acceptance of persons as resources are instances of falling. And falling, as a dimension of care, is inescapable. However,

[9] "In general, we are involuntarily linked to technique, whether we passionately affirm it or passionately deny it" (VA, 13).

[10] In this sentence I use "success" in a popular sense. Seen over a longer time range, these successes may be failures even when measured by popular standards; cf. Barry Commoner, *Science and Survival* (New York: Macmillan Co., 1963).

the falling which loses transparency, which loses sight of its direction of movement, so to speak, is the falling of inauthentic Dasein. The appropriate effort is not to avoid falling but to avoid a blind and inauthentic falling.

Thus, the point is not that these non-human models of the self are unequivocally and in every respect false. All of them have their interest and scientific importance. They lead astray, however, when they become predominant and so fascinate the students of them that these students forget the powers and limitations of their own being, their Dasein. For then thrownness, human finitude, individuality, freedom, and mortality are denied or overlooked, and the appropriate price for these denials must eventually be exacted.

The most serious consequence of visualizing oneself upon the model of some non-human or non-Dasein-like being becomes evident when it is recalled that the crucial element in the structure of the world is the for-the-sake-of-which, Dasein himself. In changing his view of himself, Dasein is changing the crucial factor in the worldhood of the world; thus, he changes his world. And now he has become a "human resource" within the world rather than its determining or final factor. Consequently, the contemporary world has become a world virtually without man; at the best it is a world in which men are estranged from their own humanity.

Thus Heidegger sees the danger associated with Gestell not in science, nor even in technology nor in machines as such, but rather in man who has lost his insight into man and behaves toward himself and to others as though all were non-Dasein-like objects.

The loss of insight consequent upon accepting Gestell not as one revelation but as the total and final revelation of Being leads also to the end of philosophy. The skeleton or death which lurks within Gestell is precisely a threat to Being, in particular to man's Being. Philosophically, such a man no longer apprehends himself as mediating between the ontic and the ontological; rather, he struggles with the problem of the relation between mind and body or between subject and object, or he stands aside altogether while he clarifies the words in which such problems are sometimes phrased, or he moves on to the last stage: he serves the state by designing attractive ideologies useful for capturing and exploiting the masses.

This evaluation of the sciences and technology points to the contemporary philosophical task; this is each individual's problem of discovering where he is situated *vis à vis* the modern attunement to the world with the eventual purpose of countering the blindness with which Gestell is more and more commonly accepted. Is there then, some method for recapturing a more human, a more authentic, Being-in-the-world?

Part Seven — From Gestell to Gelassenheit

The current self and our Western convictions about human nature Heidegger seems to say, have been caught up in routines which effectively blind us to the alternative possibilities which an understanding of Dasein might reveal. Man, absorbed by Gestell, has disappeared into the object-world; his predicament repeats Hume's interpretation of the self as a series of space-like points. In his later writings, therefore, Heidegger appears to direct his consideration upon the kind of change which might lift contemporary man out of the repetition of routines now become meaningless and open the way to a more authentic existence and to a renewed vision of his fate. For example, he suggests that our energies be devoted to what he calls thought or recollection of Being (*Andenken*). This thought of Being, however, has been difficult for him to characterize. It seems to be a turn to a sort of docile contemplation of Being, a "letting be" or "releasement" (*Gelassenheit*). Releasement, I suggest, is an initial mode of attunement to the world which is quite opposite to the mood of intellectual and technical domination of Gestell. Releasement is described as the patient waiting for the silent voice of Being. This receptive waiting of psyche is held to be the appropriate function of man, for only by this waiting is Dasein effective in bringing Being to appearance. Only thus does man become the shepherd of Being. One aspect of this contemplation is difficult to understand; the initiating function seems to be taken away from man. The "thought of Being" is as much a thinking done by Being through man as it is man's thinking of Being. (In this regard, Heidegger is reminiscent of the ancient Greeks for whom the gods, to whom they had access through psyche, were as much a center as were the things of this world, to which they had access through perception assisted by the discursive mind.)

Many readers of Heidegger have trouble in following him in this turn (the *Kehre*). Some regard it as a turn to mysticism; others take it to be a decision for idealism. Heidegger's turn falls into its proper perspective, though, when placed in relation to his reading of history. Likewise a key to understanding it is provided by the three-fold structure which we have already seen in the analysis of care, and of Dasein's existential limitations.

According to my understanding, Heidegger reads Western history as a choice dating from Socrates and Plato, to regard man as the decisive factor in being. This decision remained for a long time more or less implicit until it emerged as the cogito in the philosophy of Descartes, as the I-principle (the "I think . . .") of Kant, and as the Romantic belief in the infinite productiveness and self-creativeness of the ego. In the Humean and scientific traditions this Romantic belief in the creativeness of the self is rejected as unrealistic or as outright non-sense; nevertheless, the same decision is even more effectively present in positivism and in allied philosophies, though in an altered guise. It is present as "subjectism" or the resolution to subject the whole of nature to man's technological control. The dominating assumption of this mode of attunement might be expressed in our phrase: being is identical with being as evident to the scientific mind. Now, the emphasis placed upon Dasein's receptivity, so noticeable since the *Kehre*, is to be interpreted as an explicit turn away from this characteristic decision of Western philosophy whether expressed within an idealistic, realistic, or positivistic context. Rather it is a turn toward the identification of Being as that which gives possibilities or as that from which intuitions or inspirations may be received. Heidegger rejects the anthropocentrism of tradition. The major central position is held in his philosophy by Being; although, man might still be said to be a minor center insofar as Dasein, functioning in and through him, brings Being to evidence as beings. The famous *Kehre* is simply a turn to Being as accessible through a deepening understanding of Dasein.

The analysis of this turn, which at the same time is evidence of Heidegger's continuing anti-idealism, may be carried forward by exhibiting the moments in the renewal of the care structure. The renewed and authentic Dasein shows a change in the character of his temporality. It manifests, for example, an acceptance of facticity. This acceptance is exemplified in understanding pastness as "repetition," or by way of an interpretation which uncovers and reactivates meanings previously sedimented and forgotten. Dasein's orientation to the future may be thought of, I suggest, as a new interpretation of the *Worumwillen*, the for-the-sake-of-which. The function of authentic Dasein is explicity understood to be the unconcealing of

Being. This Dasein is aware of existing as the opening in which Being, the power of world-making, comes to evidence and expression. The world is for the sake of Dasein, but authentic Dasein is for the sake of Being. This particular acceptance of facticity and this orientation to the future are united in the receptivity of "releasement" which most obviously rejects the self-centeredness of tradition and yields instead to the way possibilities are given by Being in the "moment of vision" (SZ, 292). Just as Heidegger interpreted Kant as placing thought in the service of intuition, so now Heidegger is to be interpreted as placing intuition or receptivity in the service of Being. And thus Heidegger points away from the ego-centeredness of the modern tradition (Gestell) and seeks to effect a transition to a new vision of man whose existence is centered both upon Being and upon his own Dasein function, a vision which resolutly accepts his fallingness, his finitude, and his thrownness.

How, in terms of this article, is the change in human being to which Heidegger points to be understood? Certainly his movement is not toward an idealism. Rather all three of the factors involved in this change are to be placed in the service of a Being which by no stretch of the imagination could be identified with a Hegelian absolute or with any other idealist ultimate. More positively, this contemplative waiting upon a non-objective and non-ideal Being might be described as a waiting upon inspiration. This is a receptive thought which waits and listens, hoping to recollect or to become aware of some hint or inspiration from that Being which is prior to the distinction between subject and object. It is only questionably — and questioningly — intellectualist. Rather, it seeks to include ratiocinative and mathematical thinking within a larger context of possibilities, the totality of which cannot in principle become evident to finite mind.

Consider how Heidegger describes this meditative and receptive thought or "releasement" in *Gelassenheit*. First, it can be achieved only by Dasein whose vision has been rectified by becoming authentically itself. Secondly, and especially to the present point, it is a will-less and non-representative thinking (the Scientist in the "Conversation ... about Thinking," included in *Gelassenheit*, experienced difficulty in conceiving and conceding this point). More positively, "releasement" is a waiting which is a "release into openness" (G, 44) or an acceptance of the coming forth of truth upon the initiative of Being (G, 61). And just this unconcealment of Being as intimated also elsewhere (e.g., in the essay, "What is Metaphysics") is the "naming of the holy," a naming specifically destinguished as the poetic function. But the philosophic function is said not to be the poet's.[11] Unfortunately, Heidegger does not clarify the distinction between the two.[12] Also, he does hold that both share in maintaining a docile and receptive attitude toward the coming or unconcealment of Being. Both, then, are engaged in meditative thought. In general, as it is written in *Aus der Erfahrung des Denkens* (1947), "We do not come to thinking; rather it comes to us" (ED, 11). This receptive thinking comes to us as the poetic word which is the *Da* of the renewed and authentic Dasein; "Poetically man dwells upon this earth." *Gelassenheit,* as Paul Ricoeur remarks, "is the gift of poetical life."[13]

In the terms of this article, the receptive, will-less, non-representative, respectful thought about Being in which authentic Dasein engages, is a contemplation which seems at first glance to require an identification with poetic thought. At the least it would necessitate releasement from the concern with beings which is demanded by the highly specialized and complex tasks presented by industry and research today. Thus, it would certainly put an end to fascination exclusively with problem-solving thought and its technological utilization. The emotions with which it is associated are the tranquil and contemplative emotions, opposite to those associated with the aggressive-defensive attitude of Gestell. Would a poetic self-surrender such as this also require a surrender of philosophy?

If the philosopher were resolved altogether to forget the discipline of precision and to listen only for the non-representative voice of Being, would not philosophy have reached its end? Here is the mystical strain which some critics find in his later writings. And it must be admitted that of late, Heidegger speaks primarily for Being and as a representative of poetic thinking. It is sometimes difficult to find the relation of this kind of thinking to precise and communicable doctrine. At least to this extent there is some color to the accusation of mysticism. However, the *Kehre* is not altogether

[11] "The thinker utters Being. The poet names what is holy" (WM, 51).

[12] A point made also by L. Landgrebe in *Major Problems in Contemporary European Philosophy,* tr. K. Reinhardt (New York: Ungar Publishing Co., 1966), p. 143f.

[13] "The Critique of Subjectivity and Cogito in the Philosophy of Martin Heidegger," in *Heidegger and the Quest for Truth,* ed. M. S. Frings (Chicago: Quadrangle Books, 1968), pp. 62-75.

a turn away from the earlier and non-mystical philosophy. It is a turn toward a thinking which is complementary to objective and ratiocinative thinking. If Heidegger were charged with not working out the detail of the relation between these two kinds of thought, perhaps he might reply that not all tasks can be accomplished at once, or that much of this detail is already present in his writings. Still the question is difficult and commentators are divided.[14]

I shall go no further than to observe that Heidegger points the way from Gestell to *Gelassenheit,* but it is difficult to discern all the steps which must lie along this way. To describe "releasement" so as to eliminate the unintended overtones of mysticism, perhaps of "misology," to clarify the movement of transcendence from Gestell to this releasement, and to specify the relation between the use of mind characteristic of Gestell and that characteristic of releasement, these are the tasks which require completion if a philosophical point of vantage is fully to be gained from which the human world may be envisaged and if the danger which lurks in Gestell is to be seen clearly and neutralized.

[14] W. J. Richardson, in *Heidegger: Through Phenomenology to Thought* (The Hague: Nijhoff, 1963), p. 241ff., says this turn involves something new yet coherent with Heidegger's development. But other views are also to be found, cf. Demske, *Sein, Menschen, und Tod* (Freiburg: K. Albert, 1963), chap. 5; also John Sallis, "La différence ontologique et l'unité de la pensée de Heidegger," *Rev. Phil. de Louvain,* 65 (1967), 192-206. Cf. also Heidegger's letter contained in Richardson, *op. cit.,* p. xvi.

Truth as Art: An Interpretation of Heidegger's *Sein und Zeit* (Sec. 44) And *Der Ursprung Des Kunstwerkes*

C. D. Keyes

" 'Art and nothing but art', said Nietzsche, 'we have art in order not to die of the truth'." — Camus.[1]
"For the true sublime, by virtue of its nature, elevates us: uplifted with a sense of proud possession . . . as if we had ourselves produced the very thing we heard." — Longinus.[2]
"All art as such is essentially poetry." — Heidegger (HW, 59).

The view that art is a disclosure of truth is traditional in aesthetics. Yet the ontological basis for this connection between art and truth has not always been clarified even when it has been affirmed. In fact, as Heidegger suggests, the meaning of truth (SZ, 214-20, 224-26) and art (HW, 66) alike has been obscured. Truth has often been treated as if it were a correct correspondence between the mind and facts. And art has accordingly been treated as if it were a reproduction of the factually-present world (HW, 25 f., 30) or as if an appreciation of art could be reduced to criteria like "pleasure" (HW, 67). Or to put it another way, the questions of art and truth have ordinarily been treated "inauthentically."

---

[1] Albert Camus, *The Myth of Sisyphus and Other Essays,* trans. J. O'Brien (New York: Random House, 1955), p. 69.
[2] Longinus, *On the Sublime,* trans. W. H. Fyfe, VII. 2, in "The Loeb Classical Library" (London: Heinemann, 1965), p. 139.

It is necessary to try to disclose the ontological foundations of art and truth in order to think them together and in order to allow them to come into their authenticity. Our existence itself demands that we do this. Just as man is the only being (*Seiendes*) that can be concerned with his Being (*Sein*) (SZ, 5-8) and because this concern is radically his own (*Jemeinigkeit*) (SZ, 42), even so the creation or "preservation" (*Bewahrung*) (HW, 54–56) of an art-work is an aspect of the same truthful concern. Truth frees man, and art is the most profound truth, for it can disclose more than the ordinary way of looking at life. Whether aesthetic[3] creativity or sensitivity is affirmed because it is the only justification of existence in a universe without God (Nietzsche,[4] Camus[5]) or whether it is understood as a moment of the dialectic that leads to God (St. Bonaventura[6]) or the Absolute (Hegel[7]), art is nevertheless a matter of ultimate importance.

Of course, philosophy may trivialize itself and refuse to think the ultimate questions, renouncing even the courage to give them negative answers. In the same way art and human existence can be trivialized, and triviality can be enshrined by ages and institutions and mistaken for sophistication. Still, our radical contingency (*Geworfenheit*) and our Being-towards-death, if truthfully and authentically apprehended, can destroy the triviality and force us into the domain where art and its truth disclose their "weightiness." In this way, the truthfulness of authentic thinking can be compared (ontically) with what Longinus wrote about "great style" and "weightiness":

> For it is impossible that those whose thoughts . . . are
> petty and servile should flash out anything . . . worthy of
> immortal life. No, a great style is the natural outcome of

[3] According to Heidegger (HW, 66-68; cf. 15), "aesthetics" is a misleading term because it implies that man stands in a subject-object relation with an art-object which results in "sense apprehension" (*aisthesis; Sinnlichen Vernehmens*) or "experience" (*Erlebnis*) of such an object. Cf. SZ, 33, 226.

[4] F. Nietzsche, *Birth of Tragedy*, trans. W. Kaufman (New York: Random House, 1967), Sec. 5, p. 52; Sec. 24, p. 141.

[5] Camus, *Sisyphus*, pp. 69-87.

[6] St. Bonaventura, *The Mind's Road to God*, II. 5, trans. G. Boas, in Vol. 32 of "The Library of Liberal Arts" (New York and Indianapolis: Bobbs-Merrill), pp. 16f.

[7] G. W. F. Hegel, *Phänomenologie des Geistes*, ed. D. J. Schulze, in Vol. 2 of *Werke* (Berlin: Duncker und Humblot, 1832), pp. 527-61.

weighty thoughts, and sublime sayings naturally fall to men of spirit.[8]

The purpose of this essay is to discuss the ontology of art and truth in relation to one another and to raise a question in conclusion about the nature of philosophical thinking in relation to art. The method will be to give an interpretation of Heidegger's (1) *Der Ursprung des Kunstwerkes* (henceforth "KW") and of (2) Sec. 44 of *Sein und Zeit* (henceforth "SZ"), (3) suggesting how the dialectic which is common to KW and Sec. 44 of SZ can be subsumed into the structure of *Sorge*,[9] before (4) asking finally whether philosophical thinking itself can be regarded as thought's art-work.

(1) The Origin of the Art-Work

In order to think the truth of an art-work it is necessary for thought to discover the significance of art at a more primordial level than the subject-object dichotomy. Expressed simply, this will involve two things: First, it will require bringing into view the "work-character" of an art-work. Second, it will mean thinking the truth (or "origin"[10]) of such an art-work.

The Work-Character of an Art-Work

An art-work for Heidegger is a "symbol" because something that has been made is "brought together" (*symballein*) with more than itself. That which is "more than" the thing that was made is "truth" in the sense that will be indicated later. At the moment, however, it is necessary to show how the art-work *functions as a thing* before thinking the manner in which truth is originated in relation to it. Considered *as* a thing an art-work is a "functional-instrument" (*Zeug*) in the sense that it is not a mere object but rather an object

[8] Longinus, *Sublime*, IX. 3f., p. 145.

[9] "Sorge", English "care" (Latin "cura"), is not translated in the text in order to call attention to the fact that Heidegger uses the term in a special way. The term does not refer primarily to the content of actual experience of "care", but instead it refers to the underlying, *a priori*, ontological structure that makes such (ontical) experiences possible.

[10] "Was das Wort Ursprung hier meint, ist aus dem Wesen der Wahrheit gedacht" (HW, 67; cf. HW, 7): "Ursprung bedeutet hier jenes, von woher und wodurch eine Sache ist, was sie ist und wie sie ist. Das, was etwas ist, wie es ist, nennen wir sein Wesen. Der Ursprung von etwas ist die Herkunft seines Wesens."

which serves a purpose. In fact, any functional-instrument (e.g., a pair of shoes) has more in common with an art-work than a mere thing (e.g., a block of granite) has, precisely because an art-work and a "functional-instrument" are *produced to function*:

> Therefore, a functional-instrument is half thing, because it is determined by the character of a thing, and yet it is more than this. At the same time, it is half art-work, and yet it is less than this, because it lacks the self-sufficiency of an art-work. A functional-instrument occupies a peculiar position between a thing and a work .... (HW, 18).

In order to illustrate the connection between a "functional-instrument" and an art-work, Heidegger uses the example of a painting by Van Gogh that shows a peasant woman's shoes. The actual shoes themselves *functioned* for the woman who wore them and were "reliable" for her because they were instruments that she *used* to admit her to a whole context of actions. The painting by Van Gogh is not an art-work because it described the shoes factually as if they were something "tangibly-present" (*Vorhandenen*) (HW, 22–25; cf. 30f.). Instead, it is an art-work because it is a truthful disclosure that reveals what the shoes *are in their function*: "The art-work announced what the shoes as functional-instruments are in truth . . . . Van Gogh's painting is the opening up of what the functional-instrument, the peasant woman's pair of shoes, *is* in truth" (HW, 24f.). In other words, the art-work truthfully *opens* the function of something, by disclosing the Being of the being that functions: "Therefore, the essence of art could be stated this way: the truth of beings setting-itself-into-a-work" (HW, 25). At the same time, the thing-character of an art-work is such that, as a functional-instrument, it points beyond its thing-character to give priority to the ontological disclosure that it expresses: ". . . we now no longer ask the question of the thing-like properties in a work [of art]; for as long as we ask about that we immediately interpret a work [of art] just as a tangibly-present (*vorhandenen*) object" (HW, 56; cf. 52).

Expressed as simply as possible, an art-work is a functional-instrument that functions to point to more than functionality. Its function is to disclose Being, a function that also causes us to distinguish between beings and Being. The ontological disclosure that an art-work functions to produce in respect to a being is "truth":

This being comes forth in the disclosure (*Unverborgen-heit*) of its Being. The Greeks named this disclosure of beings truth (*aletheia*) (HW, 25; cf. 39). The art-work, in its own way, opens up (*eröffnet*) the Being of beings ... i.e., the revelation (*Entbergen*), i.e., the truth of beings (HW, 28).

The same idea can also be expressed another way by saying that an art-work functions to establish "World," i.e., the "ontological context" in which a "functional-instrument" *is*: "The establishment of a World belongs to the Being of a work [of art] (HW, 34). Therefore, "truth", "disclosure" (*Unverborgenheit* and its related context of terms), the distincition between Being and beings, and "World" are all a single context of phenomena: "The work [of art] holds open the openness of the 'World' " (HW, 34). It is this context that the work character of an art-work functions to institute.

The Truth of an Art-Work

Just as an art-work is not primordially an object that a subject experiences in the subject-object relation, neither is truth exper-ienced primordially in such a relationship, but instead both truth and an art-work have their "origin" in the ontological disclosure, an origin that is more basic than the subject-object distinction. By the same token, beauty cannot be comprehended as something that a subject perceives objectively in an art-work. Instead, beauty is the *appearing* of truth, i.e., the disclosure of Being: "Truth is the dis-closure of beings as beings. Truth is the truth of Being .... If truth sets itself in a work [of art], it appears. This appearing (*Erschein-en*) is ... beauty" (HW, 67; cf. 44). When truth is thus established in an art-work, a being is disclosed in a unique and unrepeatable way: "The institution of truth in a work[of art] is the bringing forth of such a being in a way that never was before and never will be again" (HW, 50).

Yet at the same time, the unrepeatable ontological disclosure which constitutes an art-work is established in such a way that an-other person can "stand in" the "preservation" and thereby enter into its original truth: "The preservation of a work [of art] means this: standing in the openness of beings which happens in a work [of art]" (HW, 55). Heidegger compares this entrance into the truth of an art-work with *Dasein*'s coming into its authentic resoluteness (*Ent-schlossenheit*), namely the condition in which *Dasein* realizes its "ontological disclosure" (*Unverborgenheit des Seins*):

> In 'Sein und Zeit' what is meant by authentic resoluteness is not an action a subject decides upon, but *Dasein's* opening up from constraint among beings to the openness of Being ... the essence of existence (*Existenz*) is standing outside [of constraint by] standing in the essential divergence [from the ordinary that is constitutive] of the lighting up of beings[11] (HW, 55; See also SZ, 299-301, 305-10, 349f.).

When both the creation and the "preservation" of an art-work are taken into account we can come to a clearer definition of the truth of art. It is at once the "setting into work" of the ontological disclosure of beings (*Unverborgenheit des Seienden*) as well as the preservation of the disclosure: "Thus art is: the creative preservation of truth in a work. Art, then, is a becoming and happening of truth" (HW, 59). Art brings us to the nihilation of all that is merely factual (*Vorhandenen*) and ordinary. It produces a "clearing" (*Lichtung*) (HW, 59).

The Dialectic of Truth and Un-Truth

To summarize the foregoing as simply as possible, (1) an art-work is a "functional-instrument" whose function is (2) to disclose truth (and its related context of phenomena), i.e., to produce the "ontological openness" of the "clearing." But the truth of an art-work also has an ironic quality: It is not merely ontological openness; it is the openness which has been achieved in a dialectical relation with its opposite, even in a strife with its opposite. The truth of art is not merely the truthful disclosure of Being, but it is a truthful disclosure that has taken "un-truth" into account. The most extreme expression of this idea is that "truth is un-truth" or that truth is strife (HW, 49). The strife of truth with its opposite is what produces the "clearing" or "ontological opening" (*Offene*). It is a strife that knows at once the authentically nihilating effect of Nothing-

---

[11] "Die in 'Sein und Zeit' gedachte Entschlossenheit ist nicht die decidierte Aktion eines Subjekts, sondern die Eröffnung des Daseins aus der Befangenheit im Seienden zur Offenheit des Seins ... das Wesen der Existenz ist das ausstehende Innestehen im wesenhaften Auseinander der Lichtung des Seienden" (HW, 55).

ness (to all that is merely factual and trivial[12]) as well as the totality of Being[13] that Nothingness entails. "World" is the context in which this occurs, for it is where the "clearing"[14] takes place and the context in which the strife is held. World is the context of the dialectic of an art-work's truth. But the context of this dialectic, namely "World," also has its own dialectic with its interdependent opposite called "Earth."[15]

When World and Earth are contrasted, the former is a tendency to openness, and the latter is a tendency to concealment ("self-closing").[16] But the dialectic of Earth and World is more subtle than that, for the two are also dependent upon one another and inter-penetrate each other,[17] and both give rise to the truthful disclosure since they cooperate with one another in producing the ontological opening.[18] The strife of Earth and World by which the truthful onto-logical disclosure is brought forth is called a "Riss,"[19] a term that A. Hofstadter[20] translates as "rift-design" (in order to cover an other-wise untranslatable ambivalence in the German word). Of the var-

---

[12] "Dann entsteht die Wahrheit aus dem Nichts? In der Tat, wenn mit dem Nichts das blosse Nicht des Seienden gemeint und wenn dabei das Seiende als jenes gewöhnlich Vorhandene vorgestellt ist, ... Aus dem Vorhandenen und Gewöhnlichen wird die Wahrheit niemals abgelesen" (HW, 59).

[13] "Inmitten des Seienden im Ganzen west eine offene Stelle. Ein Lichtung ist. . . . Diese offene Mitte ist daher nicht vom Seienden umschlossen, sondern die lichtende Mitte selbst umkreist wie das Nichts, das wir kaum kennen, alles Seiende" (HW, 41).

[14] See Otto Pöggeler, *Der Denkweg Martin Heideggers* (Pfullingen: Neske), p. 249f., and John C. Sallis, "Art Within the Limits of Finitude," *International Philosophical Quarterly*, 7 (1967), 285-97, p. 295.

[15] Pöggeler, *Denkweg*, 247-67. Cf. FW, 3 and VA, 50-55.

[16] "Die Welt ist die sich öffnende Offenheit. . . . Die Erde ist das zu nichts gedrängte Hervorkommen des ständig Sichverschliessenden und dergestalt Bergenden" (HW, 37).

[17] "Welt und Erde sind wesenhaft von einander verschienden und doch niemals getrennt. Die Welt gründet sich auf die Erde, und Erde durchragt die Welt" (HW, 37).

[18] "Zum Offenen gehört eine Welt und die Erde. Aber die Welt ist nicht einfach das Offene, was der Lichtung, die Erde ist nicht das Verschlossene, was der Verbergung entspricht" (HW, 43).

[19] "Der Streit ist kein Riss als das Aufreissen einer blossen Kluft, sondern der Streit ist die Innigkeit des Sichzugehörens der Streitenden" (HW, 51). "Das Gesehen-haben ist ein Entschiedensein; ist Innestehen in dem Streit, den das Werk in den Riss gefügt hat" (HW, 56).

[20] A. Hofstadter, trans. of M. Heidegger, *The Origin of the Work of Art*, in pp. 649-701 of A. Hofstadter and R. Kuhns, eds., *Philosophies of Art and Beauty: Selected Readings from Plato to Heidegger*, "Modern Library" (New York: Random House, 1964), p. 686, n. 2.

ious things that the "rift-design" signifies, two points seem to be especially significant in the present interpretation, the first of which is somewhat less textually explicit in KW than the second: (1) The "*rift*-design," by implication, is the differentiation[21] by which Being and beings are distinguished (Cf. SZ, 5–8), a distinction which, ironically, is the presupposition for allowing the being (whose Being was thereby disclosed) to be "self-closing" as well as "opening": "When a World opens itself the Earth comes to tower up. It manifests itself as the sustainer of all things, as that which in its law is safely hidden (*Geborgene*) and continually self-closing" (HW, 51). (2) The "rift-*design*" is also the mark of createdness which is left by the truthful ontological disclosure: "Being-created discloses itself as a strife Being-established in a figure (*Gestalt*) through a rift-design" (HW, 54). To leave the mark of createdness in this way (and thereby to bring truth into the open) is *to make use of* the self-closing tendency called Earth and to allow it to function as a thing (*Ding*) or "instrument" (*Zeug*) (HW, 57) (although not a "functional-instrument" that is absorbed into mere servicability, HW, 52) that expresses truth. In this way the analysis has run a full circuit, and the work-character of an art-work is restated, but this time not only from the standpoint of its function to express truth but also of truth's expressing itself in the World-Earth dialectic. This means that the functional character of an art-work can be grounded in the ontology of truth's disclosure. But something else can also be concluded. Because the truth of an art-work has the character of a "functional-instrument," art is something "invented" (*gedichtet*). That is to say, art is essentially "poetry" (*Dichtung*): "Truth happens as the lighting up (*Lichtung*) and concealing (*Verbergung*) of beings in that it is invented (*gedichtet*). As letting the advent of the truth of beings happen, all art as such is essentially poetry (*Dichtung*)" (HW, 59).

The Transition Back to "Sein und Zeit"

In KW Heidegger specifically cites SZ in the context of his dis-

---

[21] "Das Sein ist die Offenheit des Seienden: ein Seiendes kommt in sein Sein, wenn es eigens als das genommen wird, das es ist. Wird ein Seiendes *als* Seiendes genommen, dann entsteht in ihm ein Riss: . . . Der Riss reisst den Unterschied zwischen Sein und Seienden auf; . . . . So erfährt er als das Zugleich von Entbergen und Verbergen, als das Ereignis der Unverborgenheit." Pöggeler, *Denkweg*, p. 249.

cussion of the strife of truth and un-truth (HW, 49). Accordingly, truth[22] (and its context of related terms) and un-truth[23] (and its context of related terms) play an obviously important part in Sec. 44 of SZ as well as in KW, but it will be shown in the following discussion that the dialectic of truth and un-truth in SZ Sec. 44 is the same type of dialectic that was found in KW. Also, Heidegger speifically refers to SZ another time in KW (HW, 55) when he compares the entrance into the truth of an art-work with the authentic resoluteness *(Ent-schlossenheit; cf. Erschlossenheit)* of SZ. And, in at least still a third place, the language of KW seems more or less directly reminiscent of the language of SZ: "Truth is never gathered out of the tangibly-present *(Vorhandenen)* and ordinary. On the contrary, the opening up *(Eröffnung)* of the opening *(Offenen)* and the lighting up of beings happens only in that the openness which makes its appearance in radical contingency *(Geworfenheit)* is projected *(entworfen)*"[24] (HW, 59; cf. SZ, 223).

Whether or not KW represents, as Fr. Richardson observes, a "level that is attainable only by Heidegger II, where Being has assumed the primacy over There-being,"[25] it is still clear that all the elements of the dialectic of the truth of an art-work can be found in SZ. The point, however, is not only that KW and SZ share the same dialectic (that we are still within the same "hermeneutic circuit") but that this dialectic which SZ and KW share also permeates the unity of *Dasein* (through the *Sorge*-structure) in SZ. If SZ is indeed poetry, it is poetry in the sense that it is the ultimate art because it wins truth from a context that includes authenticity's dialectic with its opposite and because its "authentically truthful discourse" *(Rede)* can issue forth in word and speech that *function* to disclose truth.

---

[22] "Das Wahrsein des *logos* als *apophansis* ist das *aletheuein* in der Weise des *apophainesthai*: Seiendes — aus der Verborgenheit herausnehmend — in seiner Unverborgenheit (Entdecktheit) sehen lassen" (SZ, 219).

[23] "Den Unverständigen dagegen *lanthanei*, bleibt in Verborgenheit, was sie tun; *epilanthanontai*, sie vergessen, das heisst, es sinkt ihnen wieder in die Verborgenheit zurück" (SZ, 219; see also SZ, 166-80).

[24] "Aus dem Vorhandenen und Gewöhnlichen wird die Wahrheit niemals abgelessen. Vielmehr geschieht die Eröffnung des Offenen und die Lichtung des Seienden nur, indem die in der Geworfenheit ankommende Offenheit entworfen wird" (HW, 59).

[25] William J. Richardson, *Heidegger: Through Phenomenology to Thought,* 2nd ed. (The Hague: Nijhoff, 1967), p. 417.

(2) Section 44 (a, b) of "Sein und Zeit"

Authenticity and inauthenticity are, of course, correlated respectively with the "ontological openness" context of terms and with
the "ontological concealment" context of terms. The over-all *a priori*
structure that includes *both contexts and their interrelation* (i.e., the
structure that is the fullest expression of *Dasein's* Being-in-the-
World) is the *Sorge*-structure:

> The existential *(existenzial)* ontological condition by
> which Being-in-the-World is defined through 'truth' and
> 'untruth' lies in *the* ontological composition of *Dasein* that
> we designate as *radically contingent project (geworfenen
> Entwurf)*. It is an intrinsic element of the structure of
> *Sorge*"[26] (SZ, 223; cf. HW, 59).

It is within the *Sorge*-structure that truth and its opposite have their
dialectic. Yet it is also within the *Sorge*-structure that the truthful
disclosure is won, as Heidegger suggests in another context (Sec.
69): "In it [*Sorge*] is grounded the full truthful disclosure of the
Da [*of Dasein*]" (SZ, 350). The truth of authenticity (SZ, 307-10,
316) and the un-truth of inauthenticity (SZ, 127) in SZ therefore
have a relationship with one another that is similar to the dialectical
relation of truth and un-truth in KW in the sense that the truth of
authenticity and the truth of art alike are won through a conflict
with their respective opposites. It is necessary now to show how
this dialectic operates in SZ Sec. 44 after first establishing the context of that section.

Sec. 44, "Dasein, Erschlossenheit and Wahrheit," comes at the
end of the First Division of SZ as well as at the end of Ch. 6, "Die
Sorge als Sein des Daseins." This section, then, is the point at which
the pre-temporal analysis of *Dasein* ends. Its obvious purpose is to
contrast the primordial sense of truth with the objective (traditional) sense and to suggest how these are related to one another.
In the development of this contrast we discover not only (1) the
question of the relation of truth and un-truth, which has already
been noted, but also another theme common to KW, (2) the question of "functionality" and its related context of phenomena (*Zu-*

---

[26] "Die existenzial-ontologische Bedingung dafür, dass der In-der-Welt-sein
durch 'Wahrheit' und 'Unwahrheit' bestimmt ist, liegt in *der* Seinsverfassung
des Daseins, die wir als den *geworfenen Entwurf* kennzeichnenten. Sie ist die
Konstitutivum der Struktur der Sorge" (SZ, 223).

handensein, Zeug, Besorgen, etc.). These two themes will now be discussed in the order indicated.

The Dialectical Character of Truth

First, Heidegger takes Parmenides' statement "to gar auto noein estin te kai einai" as his point of departure in showing that the question of truth is an ontological question. The traditional and the primordial senses of truth are distinguished in this way: The traditional senses are those that presuppose a subject-object dichotomy, i.e., the view that (1) truth is the "assertion" (*Aussage*) of a judgment (*Urteil*), or that it (2) lies in the agreement (*Übereinstimmung*) between the judgment and its object, or that (3) it is simply "agreement." Even though these definitions of truth (as well as the "adaequatio intellectus et rei" that derives from them) are "inauthentic" because they have "objectified" truth, they nevertheless arise from the primordial sense of truth (as the next subdivision of this essay will suggest) and provide clues as to its meaning. In other words, they raise ontological questions which they cannot solve. For example, if we say that truth is "assertion," then we have implicitly raised a question about the kind of Being that assertion is. Or if we say that truth is "adaequatio intellectus et rei," then we have implied, but have not answered, a question about the "relational totality" (*Beziehungsganze*) of Being in which "adaequatio" is supposed to take place (SZ, 214–18).

The primordial sense of truth is more basic than any of the traditional senses because it is more basic than the subject-object dichotomy upon which the traditional senses are founded. The primordial sense of truth must be sought in terms of the phenomenon of Being-in-the-World as the ontological context of *Dasein*'s Being and knowing and of its relations. Within *Dasein*'s Being-in-the-World, the most primordial meaning of truth is the "quality of discovery" (*Entdecktheit*). It is "Being-discovered" (*entdeckt-sein*) that determines the truth of assertions because it is what allows a being to be brought out of concealment (*Verborgenheit: lanthanei*) into disclosure (*Unverborgenheit: a-letheia*): *"The existential-ontological basis of discovering (Entdeckens) is that by which the most primordial phenomenon of truth first makes its appearance"* (SZ, 220).

This discovering of truth in the primordial sense involves both (a) the discoverer (*Dasein*) and (b) that which is discovered

(*Seiende*), i.e., respectively (a) "Being-discovering" (*entdeckend-sein*) and (b) "Being-discovered" (*entdeckt-sein*). It is possible for beings (*Seiende*) to have a relation to the "quality of discovery" only because "Being-discovering" is a dimension of the discoverer's, *Dasein*'s, ontology: "Being true as Being-discovering is a way of Being for Dasein . . . . Discovering is a way of Being for Being-in-the World. Functional . . . concern *(umsichtige . . . Besorgen)* discovers beings within the World" (SZ, 220). The fundamental and primary sense of truth therefore belongs to *Dasein*'s ontology as Being-in-the-World, but there is an additional implication in the last quotation: The relationship of *Dasein* to a being it discovers within the World (*entdecken innerweltliches Seiendes*) (SZ, 66–84) is characterized by "functional concern" (*umsichtige . . . Besorgen*) which means that the discovering of truth in the primordial sense entails the functional-presence (*Zuhandensein*) of the being in question as a "functional-instrument" (*Zeug*). This observation will be of primary concern in the next sub-division of the essay, while the main concern now is the observation that *Dasein*'s discovering truth is a dimension of its ontology and that the obscuring of truth is also a dimension of *Dasein*'s ontology. It is *Dasein*'s "falling" (*Verfallen*), a term used to describe inauthenticity, that is the ontological condition for concealment and un-truth: "*Because it is essentially falling (verfallend) Dasein's ontological composition is accordingly in 'untruth'*" (SZ, 222).

This suggests that *Dasein* constitutes and is constituted by "truth" and "un-truth" at the same time. And it also implies that truth must be discovered from within the same ontological context by which both truth and un-truth are constituted, i.e., that truthful discovery has to involve itself in a dialectic with un-truth: "Truth (the quality of discovery) must always first be wrested from beings. Beings (*Seiende*) are torn from concealment. The . . . quality of discovery is always like a *robbery*" (SZ, 222). This implies that both SZ Sec. 44 and KW are able to reach the same essential conclusion, namely that truth is a negation of the opposite of truth (hence, the Alpha-privative in *a-letheia*). Truth depends upon *Dasein* (SZ, 220, 222, 226, 230), and *Dasein* is the discoverer, but the truthful discovery can take place only because truth and un-truth are dialectically related.

"Functional-Presence"

Second, as it was noted in the next to the last paragraph, the discovering of truth entails a functional relation with "beings within the World" (SZ, 220). This means that the truthful discovery is not only a dialectical negation of un-truth, but it also means that the same dialectic is involved with functionality as in KW where an art-work's truth uses a "functional-instrument" to symbolize that which transcends functionality. However, in the present context this dialectic between functionality and the discovering of truth is also the basis, in part, for the transmutation of the primordial sense of truth into the views that truth is "assertion" or "adaequatio." Assertion has a link with the primordial sense of truth as "Being-discovering" : "The *Being true* (*truth*) of assertion must be understood as *Being-discovering*" (SZ, 218). At the same time, assertion is also "functional": "Assertion is an instance of functional-presence" (SZ, 224). Truth is given expression through functional-presence because *Dasein*'s fundamental relation with the beings which are discovered in a relationship of concern (*Besorgen*), and the origin of *Dasein*'s ability to discover and to make truthful assertions is founded upon "understanding" (*Verstand*) (SZ, 223). Yet when an assertion is made about the "quality of discovery" (*Entdecktheit*), *Dasein* must communicate the discovery *about something* in such a way that the truthful discovery is established: "An assertion which is expressed contains ... the quality of discovery of beings. This is preserved in the expression. It is as if the expression became an instance of functional-presence within the World which can be taken up and stated again" (SZ, 224).

Dasein must establish its truthful discovery by expressing its assertion in the mode of functional-presence. In this way the expression can acquire an ontological structure in its own right, and such a structure can have its own relation to the same beings that *Dasein* has truthfully discovered. We have already noticed assertion's connection with "functional-presence," but the relation between the assertion and the beings about which the truthful discovery was made in a relation of "objective-presence" (*Vorhandensein*): "The quality of discovery about [something] becomes an objectively-present conformity of one instance of objective presence (the expressed assertion) *to* [another] instance of objective-presence (the being under discussion)" (SZ, 224). The discovery of truth itself is an authentic existential discovery, and yet the irony of discovering truth is that the discovery can be in-authentically transformed into "objective truth" characterized by "objective-presence" and an objectively-present relation between "intellectus" and "res."[27]

It is in this way that truth and un-truth have their dialectic with one another. Not only does *Dasein* have to grasp truth from a dia-lectic with its opposite, but truth once grasped can itself be leveled off, as the last quotation suggests in its account of the advent of the traditional sense of truth from the primordial sense. Incidentially, the advent of the traditional sense of truth shows that "functional-presence" can have a double significance; it can either conceal (in the sense that it leads to the objectifying of truth, SZ 118–21, 424; cf. 325–56) or it can reveal (in the sense that truth is initially sym-bolized by means of a functional-instrument, SZ 76-88, esp. 84f.; cf. 352–56). Perhaps, as a matter of degree, it is the former tendency that dominates SZ Sec. 44, while the latter (the revelatory tendency of functional-instruments) dominates KW. The essential point, how-ever, is that in both works truth is inevitably wrested from a con-text that includes its opposite and, further, that the procedure of expressing truth involves "functionality" and the entire range of phenomena connected with it.

Summary

In SZ Sec. 44 and KW alike, truth and un-truth are dialectically related: "Primordially, *Dasein* is in truth and un-truth alike" (SZ, 223). Earlier it was noted that the *Sorge*-structure is what gives *Dasein* the capability of existing in such a way that its Being involves both truth and un-truth. The fact that this dialectic of truth and un-truth is expressed in terms of *Sorge*, however, has an additional significance. It means that the same dialectic permeates the totality

---

[27] *"Die Entdecktheit des Seienden rückt mit der Ausgesprochenheit der Aussage in die Seinsart des innerweltlich Zuhandenen. Sofern sich nun aber in ihr ALS ENTDECKTHEIT VON . . . ein Bezug zu Vorhandenem durchhalt, wird die Entdecktheit (Wahrheit) ihrerseits zu einer vorhandenen Beziehung zwischen Vorhandenen (intellectus und res). . . . Wahrheit als Erschlossenheit und entdeckendes Sein zu entdecktem Seienden ist zur Wahrheit als Übereinstimmung zwischen innerweltlich Vorhandenem geworden. Damit ist die ontologische Abkünftigkeit des traditionellen Wahrheitsbegriffes aufgezeigt"* (SZ, 225).

of *Dasein's* Being because the four elements (SZ, 221f.) by which *Dasein's* relation to truth is summarized are the same elements that designate *Dasein's* totality (as will be shown in the next division of this essay): (i) the "truthful disclosure" (*Erschlossenheit*), (ii) "radical contingency" *(Geworfenheit)*, (iii) "project" *(Entwurf)*, and (iv) "falling" (*Verfallen*). The first of these elements pertains to the totality itself of *Dasein's* Being, while the last three elements articulate that totality. These three can be set out in the following scheme (by reversing the order of "project" and "radical contingency" in order to show more easily their affinity with the temporalized elements of the *Sorge*-structure) in what will be called "Diagram I":

(1) "Project" (*Entwurf*): This is the ontological structure
 (a) of *Dasein's* "ontological possibilities" *(Seinkönnen)*
 (b) in which we find the primary *locus* of authenticity or "the truth of existence" *(die Wahrheit der Existenz")*.
(2) "Radical Contingency" (*Geworfenheit*): This is the givenness of the ontological structure
 (a) of *Dasein's* relation to "beings within the World" (*innerweltlichen Seienden*), and
 (b) of the "facticity" of truthful disclosure: "Truthful disclosure is essentially factical" *(Die Erchlossenheit ist wesenhaft faktische)*.
(3) "Falling" (*Verfallen*): This is the ontological structure
 (a) through which *Dasein* relates itself to "beings within the World" (*innerweltlichen Seienden*) in such a way that they are inauthentically objectified, and is thereby the structure
 (b) in which we find the primary *locus* of inauthenticity by which "*Dasein* is in un-truth" (*Dasein ist in der Unwahrheit*).

These three elements of Diagram I (plus the fourth element, *Erschlossenheit*, that arises out of the unity of the others) are expressive of the same dialectic as the truth of an art-work in KW because both Diagram I and the dialectic of KW involve (a) the interrelation of truth (*Wahrheit*) and un-truth (*Unwahrheit*) in the discovery of truth (*Erschlossenheit*), and both involve (b) truth's relation to the functionality context (*innerweltlichen Seienden*). Beyond this, however, the way these three elements also articulate the totality of *Dasein's* Being can be clarified by showing explicitly how they are dimensions of *Sorge* and, accordingly, how *Sorge* is temporalized. This can be done in the following manner:

(3) The "Sorge"-Structure and "Dasein's" Unity

Heidegger gives his specific definition of *Sorge* in Sec. 41 of SZ: "Self-anticipatory-already-Being-in-(the-World-) as Being-with (beings encountered within the World)"[28] (SZ, 192; see also, 220). This definition itself can be broken down into its constituent elements thus:

(1) "Self-anticipatory-"
(2) "already-Being-in-(the-World-)"
(3) "as Being-with (beings encountered within the World)."

Furthermore, these three elements which constitute the specific definition of *Sorge* can be correlated with what Heidegger calls *Dasein*'s "three fundamental characteristics" (SZ, 249f.) and with the "three ecstases of time" (SZ, 327ff.) in order to arrive at a single scheme which will be called "Diagram II":[29]

Elements of "Sorge"	"Dasein's" Characteristics	Modes of Time
(1) "Self-anticipatory—"	(1) "Existence"	(1) "Future"
(2) "already-Being-in-(the-World—)"	(2) "Facticity"	(2) "Past"
(3) "as Being-with (beings encountered within the World)."	(3) "Falling"	(3) "Present"

Since "project" and "existence" are correlated terms (SZ, 145, 147, 221, 249f., 264, 325), and since "radical contingency" and

---

[28] "Sich-vorweg-schon-sein-in-(der-Welt-) als Sein-bei (innerweltlich begegnendem Seienden)" (SZ, 192).

[29] Elements of "Sorge"	"Dasein's Characteristics"	Modes of Time
(1) "Sich-vorweg-"	(1) "Existenz"	(1) "Zukunft"
(2) "schon-sein-in-(der-Welt-)"	(2) "Faktizität"	(2) "Gewesen-heit"
(3) "als Sein-bei (innerweltlich begegnendem Seienden)."	(3) "Verfallen"	(3) "Gegen-wärtigen"

This diagram is taken from C. D. Keyes, *From Nihilism to Comedy: A Phenomenological and Systematic Study in Philosophical Theism* (Pittsburgh: Duquesne University unpublished Ph.D. dissertation, 1968), p. 37.

"facticity" are also correlated with one another (SZ, 135, 179),[30] the three elements of Diagram I that describe the dialectic of truth and un-truth are therefore capable of being subsumed respectively into the corresponding elements of Diagram II:

Diagram I	Diagram II
(1) "Project"	(1) "Existence"
(2) "Radical Contingency"	(2) "Facticity"
(3) "Falling"	(3) "Falling"

The three elements of Diagram I that describe the dialectic of truth and un-truth are dimensions of *Dasein's* ultimate composition because, as structures of *Sorge* (i.e., as capable of being subsumed into Diagram II), their articulation is therefore *temporal*:

> The totality of the *Sorge*-structure does not emerge first as a linking together; nevertheless it is *articulated* . . . (SZ, 317). *Temporality reveals itself as the sense of authentic Sorge* (SZ, 326). . . . *The most primordial unity of the Sorge-structure lies in temporality* (SZ, 327).

It is *Dasein's* temporal articulation that constitutes its Being as a dialectic of truth and un-truth: "The truthful disclosure of the *Da* [of *Dasein*] and the basic experiential (*existenziellen*) possibilities of *Dasein*, authenticity and inauthenticity, are founded in temporality" (SZ, 350). Both "truthful disclosure" (*Erschlossenheit*) (SZ, 223) and "authentic resoluteness" (*Entschlossenheit*) (SZ, 301) must be won through the same totality of the temporal ecstases. Just as the articulation of each temporal ecstasis demands the others, and thereby calls upon the totality of *Dasein's* Being, even so the dialectic of truth and un-truth which calls upon each mode of time can lay claim to *Dasein's* totality as temporalized *Sorge* in the most basic possible way. This means that the ontology of an artwork, i.e., the winning of truth within a context that involves both truth and un-truth, is not an isolated ontology but lies, instead, at the heart of *Dasein's* Being. It is in this way that the link between art and truth is finally justified. They are both grounded in the same primordial existential phenomenon and share the same dialectical

---

[30] Cf. SZ, 222: "Zur *Faktizität* des Daseins gehören Verschlossenheit und Verdecktheit." In this quotation Heidegger is apparently speaking of one of the ways *Faktizität* can be expressed, i.e., as *Verfallen*, in the same way that Being-in-the-World has inauthenticity as one manner in which it can be expressed. Thus, (see above, n. 29), line 2 can be formulated into line 3.

subtlety. In the simplest terms possible, *Dasein* is the dialectic of an art-work, and an art-work is the dialectic of *Dasein*.

(4) Can Philosophy Be Thought's Art-Work?

How can this be thought? In fact, how can any of the questions under consideration be thought? Does the thinking of them not constitute a single context with what is thought? Is the same dialectic by which an art-work is constituted not also present in the thinking of that dialectic? Asked another way, is philosophical reflection not in some sense an art-work in itself? Can philosophy's truth not be regarded as the truth of art? That is the concluding question of the essay. The raising of such a question in this particular way goes beyond the explicit concerns of the texts which have been under consideration. Yet perhaps a clue is present in KW and SZ. In KW philosophy is understood as the concern for the truth of beings (HW, 50), and in Sec. 7 of SZ "authentically truthful discourse" *(Rede)* is the *logos* of phenomenology (SZ, 33; see also, 154-60, 223-26).

Authentically Truthful Discourse

Since philosophy's concern is the truth of beings and since truth is the ontological openness to which "authentically truthful discourse" attests as *logos,* it is reasonable to try to think the meaning of philosophy and "authentically truthful discourse" together. To do this, however, is to think the meaning of philosophy on the same foundation as the temporalized unity in which the dialectic of an art-work is expressed as constructive of *Dasein's* total Being, for both are grounded in the same unity: "Therefore authentically truthful discourse does not temporalize itself primarily in one ecstasis [of time]. . . . Authentically truthful discourse is . . . grounded in the ecstatical unity of time" (SZ, 349; cf. 163). "Authentically truthful discourse" is, in other words, grounded in temporalized *Sorge* (SZ, 350; cf. 277) and thereby involves itself in a dialectical relationship with the dimensions of un-truthfulness (or inauthenticity) that are included in the apriority of *Sorge.*

The dialectical character of "authentically truthful discourse" can be illustrated in this way, for example: In the call of conscience (SZ, 271) "authentically truthful discourse" brings *Dasein* to its authenticity and to the Nothingness that at once negates the triviality of conformity to The Group (*das Man*) and gives *Dasein* its truth totality as Being-in-the-World: "What could be more alien to The Group (*das Man*), which is lost in the functionally-concerned (*besorgte*) and diverse 'World', than the Self which is individualized, alone, uncanny, and thrown contingently (*geworfene*) into Nothingness?" (SZ, 277). In other words, "authentically truthful discourse" is truthful and authentic because it *negates* a negation, namely the un-truthfulness of inauthenticity and the "trivial small talk" (*Gerede*, SZ, 167-70) of The Group. "Authentically truthful discourse" gains its truthfulness, as the truth of an art-work does, through a relation with un-truth.

"Authentically truthful discourse" is similar to the truth of an art-work in respect to functionality also, for as the truth of art demands a "functional-instrument" through which it can be symbolized, in the same way "authentically truthful discourse" can turn into speech. In itself "authentically truthful discourse" is not the same as speech (or any other ontically definable condition). Instead, it is the existential-ontological foundation of speech (SZ, 160) which can issue forth in speech whose words are *functional*: "The outward expression of authentically truthful discourse is speech. This totality of words, . . . thus comes to be like an instance of functional-presence which one can meet" (SZ, 161).

"Authentically truthful discourse" is as ironic as the truth it expresses because it must call *Dasein* from its inauthentic relation to "functional-presence" (SZ, 187), and yet if it should issue in speech, the words themselves become "functional", just as (in KW) an art-work is a revelatory "functional-instrument" which is invented (*gedichtet*). This means that Heidegger can say that the essence of art is "poetry" (*Dichtung*) (HW, 60). Both an art-work and "authentically truthful discourse" which has issued in speech, therefore, must be considered revelatory in their functional character. By the same token (in SZ, 162), "authentically truthful discourse" itself can also be "poetic": "The communication of the existential possibilities of ontological sensitivity (*Befindlichkeit*), namely the disclosing of existence (*Existenz*), can become the particular goal of 'poetic' (*dichtenden*) authentically truthful discourse."

The Question

An art-work brings truth to light, just as "authentically truthful discourse" does. Both have won truth in a conflict with un-truth. Both are "poetic", and both have arisen from a dialectic that can be expressed as belonging to the totality of *Dasein*. If indeed authentically truthful discourse is the very language of philosophy and can issue forth in symbols that function truthfully, then can philosophy itself not be regarded as a type of art-work? Is it not possible that the historic branch of philosophy called "aesthetics" can now be regarded as the foundation? Can a metaphysical system itself not be regarded as an aesthetic creation differing from a given art-work only in the sense that it is a comprehensive structuring of many art-works (conceptual symbols)? If so, speculative philosophy will have superseded the contemporary critique of metaphysics and at the same time will have reclaimed its perennial task of disclosing truth. On such a foundation the truth it can disclose is the deepest truth, the truth of art, truth that has its own way of announcing its necessity: "It is only as an *aesthetic phenomenon* that existence and the world are eternally justified."[31]

[31] Nietzsche, *Tragedy*, Sec. 5, p. 52.

The Language of the Event:
The Event of Language

Theodore Kisiel

With the recent publication of the already well-known lecture of January 31, 1962 entitled "Time and Being," Heidegger's thought seems to have at last officially come full circle, and appears to bring some degree of completion to all that Heidegger had announced he would undertake in his prospectus in *Being and Time* (SZ, 39), though not exactly as it was announced there. The second part of this prospectus, dealing with the "phenomenological destruction of the history of ontology," has proliferated far beyond the announced three divisions, notably in the Nietzsche volumes and including some of the lectures and essays most recently collected in *Wegmarken*. The outstanding omission has always been the third division of the first part, entitled "Time and Being," which was to have completed the chain begun by the two divisions published as *Being and Time*. These two divisions, which concluded by showing that temporality was the Being of the being which understands Being, of Dasein, was to have been completed by "the explication of time as the transcendental horizon of the question of Being." In the *Letter on Humanism*, Heidegger explains that this division was withheld because the available language of metaphysics (presumably including such phrases as "transcendental horizon") was inadequate to express the turn from "Being and Time" to "Time and Being" (PW, 72). This is not to say that no breakthrough to the

85

articulation of this turn was made until the recent lecture on the issue. In the same letter, Heidegger indicates that the lecture *On the Essence of Truth* (1930–1943) already gained a measure of insight into this turn. And according to Heidegger, the pivotal "concept" of this turn, *das Ereignis* (the appropriating event), was already at work in his thought during this period (US, 260), appearing thematically in the Hölderlin essays and in *The Origin of the Artwork* (1936), although it received no sustained treatment in his publications until *Identity and Difference* (1957) and *Underway to Language* (1959).

The incubation period was evidently necessary in order to develop a language suitable to express the issues and relationships involved in the turn. Not that the long preparation and waiting period for the necessary transformation is over. Heidegger continues to reiterate that he is still "underway to language." The 1962 lecture still proceeds "cautiously" and "with foresight" (ZS, 20), without hindsight back to metaphysics and its readily available language, groping its way toward a remarkable realm that does not readily yield to articulation. Not that an entirely new language of neologisms must be invented to bring the domain of the appropriating event to the fore. Rather, what Heidegger seeks is "a transformed relationship to the essence of the old language."[1]

Heidegger's use of language has long been a philosophical notoriety. Carnap's parody of Heidegger's "propositions" on Nothing has become a stock in trade in the positivistic debunking of metaphysics. Heidegger's response to such critiques are characteristically comprehensive. For him, the linguistic standards of logical positivism are simply the natural conclusion of a long tradition of the metaphysical approach to language, and hence themselves metaphysical. The first step in transforming our attitude to language is then to "destroy" the logical-grammatical interpretation of language, centered on the proposition and its subject-predicate relationship, that a metaphysics of substance and of subject has conveyed to us, in order to clear the way for orienting language to the pre-predicative realm which is its source. It is in this re-orientation that Heidegger looks for new possibilities of expression that would hold themselves closer to this source. It is to some of these linguistic strategies

[1] According to his letter published in the preface to William J. Richardson, *Heidegger: Through Phenomenology to Thought* (The Hague: Martinus Nijhoff, 1963), p. XXIII.

that at once turn from metaphysical ways of speaking and toward a more fundamental penetration of the origins of language that we wish to address ourselves here. The choice of possibilities are manifold, e.g., Heidegger's interest in poetry and in Oriental ways of speaking, but the focus of our attention will be on the language of the event. Since the appropriating event lies at the very center of Heidegger's thought, the most basic traits of the transmutation of language that he seeks are to be found here. A more detailed characterization of the background and the approaches to this domain will help point the way in our investigation. Special emphasis will be placed on the linguistic devices used in these approaches, the first of which is the vicarious role which the "and" plays in Being "and" Time.

On the "And" in Being and Time

It is often said that Heidegger is a man of one thought: Being. To say this relates him to a long tradition of Western philosophy, but it does not truly indicate what his unique question is. What we must do is to get a glimpse of his central concern, of that one thought which has troubled him from the beginning, that draws him over and over again to the effort of thinking and that gathers all of his reflections together. What we are after is what Heidegger himself calls *die Sache*, "that which concerns thought, that which for thought never ceases to be a question, that which is the very point of the question" (FP, 183).

His answers to Fr. Richardson's questions concerning his *Denkweg* are particularly enlightening on this point. Referring to the Aristotelian statement that "being is said in many ways," which opens Brentano's inquiry into the manifold sense of being in Aristotle, the book which led him from the gymnasium into philosophy, Heidegger tells us that "latent in this phrase is the question which determined my *Denkweg*: what is the pervasive, simple, unified determination of Being that permeates all of its multiple meanings?"[2] But before the "common origin" of the polyvalence of Being can be established, a prior question must first be answered, namely, "whence does Being as such (not merely being as being) receive its determination?"[3] The phenomenological character of the

[2] *Ibid.*, pp. X-XI.
[3] *Ibid.*

quest for the source of the *Sinngebung* implied in this question only
came to the fore later when Heidegger came in contact with the
phenomenological "method," which he interprets for himself in
terms of the basic Greek senses of *phainesthai* (to show itself) and
logos (to make manifest). This he identifies as the first of three
decisive insights that clarified the venture of considering the Being-
question as a question which seeks the sense (*Sinn*) of Being. The
second was the interpretation of *aletheia* as unconcealment, gleaned
from reading Aristotle, and the third the recognition that presence
is the fundamental trait of Being as *ousia*. And Being as presence
develops into the question of Being in terms of its time character.

Such is the complex of questions and insights which sets the
stage for the problematic of Dasein posed in 1927 under the title
Being and Time, in which "the 'and' in this title holds within itself
the central problem. Neither Being nor time have to give up their
hitherto constituted meanings, but a more original interpretation
must establish their justification and their limits" (KM, 219). That
Being is related to time is already contained in "the possibilities
prepared for us by the 'ancients,'" (SZ, 19) who conceived Being as
permanence in presence (*aei on, ousia, parousia*) and the whatness
of beings as "that which has always been," which in turn was one
form of *a priori* and hence "earlier" (KM, 216-17). And time has
long functioned as a criterion for distinguishing realms of Being into
the temporal, atemporal and supratemporal, so that even eternity
was interpreted as a *nunc stans*, a permanent now. And yet why
Being should spontaneously be conceived in terms of time has never
really been made an explicit theme of philosophical inquiry. In opposition to this obliviousness, Heidegger sets himself the task of
showing "that and how the central problematic of all ontology is
rooted in the phenomenon of time, when rightly seen and rightly
explained" (SZ, 18). In order for metaphysics in its entire history to
be properly founded, one must make explicit the hidden relations of
Being and time, the terms in which the very first thinkers of the
question spontaneously expressed the issue, in which terms present
thinkers continue to express themselves, manifesting that "the understanding of Being in Dasein almost of itself projects Being upon
time" (KM, 219). The most apparent juncture of Being and time,
at least in 1927, is then *Dasein* itself.

The issue of Being and time seems to resemble the well-known metaphysical distinctions of Being and becoming, Being and appearance, and Being and thinking. But the "and" of the metaphysical distinctions is disjunctive: Being *and not.* . . . It serves to introduce something other than Being, which delimits Being and still somehow belongs to it. But "in the formula 'Being and time', 'Being' is not something other than 'time' inasmuch as 'time' is named as the forename for the truth of Being, where truth is the essencing of Being and therefore Being itself" (WM, 17). Therefore, the essence of time considered within the question of Being points toward a completely different realm of inquiry than the metaphysical distinctions (EM, 157). And yet the most consequential of these metaphysical distinctions, Being and thinking, can be turned in the very same direction by investigating thinking not as a power of men but as a power of aboriginal Being, as the first essay in *Identity and Difference* does.

All of Heidegger is then an attempt to read Being and time into one another. Being and time are "convertible" terms, i.e., they "turn together." And the thrust of the later Heidegger converges on a focus of thought in which Being "and" time are read into one another to such a degree that they become One in a simple center which is the source of both. This "and," left unspecified by the early Heidegger, is now given the singular and proper name of *das Ereignis* and described as the e-vent that appropriates Being and time, the It that gives both, the third that has always been first, and as such, the secret power hidden in both Being and time and holding the two in a relationship of reserve. But the two terms being unified have also developed in the course of the *Denkweg*. Hence he now states that "the task of thought better perceived now needs a more appropriate determination of the theme which had otherwise been indicated under the title *Being and Time*. The title ought now to read *Presence and Clearing (Anwesenheit und Lichtung)*" (FP, 173).

It is in these deepened terms that Heidegger finally understands his preliminary question, "Whence does Being as such receive its determination?" and its answer: "Being is determined by the reach of time." And in reply to the first question, it appears that the simple unified "determination" of Being, the "common origin" which pervades all of its multiple meanings is now the event out of which Being as presence and time as clearing become apropos to each other.

If instead of "time" we substitute: clearing of the self-
concealing of presenting (*Anwesen*), then Being is determined by the reach of time. This comes about, however,
only insofar as the clearing of self-concealing assumes in
its want a thought corresponding to it. Presenting (Being) belongs in the clearing of self-concealing (time).
Clearing of self-concealing produces presenting (Being).
. . . this belonging and producing rest in an ap-propriation
and are called event.[4]

Presenting and Clearing

Now that the direction of Heidegger's thrust into the "and"
has been pointed out, we must follow through with a brief development of the content of its two poles. As already indicated, the two
terms cannot be considered different from one another. Both refer
to the essence of time. Both describe the process of unconcealment,
the truth of Being. Both accordingly bear a reference to the ultimate
concealment. The presenting process (*Anwesen*) is at once an ab-
senting process (*Abwesen*). Essence (*Wesen*) for Heidegger is accordingly understood verbally in terms of an interplay of presence
and absence. And clearing is always understood in terms of the
background of obfuscation from which it frees itself.

But each of the terms makes it appearance in the Heideggerian
opus in a different way, from a different source, in different contexts, and therefore carrying differing nuances, which is precisely
the source of the difficulties of bringing them together in the turn.
Presence and its presenting process are the temporal terms for
Being which Heidegger finds in the Western tradition and accepts
as such, while constantly mulling the secret essence of time which
lies hidden and unthought in these terms. Presence more often than
not is used as a variant expression of the ontological difference of
Being and being, *viz.*, the presenting of what is present, which emphasizes its association with a long tradition of metaphysics concerned with beings to the neglect of Being. And the various missions
of presence sent by the appropriating event constitute the history of
metaphysics.

Clearing, on the other hand, is that within which beings can present themselves, the free and open space which grants us access to

[4] *Ibid.*, pp. XX-XXI.

the beings which we are not and to the beings which we are, the leeway and playing field of the world. More basically, when verbally understood, clearing is the regioning of a region, the expansive opening which permits an outlet for free play and enables presenting to take place and thus lets being be. As the enabling element, the clearing is not only that within which beings present themselves, but also that by which things appear. As the site of openness, it is the here of Being, Da-sein.

Dasein was the preliminary pivotal concept of the first part of Heidegger's original prospectus for executing the turn to the event, just as its second part was to "destroy" the traditional conception of time in order to prepare the ancient conception of *Anwesen* for the turn. In *Being and Time*, Dasein as Being-in-the-world is identified with the clearing, in the introduction to the well-known sections which elaborate the constitution of the here as the thrown and projected linguistic realm of meaning which is man's understanding of Being (SZ, 133). Here, it is also pointed out that a long tradition of *Lichtmetaphysik* has described this understanding figuratively as a *lumen naturale*. But the light of reason interpreted as a reified power somehow implanted in us is precisely what Heidegger from the beginning strives to surpass, in order to establish the ontological ground for any act of illumination or intuitive seeing. Such a backtracking ultimately leads to a reading of the traditional definition of man, the living being possessing *logos*, instead as the being possessed by *logos*, where *logos* is now (among other things) the indigenous field of language in which he lives, moves and has his Being.

Furthermore, even though *Lichtung* suggests *Licht* and hence has been translated as "lighting-up process," Heidegger strives to surpass the *Lichtmetaphysik* from Plato on and to backtrack into the ground that precedes as well as makes possible such an interpretation. The clearing as such is neutral with regard to its medium and mode of reception, and sets free sounds, for example, as well as sights. For Heidegger, even more basic than the *Licht* of *Lichtung* is its metaphorical reference to a clearing in the wood which is first cleared by a process of lightening rather than lighting, a thinning of the thicket (FP, 170-71, 190-91). Obstacles must first be cleared *away* before obscurities can be cleared *up*. The disencumbering disclosure is first necessary to release the clearing for illumination. Parenthetically, it may be noted how the spatial metaphor which permeates language through and through continues to crop up in any attempt to discuss time, where, for example, the clearing continues to be described as a "temporal playing field" (*Zeit-Spiel-Raum*).

From the beginning, the clearing process was conceived as temporal through and through. *Being and Time* concludes that it is ecstatic temporality which originally clears the here of Dasein and which unifies its articulated structure in terms of the three dimensions of time (SZ, 351). As the *ekstatikon* pure and simple, temporality is the condition of the possibility of the ex-sistence that Dasein is. Time is the primordial "ex" that extends Dasein in its scope and limits, which determines the kind of understanding of Being which man has, appropriate to his time. "With the disclosure of the 'here' grounded in ecstatically stretched temporality, a 'time' is allotted to Dasein" (SZ, 410).

This tensile character of time and its tenses is maintained in the 1962 lecture "Time and Being" in the way time is given in the event, as an offer of presence that reaches (*Reichen*) and that thereby defines the reach (*Reichweite*) of a region (*Bereich*). The three time dimensions constitute three different modes of reaching and of offering presence. In reaching to one another, the three dimensions of time not only establish a play of presence and absence, but clear for themselves a temporal playing field. This reciprocal interplay is under the sway of a fourth dimension in which the unity of authentic time reposes, an incipient offering and reaching-extending which clears the three dimensions by holding them apart and together in proximity, a proximating proximity which at once denies what has been and restrains what is to come and so conceals as well as clears, and clears only when the time is "ripe," appropriate (ZS, 46-49). For "the proximity which proximates is itself the appropriating event" (US, 196).

And its last word is silence. For the event is not a permanent presence, but instead gives itself by withdrawing itself. It is this withdrawing mystery which provides the permanent origin of all clearing. Accordingly, the clearing itself is not a fixed stage with its curtain always raised where the play of beings runs its course, but a shifting scene that fades into the background only to emerge anew. Because the event withdraws, it is still the indeterminate "There is" of the Ur-phenomena of Being and time, the *Lethe* at the very heart of *aletheia* that continues to draw thought forward.

To Describe the Indescribable

With its principle of *zu den Sachen selbst*, phenomenology has acclimated us to a movement of radical regression which strives to undercut the constructions of the natural attitude, science and metaphysics in order to manifest the fundamental experiential structures that found them. The most fundamental and all-pervasive structure is that of intentionality, at once constituting and intuitive, productive and revelatory, active and receptive, and variously described by Husserl as a transcendental life experiencing the world in a "living present," by Heidegger as the event of unconcealment in which thinking and Being are the "same" in a point of intimacy between Being and man which precedes all distinction, by Sartre as a pre-reflective action of revealing the world, by Merleau-Ponty in terms of the active human body perceiving a world of ambiguity. Not that these formulations exhaust the issue. As Heidegger puts it in his foreword to Husserl's lectures on time constitution, "the term 'intentionality' is no all-explanatory word but one which designates a central problem." In Husserl's words, we are standing before "the deepest essential bonds between reason and being in general, the puzzle of all puzzles."[5]

The regress takes us to the root of human experience itself, in a radical effort to get to the bottom of things which ultimately reaches a point where the bottom falls out and gives way to an abyss *(Abgrund)*, an undifferentiated and indeterminate chaos, "the chasm out of which the Open opens itself" (HD, 61). Chaos here is thus not to be taken in the static sense of sheer disorder and confusion, but as a "drive, flow, and motion, whose order is *hidden* and whose law is not immediately known" (N, I, 566), "the hidden, self-overflowing, unmastered excess of life" (N, I, 568). We are before a radical beginning that posits itself beyond all distinction, as the immediate, the simple, the element, the *Lethe* of *aletheia*.

The drive to grasp experience by its umbilical cord takes us back to the moment of incipient pregnancy where meaning first takes hold in human experience, the original upsurge of "reason" in experience, a fullness of meaning to be found in the very immediacy of experience, the ultimate *Sinngebung* whose immediacy and spontaneous genesis of meaning at once find their apt expres-

[5] Edmund Husserl, *Die Krisis der Europäischen Wissenschaften und die Transzendentale Phänomenologie*, Husserliana VI, ed. W. Biemel, 2nd ed. (The Hague: Nijhoff, 1962) p. 12.

sion in the double-entendre of the German *Es gibt*. Following what
he considered to be a more faithful adherence to the phenomenological prescription *zur Sache selbst*, it was Heidegger who radical-
ized Husserl's quest for the most original givenness of beings into
the question of the origin of givenness pure and simple.[6]

And yet this region of absolute giving is itself not given. "The
immediate, therefore, is never and nowhere 'given'; it must always
be reconstructed; and to 'ourselves,' that is to our most intimate life,
we have no access."[7] "For the 'primal experience,' upon which our
experiences are grounded, has always passed irrevocably away by
the time our attention is directed to it."[8] Here is the essence of the
finitude of man, to whom life poses "the colossal aporia, the insol-
uble dilemma"[9] of glimpsing an immediate which is never accessible immediately (HD, 59-61). For consciousness always arrives too
late to seize that which seizes it, the immediate present. "Consciousness is senescence and a quest of things past."[10]

And yet the immediate in its withdrawal is precisely what draws
thought by calling out to be thought. The draw of its unthought is
the very food for thought. It "wants" thought, and "gives" thought
its sustenance, and in this way "uses" thought to reveal itself. The
lure of the ineffable, the call of the wild and aboriginal is the very
provocation of thought. It is what sets thought on its way, its very
incipience. It evokes thought, appeals to be thought — and therefore "speaks"! Though it always holds itself in reserve, its silence is
infinitely suggestive. Its draw is like the gesture of a finger pointing
the way to the secret of our Being, of our time, of what is most
appropriate to us. Accordingly, in its gestation of what is most timely
and original for us, it guides the course of our thought and of our
history. And yet all this goes on surreptitiously, behind the scenes,
as it were, outside of the arena of earth-shaking historical occurrences. The inaugural event of Being is not newsworthy. For, as the
most immediate and comprehensive of our experiences, it is always

[6] Ernst Tugendhat, *Der Wahrheitsbegriff bei Husserl und Heidegger* (Berlin: Walter de Gruyter and Co., 1967) p. 242.

[7] G. Van Der Leeuw, *Religion in Essence and Manifestation: A Study in
Phenomenology* (New York, Harper Torchbook, 1963) vol. II, p. 672. The
chapter being cited is entitled "Phenomenon and Phenomenology."

[8] *Ibid.*, p. 671.

[9] *Ibid.*, p. 672.

[10] Emmanuel Levinas, "Intentionalité et sensation," *Revue Internationale de
Philosophie* (1965) nos. 71-72, pp. 34-54. Cf. p. 47.

with us as the element and background of all of our particular experiences, and in this sense quite ordinary. "Nothing" really happens in this event (N, II, 485) — which is why it is the most extraordinary and potentially devastating of our experiences when it does come into the foreground. Consider, for example, this description of the poet's venture into the ineffable immediacy ("the holy"): "The shock of chaos, that offers no support, the terror of the immediate, that frustrates all intrusion, the holy is transformed through the tranquillity of the shielded poet into the mildness of the mediate and mediatizing word" (HD, 68-69).

But how does this event of language come about, if the immediate itself is ineffable, and can never be apprehended immediately? Even though the immediate is inaccessible in its immediacy, as the comprehensive event which permeates all particular experiences, it is at once the mediation of all mediated beings, and so can be glimpsed in and through its mediations. It is the word which articulates these relations among everything actual, and so itself is the mediation which holds and retains beings in Being. "Without the holding and relating word, the totality of things, the 'world,' sinks into darkness" (US, 177). Language accordingly institutes the network of relations which is our historical world in its particular differentiations and bounded by its particular horizon. Its welcome capacity to domesticate the aboriginal in the "mildness" of the word can nevertheless tranquillize the elemental power of its mediating ground into oblivion, as the current technological modulation of language has done. But it is always possible to revive the relationship of the event, "the relation of all relations, the hold of all holds" (US, 267), since the horizon of our linguistic world "is not a wall that encloses man; on the contrary, the horizon is *transparent*, it points as such to the non-established, becoming, and capable of becoming, to the possible" (N, I, 574). "The horizon throughout its transparent permanence lets the chaos appear as chaos" (N, I, 575). Accordingly, the existing languages in which we find ourselves "thrown" are always open to orientation toward this aboriginal language which "speaks" in silence. And it is to our creative poets and thinkers that we look to find the words which somehow intimate the ineffable, old and familiar words long in use made to speak anew their relationship with the very source of language. This process of listening for the unsaid to be said in what has already been said has long been called hermeneutics.

To summarize, "the intangible experience in itself cannot be apprehended nor mastered, but it manifests something to us, an appearance: says something, an utterance. The aim of science, therefore, is to understand this logos; essentially, science is hermeneutics."[11] The mediatizing immediate which itself is unmediated, the ground which itself is an ungrounded abyss, the differentiating, articulating, unconcealing process which itself is undifferentiated, ineffable and concealed, such is the ultimate character of Being in its most archaic sense. Its concealment (*Verbergung*) is the very shelter *(Bergung)* of the aboriginal language, which speaks in its own time and its own unexpected way, according to which the hermeneute must bide his time.

Hermeneutical Language

The language which orients itself to the silent event thus warrants being called a hermeneutical language. *Being and Time* situated the hermeneutical "as" in a pre-predicative involvement in the referential relations of the world of gear preceding the theoretical predications of the apophantic "as." Later, the "as" structure of "something as something" appears again in the history of the metaphysical interpretations from Being as idea to Being as will. But "the hermeneutical does not first signify the explicit interpreting that lays out, for even before this there is the bringing of the message and tidings" (US, 122). The hermeneutical language most basically is oriented to the "primal tidings" of the aboriginal event, which "speaks" silently, by withholding itself. To be true to its ineffable source, such a language leaves more unsaid in what it actually says. Its seminal, germinal, suggestive probing calls for a *logos* oriented to silence, a "sigetic" logic.[12] "Every incipient and authentic naming utters the unspoken, and indeed in such a way that it remains unspoken" (WD, 119). The unsayable is somehow said!

Such a hermeneutical language necessarily reaches beyond the resources of the current logical and grammatical conception of language, whose final court of appeal is the judgment and whose basic structure is the subject-predicate relation. For that about which one speaks here is no longer the self-givenness of a subject, but the self-

[11] Van Der Leeuw, *op. cit.*, p. 676.
[12] Otto Pöggeler, *Der Denkweg Martin Heideggers* (Pfullingen: Neske, 1963) p. 276.

withdrawal of the event. We are no longer dealing with the *An sich* of things on hand, but the *Ansichhalten,* the holding-to-itself of the basic mystery. Whereas the apophantic language arrives at a predicate which bestows a definite character on a subject that already stands out, the hermeneutical language, groping in the most primordial pre-predicative realm, culminates in the "saying that does not say" (*sagenden Nichtsagen*) (ID, 72). In it, purely declarative sentences are no longer possible, its assertions take on a peculiarly non-assertive character, its propositions amount to a leap[13] to which the usual logic of the substantive does not apply. It is no wonder that Carnap found in Heidegger a particularly rich source of what for logical positivism can only be meaningless assertions or pseudo-statements, like "nothing itself nothings." "A sequence of words is meaningless if it does not, within a specified language, constitute a statement."[14] It is precisely such a closed system of language, with its strictly defined rules of formation and rigidly fixed vocabulary, that Heidegger seeks to "destroy." How he does this, what linguistic strategies he employs, is what we now wish to examine.

Generally speaking, it can be prefatorily stated that Heidegger's resorting to these peculiarly non-assertive assertions arises from his attempt to think Being *itself,* Being *as such.* The following quotation strikes the pervasive keynote: "Yet Being — what is Being? It is itself. This is what future thinking must learn to experience and to say. 'Being' — it is not God nor a world-ground. For being is further than any being, be it a rock or an animal, a work of art or a machine, an angel or God. Being is the nearest. Yet the near is what is farthest for man" (PW, 76). And later: "The appropriating event is the most unpretentious of the unpretentious, the simplest of the simple, the nearest of the near and the farthest of the far, within which we mortals sojourn and live our temporal life" (US, 259). As the simplest of the simple which is nearest in immediacy and farthest in accessibility, Being as such signalizes a new principle of identity toward which all converges and out of which all emerges, the *self*-given in a strictly terminal sense, at once *self*-withdrawn.

---

[13] Heidegger often plays on the German *Satz,* which means both "proposition" and "leap."

[14] Rudolf Carnap, "The Elimination of Metaphysics Through Logical Analysis of Language," tr. Arthur Pap, in *Logical Positivism* (Glencoe: Free Press, 1959) pp. 60-81. Cf. p. 61.

Thus, echoes of the old tautological A *is* A are constantly heard in Heidegger's meditations. These apparent tautologies serve as bases for a leap into a new dimension of identity which in its immediacy defies articulation. Accordingly, we are told that the sentence "language is language, speech is speech," apparently "a tautology which says nothing" (US, 12) and its verbal iterative, "speech speaks," can lead us to an abyss which opens onto the place of the essence of speech and of the speaking being, man. Far from being a meaningless tautology, such an iterative sentence serves to turn us away from thinking about language in terms other than itself, as an externalization of inner feelings or as an activity of man, for example, in order that we may consider language as language, in terms proper to it as such. It thus turns our attention to the power of language itself to reveal, to let beings be, and more profoundly, to the silent source of this power, to whose "air" we as speaking beings are called upon to listen, to whose elemental modulation we already find ourselves attuned.

Speech speaks in order to summon the world and things to their essence, whereby the world worlds and the thing things. In thinging, the thing draws the world near and gathers it. The world in turn worlds by granting the thing its nexus for gathering. In reciprocal intimacy and with the articulation of the difference between them, each comes into its own. Issuing out of the e-vent of appropriation, each receives its unique essence.

Speech speaks — the world worlds — the thing things — why these verbally iterative sentences (to which others can easily be added from the Heideggerian opus)? For one thing, such iterations stress the verbal over the substantive, and develop a series of iterative verbs designed to overcome the static permanence which the "is" has acquired. Moreover, we are in the proximity of a family of phenomena to which the "is" is to a large extent not applicable, for Being "is" not a being, nor "is" time. Finally, such a linguistic strategy serves to emphasize the phenomenon itself (*die Sache selbst*), "as such," in its unique essence and essential uniqueness. From his early interest in Scotus' notion of haecceity to his ultimate selection of *Er-eignis* as his theme-word, Heidegger's concern for a uniqueness which is at once universal is everywhere apparent, as in the concreteness of the "here" and the temporal riddle of uniqueness. All of these iterative verbs therefore seek to express how the "proper" nouns, speech, the world, the thing, etc., "essence." In opposition to a tradition of static and eternal essences, Heidegger seeks to develop a verbal conception of essence. The iterative sentence accordingly points to an identity and sameness which permits difference, to an essence which is self-changing and historical, appropriate to its time.

This transmutation in the conception of essence is especially expressed in the following two turning sentences:

The essence of truth is the truth of the essence (WW, 26).
The essence of speech: the speech of the essence (US, 200).

In each case, the first essence is understood traditionally as quiddity, while the second is taken verbally and refers to the enduring abiding that makes way, i.e., the appropriating event. The other terms follow their contextual suit in the turn of phrase. Accordingly, the turning sentences now read: what truth as knowledge is emerges from the unconcealment of the event that appropriates; speech as human activity finds its incipience in the silent saying of the event. Both turns terminate in the appropriating event. The colon which breaks the second sentence serves to symbolize the leap that is necessary to execute the turn.

The way leading to the direct articulation of the event itself also traverses a linguistic evolution. It centers on the attempt to find a suitable way of speaking of the It which gives the Being which is there when we say "there is Being." At first, the It is simply identified with Being itself in its self-giving, so that "Being gives Being" (PW, 80-81). But this way of putting it still has the disadvantage of suggesting that Being somehow "is," like a being. Later, the giving of Being is identified with the sending of the mission of presence in the history of Being, which must be considered together with the giving of time as the extending of a clearing. The substantifying effect of the It, which is now identified as the appropriating event, must then give way to the verbal impact suggested by these two modes of giving. For the event is nothing but the giving itself. It is unacceptable to say that "the event is," since it is not a being, or that "it gives the event," since all giving issues from the event. Both expressions therefore reverse the proper direction in which the event is to be thought, which in its giving always retreats into its abyss. The best that can be said is: "The appropriating event events by appropriating" (*Das Ereignis ereignet*), not as a mere sentence subject to the questioning of logic, but as a touchpoint of meditation on the mysterious comings and goings and abiding character of the central concern of thought. Even to speak of Being *as* the event, which certainly is true in its general intent, risks placing what is thought here on the same level as the metaphysical interpretations of Being as idea, as will, etc. But the event is not a kind of Being subordinated to the basic concept of Being. And the reverse is no less objectionable: Being is not a kind of event, for the event is not a generic concept to which Being and time are subordinate. Relations of a logical order say nothing to us here. Being and time disappear into the event out of which they are appropriated and thus come into their own. The "as" here is simply the giving appropriation of Being and time, the eventing of the event itself. The event events. All comes back to saying the same, going from the same and returning to the same, which at once is always different, the principle of uniqueness itself (ZS, 54-66).

Summary: A "Linguistic Analysis"

The iterative and circular "syntax" of the hermeneutical language serves to de-emphasize the predicative structure of our inherited languages, and therefore tends to concentrate our attention on its keywords within a pre-predicative context. The hermeneutical process ultimately focuses on the most fundamental words of our language, in order to listen to their changing modulations and mutual resonance. By way of summary and conclusion, an attempt will be made to unravel the strands of meaning knotted into the notion of *Ereignis* from a somewhat different perspective. And the translation of *Ereignis* as "appropriating event" has yet to be justified.

In officially introducing *Ereignis* as the very centerline of his endeavors, Heidegger rather grandiosely asserts that "it can be translated with as little success as the Greek keyword *logos* and the Chinese *Tao*" (ID, 29). If we bracket the Teutonic pomposity of this declaration, it does suggest that we can expect in this word the same manifold convergence of connotations that Heidegger himself has unraveled from the Greek *logos*. In fact, he later specifies the *Ereignis* as the one and only, unique and simple subject matter of thought, inaccessible in its simplicity, approachable only through a manifold thought, and *ipso facto* through a manifold language.[15] This accounts for the structure of the Heideggerian opus, aiming

[15] Richardson, *op. cit.*, p. XXIII.

at a single center, approached along numerous "forest trails," some of them perhaps dead-ends.

As a first approximation to this unique *Sache,* Heidegger takes the phenomenological path. Recall the great circle of Heidegger, that it is first necessary to anticipate and acknowledge what is to be explicated, namely, the total situation where emergent Being shows itself. Once in the circle comes the problem of finding a suitable language to describe this process of emergence, the relations within it between man and the Being of beings, and finally the enabling element which is the condition of the possibility for such emergence and such relations. This enabling element is ultimately termed the *Ereignis.* Difficulties to this project are soon encountered in a language rendered opaque by a long tradition of metaphysics. In the face of this, Heidegger does not suggest that we take to neologisms, but rather calls for "a transformed relationship to the essence of the old language."[16] What sort of a conversion? A phenomenological one, and to the extent that phenomenology calls for complete honesty, an ethical one as well. And if phenomenology is a matter of letting "things" speak for themselves, then its most refined phase, thought, is a matter of letting language speak for itself. Indeed, at the aboriginal level of the *Ereignis,* language and *Sache* are one for Heidegger.

In what ways then does this aboriginal language speak of itself? I submit that a manifold of major linguistic constellations can be distinguished in Heidegger's own descriptions of the *Ereignis.* If indeed *Ereignis* is the common source of emergence of the manifold senses of Being that Heidegger wants it to be, then one should expect all the heavy-duty stems of our most archaic language to tend to merge here. Heidegger's own reflections on the convergent senses of *logos, physis, aletheia,* and the other old Greek words which somehow named the unnameable prefigure our discussion here, and in some sense are to be repeated for the sake of a new beginning in the event. The process of instituting *Ereignis* as a "guiding word in the service of thinking" (ID, 29) in fact continues the reflection on the most fundamental words of our language in an attempt to approximate the archaic simplicity of the aboriginal language. What follows then is a highly condensed "linguistic analysis" of Heidegger's most basic language in terms of the main linguistic constellations that thread through his conception of *Ereignis:*

[16] *Ibid.*

1) The language of *coming and going,* used to express the dynamics between man and Being. On the basis of such descriptions, *Ereignis* becomes the event of the advent of Being overcoming man through intervention in his ventures. Certainly no ordinary event, limited to a moment or period of time, but one that is momentous and periodic, or better, that which makes events momentous and periodizes them.

2) The suggestions of intermittence in the comings and goings of *the* event are countered by a second linguistic group of *stasis* words, of standing and bringing to stand, posing and positing, setting and fixing, in which man stands out into Being in a holding attitude that holds himself and beings in ex-sistential place. This incipient state-of-affairs ultimately points back to the *Ereignis* as the "holding that holds to itself, the relation of all relations, the hold of all holds."

3) Insofar as aboriginal Being holds to itself, it holds back, withdraws, and in so doing draws man with it. We are now approaching the language of *hide and seek,* and the chiaroscuro interplay of *hide and show.* This always appears as Heidegger's last word on *Ereignis,* as the concealment.

4) Closely tied to but significantly distinct from the language of hide and show is the language of *closing and opening.* Opening as clearing constitutes a releasing, a freeing, permitting an out-let for free play. Thus appears that all important Heideggerian word, *lassen,* and *Ereignis* becomes the dimension enabling the emergence of beings and providing viability to man.

5) But the last word in Heidegger is still the closure of disclosure. That which grants access is itself inaccessible. Confronted with the ineffable opaqueness of the abyss of aboriginal Being, all that can be said is that "there IT is," or — and here English fails to keep pace with the German — *Es gibt. Ereignis* as the indeterminate "there is" which gives and promotes a language of *give and receive,* or more vehemently, in keeping with the violence of man and Being that Heidegger finds expressed in the Antigone chorus, *give and take.*

6) "To appropriate" says both give and take, as well as the all important propium (*eigen*) and adapting (*eignen*) of the *Ereignis.* Heidegger's persistent use of these cognates and their variants suggest that these connotations were uppermost in his choice of this "guiding word in the service of thinking." Evidently *Ereignis* is to

be the mutually appropriating realm of the give and take of uniqueness.

Zygmunt Adamczewski[17] has suggested "bearing" as a translation for *Ereignis*, which helps to bring out some of its further ramifications. For one thing, it intuitively brings to the fore another linguistic constellation, the language of *genesis* so time-honored in religion, philosophy and phenomenology. It thus emphasizes the perpetual pregnancy and fruitfulness of the engendering phenomenal ground. Bearing as begetting, carrying and delivering accentuates the creative character of aboriginal being, which Heidegger himself develops in his reduction of causality to a bringing forth or pro-ducere. It also suggests the carry-over and deliverance of the inheritance of tradition (*Überlieferung*). Hence no one can deny that "bearing" is a very fertile term. It furthermore suggests not only originating but also sustaining power. But here it is on a par with the holding action and staying power already indicated as proper to aboriginal Being. Likewise, some of the other nuances of "bearing" are present and perhaps better expressed in the other linguistic groups. For example: forbearance is also withstanding and the ability to "take it"; bearing as an attitude is also a stance or posture, an approach (*Angang*) or the now-cliched openness. On the debit side, bearing suggests the teleology of the originating process to such a degree that it also connotes meaning and direction (*Sinn*), so that it in fact obscures its archeological character and the concomitant concealment at the heart of the "e-vent," as an occurrence that comes from afar. And where are the closure and withdrawal that leads to degeneration and the intermittent need for regeneration? Finally, even though bearing suggests relevance, and hence implies the pertinence that belongs to the appropriate, it nevertheless verbally interrupts the profound resonance between the "ownness" or proprium of the appropriate and the owing of a debt to my own existence to which I ought to own up, so well brought out by Adamczewski in his paper.

Not that we should reject the suggestions of gestation that "bearing" brings to the understanding of the *Ereignis*. It suggests for instance that heavy-duty English root stemming from the Latin verb for "bearing," *ferre*, which gives us that all important Heideggerian term, difference. In closest harmony with the *Ereignis*, Heid-

---

[17] "Martin Heidegger and Man's Way to Be," *Man and World* (1968) vol. 1, no. 3, pp. 363-79. Cf. p. 369.

egger places the *Austrag* (ID, 10) which he roughly interprets as a "bearing out." In *Identity and Difference, Austrag* is the differentiation between Being and beings. In *Underway to Language* (22-25), it is also the gestation of the gestures of language, especially in the primordial articulation between world and thing. We are now evoking the language of *identifying and differentiating,* which conjures the most difficult of Heidegger's problems, the modulation of uniqueness, involving at once the exclusivity of selfhood, the disjunction of temporal epochs, and the historical discursivity of language.

Such is the language of the event in terms of its most primeval linguistic groups, which attempt to sound the most primeval event of language. The language of the event: the event of language. If we recall the double play of the "of" that Heidegger emphasizes in other contexts, these two turns of phrase should ultimately be one and the same, at least in the sense of belonging together and corresponding to each other. In the metaphysics of grammar, "of" is the genitive of possession; for Heidegger, it is the genesis of the proper, once again the appropriating event itself. More than once, he refers to an *Eigentum des Er-eignisses* (ID, 31; N, II, 484; US, 265; ZS, 62-64). And what we have just surveyed in terms of linguistic groups are those very "properties" of verbal essence, or better, the propia of aboriginal Being.

Heidegger: The Problem of The Thing

Thomas Langan

Introduction

The fundamental preoccupation of Heideggerian philosophy is the revelation of the essence of Being. Being is not one with the *Seienden* — with the things-that-are; however, Being happens only in the revelation of the things-that-are (*Wahrheit nur west, indem sie sich in ein Seiendes einrichtet*, HW). Being can only happen through the activity of men, but no activistic, voluntaristic act of will can force a revelation of being. We must will that Being be, but this will act is a "letting Being be" (*eine Seinsverlassenheit*) which respects both the deepest inherent sense of Being's historical coming to be and the being-in-itself of the *Seienden*.

The central problem confornting this ontology — the problem dominating the future of Heideggerian philosophy — is this: If the becoming of history has a certain sense in itself and if the things that are have a certain reality in themselves, how then does human creativity insert itself into this given, and out of the matter of the things form meaningful cultural objects and through "espousal of the deepest vectors of the historical becoming", (Merleau-Ponty's phrase) preside over its development? Kant, Hegel, and Nietzsche all realized that the *an sich* is truly *in itself*: they found it indeed hopelessly resistant to liberty. The voluntarism of Nietzsche is a refusal of the *in itself*; the "Eternal Return" its acceptance. Kant's denial of noumenal insight sets the *an sich* beyond science, but, as Ricoeur shows in his *Kantstudien* article ("Husserl and Kant"),

105

Kant does not deny its existence. Hegel, like Heidegger, wrestled to bring the *in itself* and the freedom of interpretive-creating existence together; but Hegel never freed his philosophy sufficiently from the spector of necessity ruling from within the dialectical becoming of Spirit, the freedom of the individual *Dasein* and the creativity of Being's revelations of itself are not protected.

In the present paper, through the examination of the central ontological problem as it is presented in an important work, *Die Frage nach dem Ding*, dating from 1937 but only recently published, and in the essay, "On the Essence of the Work of Art," I hope to throw some light on Heidegger's position in regard to the "in itself." It is very unKantian to speak of knowing something of things as they are in themselves. Nevertheless, I believe Heidegger wants to hold, against all Kantians, that we do. Yet, as he is influenced by the transcendental approach, the same pressure that drove the Kantians toward idealism is forever working against systematic development of Heidegger's conviction that we know something of things in themselves.

In order to show the importance of this aspect of Heidegger's thought, we shall first review some key texts in which he finds himself constrained to affirm (or at least appears to assume) some access to things as they are in themselves. But then we shall recall the presuppositions Heidegger inherits from the Kantian tradition, presuppositions inimical to any sort of realism. Finally, after suggesting criticisms of these presuppositions, we shall return to Heidegger's basic position regarding the things themselves in order to suggest that the deepest sense of the Heideggerian ontology can be saved only by an unabashed inquiry into the intelligibility of what is revealed in nature.

Part One — The In-Itself: Heidegger's UnKantian Affirmations

Heidegger's long commentary in *The Question about the Thing* on the *Critique of Pure Reason's* "System of All Principles of the Pure Understanding" is devoted to bringing out Kant's genius in discovering the empire of Being (*das Reich des Seins*) to lie in the "in between," between the knower and the things known, which is to say that Being is neither subjective nor objective. Despite Kant's greatness in having revealed this "in betweeness" of Being, the father of transcendental philosophy is no exception to the hard truth that even the most creative philosophers are limited by presuppositions inherited from their tradition. In Kant's case this means the tradition of the mathematization (in the sense Heidegger gives this notion) of the thing, with emphasis on "that in the things which we already know, that which we do not have to get from the things but rather in some way bring ourselves," (FD, 57) in short, the *a priori*. This leads Heidegger to his most important criticism, a warning to us that the question of the thing so uncritically mathematized by Kant, requires fundamental reconsideration.

> Kant overlooked questioning and determining in its own essence the Revealed (*das Offenbare*) which we encounter (*begegnen*) before any objectivisation intended to produce an object of experience (FD, 110).

When Kant discusses perception (*Wahrnehmung*) it is always from the standpoint of fully constituted experience (*Erfahrung*) in relation to which the perception is always treated as a *"noch nicht"* — without any reality in itself. This, Heidegger would call into question. Just because it can be shown that the thing receives its *full* sense only when integrated into the universe of discourse — the ultimate cultural context — it ought not hastily be concluded that what is primordially given (*das Offenbare*) is in itself totally structureless.

In *The Essence of the Work of Art* Heidegger makes this point more fully. He there criticizes first a too *a priorist* approach to the problem of understanding the nature of the thing. Then he criticizes the empiricist attempt to reduce the thing to sensed qualities. The *a priorist* approach, he says keeps the thing too far from our body, and the empiricist approach makes it too close. In order to avoid the exaggerations of both, "the thing itself must be allowed to remain in its own resting-in-itself. It is to be accepted in its own proper firmness (*Standhaftigkeit* — its own ability to stand in itself)" (HW, 16). In contrast to empiricism and *a priorism*, the traditional matter-form interpretation of the thing respects this essential aspect of the thing's own resting-in-itself; but, as Heidegger construes (I would say rather misconstrues) the position, it is so modeled on the production of a tool or art object as to obscure the mysterious but all important contribution of the matter. "A tool ... does not have that quality of possessing its own heaviness that the granite block has" (HW, 18). In the natural thing we feel especially strongly the weight of its ineluctable presence. Heidegger seeks to communicate this through his poetic conception of "the Earth," which we shall examine in a moment.

Like Husserl, Heidegger in the Kant commentary forming part of *The Question about the Thing*, stresses, as we have just suggested, the pre-predicative unity of an object which is not yet integrated into the vaster unity of rational discourse. It is important to consider how he conceives this primordial unity of the thing. Before a thing can be thought, it must *be*, that is to say, it must be presented in an intuition. Heidegger insists strongly that to be presented in an intuition is something quite opposed to being produced through a synthesizing activity out of an otherwise structureless stuff. "Intuition (viz. the act of intuiting) is a way of representing (*vor-stellen*) something, a way of access to something, a way something is given, but is not this something itself" (FD, 156).

The very way Heidegger explains the difficult Kantian notion of space as a pure intuition is a good indication of the truth of our contention, that he wishes to maintain, against most Kantian interpretations, that the act of the transcendental subject is not the all-organizing act, but rather the act of opening onto a thing which has a certain structure in itself. In *Sein und Zeit*, Heidegger had distinguished *Entfernung*, which can only be experienced, from *Abstand* which things possess in relation to one another whether or not any *Dasein* is present to experience it.[1] Similarly, in *The Question about the Thing*, the "spatial-being of space" is described as giving the self-manifesting reality the possibility to manifest itself in its own proper extension. (*Das Raumsein des Raumes besteht darin, dass es dem sich Zeigenden die Möglichkeit einräumt, in seiner Ausbreitung sich zu zeigen* (FD, 156)). In this context Heidegger hints that Kant's doctrine on space is too anthropological. "The principal difficulty (with Kant's version of the question of space) lies in his attributing space as an intuition to a human subject whose being is insufficiently determined" (FD, 156). Heidegger then refers the reader to *Sein und Zeit* to see how the last trace of subjectivity can be removed from the question of space.[2]

---

[1] SZ, 105. Things have *vorfindlichen und ausmessbaren Abstand*.

[2] Heidegger avoids explicitly the existentialist temptation to subordinate space to the lived experience of time. "Space cannot be deduced from time nor does it occupy a second position in relation to time" (FD, 13).

Lest it be thought Heidegger conceives the given only as so many extended points, I would like to call attention to his declaration in *The Question about the Thing* that in the analytic as well as the synthetic judgment the object is determining (*mitmassgebend*) through the *Begriff*, which is of experiential origin. Hence, it is what is given in experience which determines even what can be unfolded analytically from a notion (FD, 128). From this declaration I conclude that Heidegger holds there is a panoply of natural relations given in experience and offering a potential intelligibility to intuition.

Part Two — Uncriticized Presuppositions

But if Heidegger may rightly criticize even the great Kant of suffering from the limitations imposed by the most persistent (and hence least visible) presuppositions of his predecessors, we have the right, indeed the responsibility of seeking to illumine the limitations of Heidegger's own presuppositions. Perhaps the most fundamental assumption, one in conflict with the *spirit* of the remarks we have just been examining and inimical to any project of rehabilitating the things in themselves, is the notion that what is primordially given is entirely in flux and that all objectivity, in the sense of a standing, remaining, enduring something, is a product of acts of objectivisation — a making stand over against — over against the flow of experience and the restless process of the world: a *vor-stellen*, a reproduction, a re-petition. Kant is quoted (and never criticized for saying it),[3] to the effect that the understanding is the source of all rules — that which collects experience into the standing thing (FD, 147). Heidegger speaks of experience itself as an *Andrang*, as though it were a restless pressing crowd of facts. "If we men were simply open to all in the midst of which we stand, then we would not be up to this press (*Andrang*). We only become its master by serving of it in the light of some consideration, that is by letting the press stand over against us (*uns entgegenstehen lassen*), thus bringing to a stability and thereby establishing and maintaining a region of possible endurance" (FD, 148).

[3] In reading Heidegger on Kant one faces the same problem as in reading Thomas on Aristotle: to know when paraphrase implies approval, rather than just stating the fact that the philosopher held a particular position. The only way to check whether my attributions of Kantian positions to Heidegger are just is to reread the context in his Kant commentaries and decide for yourself.

It is, of course, not to be denied that experience is a flux, nor that only through intentionally directed selectivity can objects be made to stand out and thus an experience be ordered. I would contend, however, that it is necessary if anything is to be true, that within the flux of experience some aspects present themselves (as Heidegger says, "are intuited") as stable in relation to the fundamental experiential frame of reference furnished by the experiencing subject; that the less rapidly changing aspects serve as points of reference for organizing the less stable aspects; and that the self-directing selective subject can consider aspects of the total spectacle because the world presents itself as having *distinguishable* parts.

Nor does Heidegger intend to deny any of these claims, and indeed virtually all of the texts we examined in the preceding pages require such a position if they are to be intelligible. But the presuppositions of a long tradition make him nevertheless hesitate to admit that *perception* intuitively yields anything but ever changing sensory data. Those lulled by the tradition into uncritically accepting such a starting point find it impossible to imagine that any stable intelligibility should be founded in our experiential, perceptual intuition of a structure manifest as existing in the world independently of the experience which presents it. Despite his wariness of that mathematisation which places the ground of everything in the *a prioris* of the transcendental subject, Heidegger seems nevertheless unable to admit anything like the intuition of an essence in things through perception. How far this hesitation goes we can measure in the following paragraph, where although commenting on Kant, Heidegger in no way dissociates himself from what is being maintained here:

> We are receptive beings. To be sure! But a "something" and a "what" no man has ever passively encountered (*empfunden*). Through which sense organ shall anything of that sort happen? A "something" permits itself neither to be seen, nor heard, nor smelled, nor tasted, nor touched. There is no sense organ for the "what" and for a "this" or a "that." The "what-character" of the receivable must be pre-sented, pre-scribed in the circuit (*Umkreis*) and as ambiance (*Umkreis*) pre-grasped. Without reality there can be no real thing, without the real thing no receivable thing (FD, 171).

A reflection of this conviction is to be found in the reconstruction of the thing as an unperceived *Etwas X* which serves as bearer of properties which themselves are perceived. It fits with the traditional conception to take it for granted that these perceived properties are themselves always changing. Heidegger quotes Kant: "All phenomena (that is all things for us) contain the persisting substance, which is the object itself, and the changing properties, which are the determinations of the substance, i.e., a way the object exists" (*Critique of Pure Reason*, A 182, quoted, FD, 26). Heidegger then paraphrases this conception of the thing: "What then is a thing? Answer: A thing is the at hand bearer of many likewise at hand and consequently changing properties" (*Ibid.*). Any reader of *Sein und Zeit* of course knows to equate the adjective *vorhanden* with the inauthentic. Heidegger here wishes, then, to indicate that he is not content with this conception of the thing. He laboriously works us toward his conception of the thing in which, although the possibility that things might reveal themselves to us as relatively stable and thus in-themselves-for-awhile-enduring realities, is not explored, a certain stability is nevertheless explained through the enduring projections of the historical transcendental subject. I would like to indicate briefly why the very criticisms Heidegger levels against Kant in fact apply also to such a conception, and then show what it is I think blocks Heidegger from considering seriously the notion that we can intuit essential forms.

The assumption that the given as such cannot of itself stand and that all endurance in the thing is the result of the transcendental subject's making the thing stand is obviously one of those "metaphysical assumptions" of the sort the positivists are always delighted to point out cannot possibly be either proven or disproven. Moreover, so to assume is to repeat the fault of which Heidegger accuses Kant: It is to fail to examine the encountered given thing as it is intuited, prior to the objectivizing acts which integrate it into a universe of explanation.

But what then is given? An irreparable mistake is made, as Merleau-Ponty has shown, when one takes it that that which can be further analyzed cannot then be truly given as a whole, as though only parts are really given. After all, wholes composed of real parts do manifest themselves in experience. We may integrate such perceptually given wholes into a larger totality as a part of which it is not immediately given; or we may attend analytically to its parts.

Our ability thus to synthesize and analyze should, however, in no way distract our attention from the *giveness* of *this* structure which withstands the critical regard and persistently goes on manifesting its integrity even when we choose to rivet our attention on its parts. Some recent philosophers have been over-impressed by the discovery that through the anticipations which are an essential part of every perception we are led in spontaneous common sense experience to believe that more is *actually* given than critical analysis reveals to be the case. But it is groundless to react against naive realism's failure to see this by saying as the empiricist does, that only that is truly *given* which cannot be further analyzed. Those who reject the gratuitous atomism of the empiricists but nonetheless continue to confound the absolutely given with the unanalyzable are finally obliged to say that meaning is grounded only in the lived system taken as a totality. Until one is ready to explore the possibility that certain wholes, certain structures manifest themselves in experience on a level of complication above the atomic but below the unity of the whole universe of experience of which lived whole they are objective and orienting parts, then it is inevitable that the lived whole of experience itself be taken, as Merleau-Ponty does, for the only reality. But were that the case, then this whole would be without *something* of which it is the reality, there would be a world but no real things. Heidegger himself reminds us however: *"Wahrheit nur west, indem sie sich in ein Seiendes einrichtet"* (HW).

Part Three — Heidegger Before the Fullness of the Intelligibility of Nature

No one who has meditated on the poetic pages of *The Essence of the Work of Art* can fail to feel Heidegger's sacred awe before the inexhaustible intelligibility of the world. Heidegger not only agrees with the Aristotelian realist in this central regard, he far outreaches him. The whole level of historical-existential intelligibility which is most central to the Heideggerian notion of *Sein* goes beyond what the philosophers of the realistic tradition, with their attention devoted mostly to objective being, have ever been able to see.

This being the case, what has a Heideggerian to await from a realist? I make bold to say that without a firm grasp on what I believe to be the central realistic conviction, the Heideggerian enterprise will flounder. If I may be allowed to state that conviction here without, in this paper, attempting in any way to justify it, I shall be in a position to complete the present inquiry with at least an indication of the kind of exploration I believe ontologists in the Heideggerian tradition need to carry forward in order to ground adequately the Heideggerian conception of Being. The following is then that realistic conviction simply stated: Without a ground in things which manifest themselves as having their own time, their own natural history, their own inherent structures, indeed their own essences, that *Sein*, which is the cultural-historical-human destiny of the becoming horizons of interpretation, would float without direction, feed on itself, and lacking given sources of material inspiration, soon cease to create in any rich and satisfying way.

To this I can imagine a Heideggerian of the Strict Observance responding, "*Mon pauvre ami*, you have understood nothing! There can be no things in themselves, no natural histories, no essences, independent of the historical world horizons within which they are interpreted."

But that is just the question ! There can also be no world and no things within that world unless there is something out of which that world and those things are made. The world is not the earth and the earth is not the world. *The Essence of the Work of Art* insists on the inevitability of both and seeks to describe a relationship betwen them which is perfectly reciprocal. Heidegger would avoid the realist-idealist controversy by poetic suggestion of two constituent principles neither of which can really be described without reference to the other.

The question in my mind, though, is whether Heidegger in these descriptions really gives the Earth its due. Heidegger writes: "*Welt weltet* and is *seiender* as the Seizable and Understandable in which we believe ourselves to be at home" (HW, 33). I question this. And I doubt that we only *believe* we are at home in the "seizable." With the help of Heidegger's remarkable meditation on Van Gogh's painting of the Farmer's Shoes, we can perhaps approach the central difficulty here.

In those pages (HW, 22 ff) Heidegger shows that the instrumentality of the tool resides in its servability (*Dienlichkeit*) and that this in turn is grounded in the reliability (*Verlässlichkeit*) of the thing. This quality is poetically invoked in a way suggestive of the thing's reliably taking its place in a familiar world. It is contrast-

ed with the materiality of *this* instrument here, in virtue of which
this thing can get used up. It is more the earth-including idea of the
thing, which permits its renewal, its repeated re-incarnation in other
matter. Because of this "reliability" the thing enjoys its "servability,"
and it is in view of its servability that the form is chosen and moulds
its matter. In Heidegger's description of the farmer's shoes we are
made to feel the ingathering of an entire world about these homely
objects. Sleepily the farmer gropes in the grey dawn light for the
trusty shoes and without further thought of them wends his way
through the cool dew to the fields not yet warmed by the reluctant
rising sun. As we study Van Gogh's painting we feel the weary
homeward trudge of the healthily tired peasant who looks forward
to his hard bread and pork scraps. Heidegger's essential point is,
of course, vital. It has, I hope, become a part of the living philosophical tradition: The *Sein* in which the individual person's life has its
sense is *world* and *earth* — and both are historical in the sense of a
series of happenings which reinforce one another, and which are
rooted in the giveness of a vast experience, itself founded in a nature
which we do not create.

The problem, however, is that Heidegger refuses to face squarely
the difficulties which arise from according to that nature the fullness of its giveness. He is justifiably concerned to avoid having anyone think that *Sein* can be explained through an exploration of
natures. But that is no reason for underestimating the role that natures play in the *Verlässlichkeit* — the reliability — of the thing.
True, the chosen end — *die Dienlichkeit* — determines the form of the
instrument, but the natures of things propose a limited gamut of
possible ends; and the natures of materials, the possible forms which
can reach these ends. Heidegger touches on this, but always only
from the one side, from the viewpoint of the purpose as *already*
determined: "Corresponding to the servability, whether for work in
the fields or for the dance, the matter and form are other" (HW,
22).

I do not believe anything of the essential vision of *Sein* will be
lost by a franker and more concerted exposition of the role of the
giveness of natures in that "Earth" whose resisting-anchoring-
bearing-fruitfulness Heidegger so powerfully invokes. Indeed a
great deal will be gained. The richness of the fruitful earth will
stand out in all the complexity of its giveness; and the ultimate protection will be gained against that arbitrariness, that *Willkür* of

realistic voluntarism which Heidegger deplores. Through the uninhibited exploration of the intelligibility of the earth opened through the world-founding horizons, the Heideggerian philosophy will be led to its best development and to ultimate fulfillment of its mission: the revelation of the sacredness of Being.

The Late Heidegger's Omission of the Ontic-Ontological Structure of Dasein

Ralph Powell, O.P.

Part One

Sein und Zeit seeks the meaning of *Sein* through an understanding of *Dasein*: "Since the interpretation of the meaning of *Sein* is the task, *Dasein* is (not only) the first *Seiende* to be interrogated," writes Heidegger in his First Introduction (SZ, 14). *Dasein* owes this distinction (*Auszeichnung*) to its *Seinsverfassung*, its Being-structure: "To this *Seinsverfassung* belongs . . . that . . . *Dasein's* ontic distinction (*Auszeichnung*) lies in this, that it is ontological" (SZ, 12). The main labor of *Sein und Zeit* consists in explaining the ontic-ontological *Seinsverfassung* of *Dasein*.

What does Heidegger mean by *Dasein's* ontic-ontological *Seinsverfassung*? Here a note on Heidegger's terminology is required. Sometimes the couplet *ontic-ontological* is used for his analysing of *Dasein*; but usually the couplet *existential-existentiell* is used for phases of his analysing, so that the couplet *ontic-ontological* is reserved for a diversity of elements uncovered in *Dasein* by his analysing.

Walter Biemel explains the meaning of the ontic-ontological structure of *Dasein* as follows: "The ontological dimension is not entirely separated from the ontic one; it is the dimension that comprises the essential structures of the concrete (ontic) real. . . . The two dimensions, if this expression be allowed, necessarily go togeth-

116

er; the ontological is not ontological except to the degree that it has reference to an ontic existence (what Sartre calls the concrete). That is what Heidegger writes explicitly: 'The existential analytic (ontological study of the Being of *Dasein*) is in the last analysis rooted in the existentiell, that is, in the ontic'."[1] Father William J. Richardson agrees with Biemel: "It is worthwhile insisting on the fact that although existential and existentiell in There-being are distinct, they are not separate. They are different dimensions of a unique and profoundly unified phenomenon: finite transcendence. The function of the existential analysis as a re-collection of forgotten transcendence will be to discern the existential dimension which structures everydayness. It must respect the unity of the phenomenon that it analyses. The existential analysis must be rooted in the existentiell, sc. unless it discerns the existential within the existentiell, it remains groundless."[2]

In my opinion, the understanding of these two Heideggerian scholars is entirely accurate. But it brings us before a scandalous situation. Distinct dimensions that are identical constitute what was always called an act-potency composition. For such dimensions are co-principles that are distinct but which cannot exist separately.[3] For the last question to be answered by an act-potency analysis of beings is: how do the alleged components form an *unum per se*? And the answer must be: because the distinct dimensions cannot exist apart.

Perhaps the reader will balk at this conclusion because act-potency philosophy is a philosophy of substance; whereas *Dasein*

[1] "Le plan ontologique n'est nullement un plan tout à fait séparé de l'ontique, c'est le plan qui comprend les structures essentielles du réel (ontique) concret.... Les deux plans — si cette expression est permise — tiennent nécessairement ensemble, l'ontologique n'est ontologique que dans la mesure où il se réfère à une existence ontique (ce que Sartre appelle le concret). C'est ce que Heidegger écrit explicitement: 'L'analytique existentiale (à savoir la recherche ontologique de l'être du *Dasein*) est en fin de compte enracinée dans l'existentiel, c'est-à-dire dans l'ontique'." Walter Biemel, *Le Concept de Monde chez Heidegger* (Louvain: E. Nauwelaerts, 1950), pp. 88-89.

[2] William J. Richardson, *Heidegger: Through Phenomenology to Thought* (The Hague: Martinus Nijhoff, 1963), p. 50.

[3] The scholastics disputed about correlative inseparable and mutual causality of material and formal cause without explicitly mentioning substance. For a history of the opinions of the principal schools cf. John of St. Thomas, *Cursus Philosophicus Thomisticus* (Turin: Reiser edition, 1933), vol. II, pp. 223-26, 233-34. Hegel in his *Enzyklopädie der philosophischen Wissenschaften* (Glockner edition, vol. VI) also takes up matter and form (pp. 78-79) before he considers substance (pp. 88 ff.).

is not a substance, not even in SZ which still allows the existence of substances other than *Dasein*.[4] Historically, this is a well founded objection. But intrinsically, act-potency composition is not principally concerned with substance but rather with identifying a certain type of whole; namely a whole with distinct dimensions which are inseparable. Thus the difference of magnitude involved in a nerve impulse and the molecular events which underlie it exemplify what act-potency philosophy claims are diverse dimensions that are identical. The macroscopic events of the nerve impulse follow their own laws and structures: the molecular events follow another system of laws and structures at the microscopic level. But both levels constitute one identical reality, since the nerve impulse occurs only through the molecular event: yet the two levels of magnitude are distinct. These inseparable but distinct dimensions would be act-potency components according to act-potency philosophy. No question of substance need be raised in order to raise and adjudicate this general claim. For substance is only one alleged distinct inseparable dimension among others.

Hence, *Dasein's* not being a substance does not remove the act-potency character of its ontic-ontological structure in *Sein und Zeit*. But such act-potency composition is metaphysical according to the late Heidegger, whereas his thought is a step backwards out of metaphysics.[5] Whether consciously or not, any backward step out of metaphysics had to take him out of the ontic-ontological structure of *Dasein* in *Sein und Zeit*: in any case, it is missing in the late Heidegger.

But I can go further. What a philosopher consciously sets in contrast with his thought is an indispensable ingredient of his thought. But Heidegger defines his thought as a step backwards out of metaphysics,[6] which for him is a historical fate of *Sein*. Since the times of the Roman Empire, Heidegger claims, this fate is characterized as the understanding of *Sein* in terms of *actualitas* as against *potentia* or *possibilitas* (N, II, 412 ff.), which became identified with *existentia* and *essentia* (PW, 57). This "distinction of *essentia* (whatness) and *existentia* (actuality) has dominated the

---

[4] "Seiendes dessen Sein den Character reiner Substantialität hat" (SZ, 88).

[5] Back step, i.e., Schritt zurück. A phrase frequently used by Heidegger. Richardson translates it: step in reverse. Cf. the references under this phrase in the index to Richardson's work, p. 758.

[6] Cf. especially ID, 71-72.

fate of Western thought and of all thought influenced by the West"
(PW, 73). Now *actualitas* and *possibilitas* thinking is rooted in the
experience of *Sein* as cause (N, II, 415 ff.). So the late Heidegger
sees metaphysics as the intimate union of ontology that studies the
common attributes of *Seienden* and of theology that reduces all
Seienden to their First Cause (ID, 69). It is out of such metaphysics
that Heidegger's thought steps, out of the leading terms of metaphysics (*Sein* and *Seienden, Grund* and *Gegründetes*) *into "das
Wesen der Metaphysik"* (ID, 69-70). By calling his thought a backward step out of metaphysics into the "essence" of metaphysics (defined for him as *actualitas-possibilitas* thinking), Heidegger plainly
defines his thought as the contrary opposite of act-potency thinking.

Thus, Heidegger's thought must be seen not just as utterly other
than act-potency thinking. It must be seen as its contrary opposite.
This contrariety can be seen by contrasting the late Heidegger's
thought about a "thing" with an act-potency conception of a thing.
The late Heidegger's historical-phenomenological thought finds
beautiful expression in the essay *"Das Ding."* In this essay, a "thing"
is explained as the drawing near (*Nähern*) of four meaning-factors: earth, sky, the divine and mortal man.[7] The "thing" gathers
the meaning-factors and lets them tarry (*verweilen*). The meaning-
factors occur in varying (*frei*) proportions in a "thing." But the
meaning-factors constitute a simple total world-meaning: they play
into one another, but their play just happens (*ereignen*), and requires no cause. The simple total world-meaning is the world, and
the world can have no cause: *die Welt weltet.* The "thing" lets the
total simple world-meaning tarry as what-is-currently (*ein je Weili-
ges*) in the worlding of the world (*aus der weltenden Welt*). The
term *Welt*[8] here signifies *Sein* which, for Heidegger, is the historical
meaning of *Seienden*; and *Sein* is essentially involved in human nature (WM, 13-14), from which it is not even correlatively distinct.[9]

---

[7] VA, 176-79; also 153-54. Cf. also James T. Demske, "Heidegger's
Quadrate and the Revelation of Being," *Philosophy Today*, VII (1963), 245-
57.

[8] *Welt* in this text is the meaning of *Das Ding* as integrated out of the
world's four meaning factors. Usually, *Welt* is *Das Seienden im Ganzen* whereas
Sein is its meaning. Cf. Max Müller, *Existenzphilosophie* (Heidelberg: Kerle,
1964), pp. 137-38.

[9] "In Wahrheit können wir dann nicht einmal mehr sagen, 'das Sein' und
'der Mensch' seien das Selbe in dem Sinne, des *sie* Zusammengehören; denn
so sagend, lassen wir immer noch beide für sich sein" (SF, 28).

In contrast, the act-potency philosophy of a "thing" explains it merely from distinct dimensions intrinsic to the thing itself and takes no account of the tarrying of the current phase of the evolving world meaning involved in human nature. Hence Heidegger can take the doctrine of the distinction of essence from existence as a sign of the forgottenness of *Sein* (PW, 73).

Act-potency metaphysics introduces certain conceptions particularly contrary to the late Heidegger's thought. These are: man as a substance or subject (which amounts to substance according to Heidegger (WM, 16)); man as an animal subject having intellect (PW, 66-67); truth as conformity of intellect to thing (WW, 8, 20); man as consciousness (WM, 13-14); and in general, *Seienden* as the *actualitas* of their *possibilitas*, as we have already seen.

Now the key to the late Heidegger's thought is his understanding of *Sein*. For me as for Max Müller and J. M. Demski,[10] *Sein* is that fundamental historical meaning which gives meaning to all the *Seienden* of an historical epoch. Moreover, for me as for Max Müller, metaphysics is a historical presupposition of the late Heidegger's thought; and I have shown that Heidegger considers metaphysics to be act-potency thinking. Hence, if I am right, it should be possible to pass into the late Heidegger's thought by dissolving the act-potency concepts that constitute act-potency thinking as the contrary opposite of Heidegger's thought. Thus we would have an "*ad oculos*" demonstration of the step backwards out of metaphysics into the "essence" of metaphysics.

The whole burden of *Kant und das Problem der Metaphysik* was the phenomenological reduction of the faculties of intellect and sense into a common root (KM, 40-41); hence intellect as a distinct faculty disappeared. And in *Vom Wesen der Wahrheit*, truth (*veritas*) as *adequatio intellectus et rei* was rejected (WW, 8) in favor of truth (*Wahrheit*) as "the self hiding uniqueness (*Einzige*) of the once-happening history of the revealment of meaning—which we call *Sein*" (WW, 24). But the fundamental motive for stepping back from man as having intellect and from truth as *veritas* consisted in his stepping back from the notion of man as consciousness and in his contrary understanding of *Sein* as involved in the existential nature of man: "Unhiddenness may well be more original than truth in the sense of *veritas*. *Aletheia* may well be the word that

[10] Cf. note 7 above.

gives an as yet unexperienced insight into the unthought essence of *esse*" (WM, 11). And taking up the same idea two pages later, Heidegger explains:

> The yet to be vindicated experience of the forgottenness of *Sein* includes the conjecture that in accordance with the forgottenness of *Sein*, the relation of *Sein* to the essence of man belongs to *Sein* itself. Yet how could the experienced conjecture even grow into an express question before straining every effort to extricate the essential notion of man out of subjectivity and especially out of that of *animal rationale*? In order to hit off in a single word and at the same time the relation of *Sein* to the essence of man and the essential relation of man to the openness (there) as such of *Sein*, the word *Dasein* was chosen for the essential realm in which man as man stands . . . . Hence any re-thinking of *Sein und Zeit* misconstrues it if one assumes that the word *Dasein* was used in place of consciousness (WM, 13-14).

And two pages later Heidegger tells us just where to look in *Sein und Zeit* to find his step back out of the metaphysical notion of man as conscious subject into the ex-sistential nature of man: "Yet because metaphysical thinking gets its notion of the self-being of man from substance or, from what amounts to the same thing, from the subject, therefore the first road that leads out of metaphysics into the ecstatic-existential essence of man must lead through the metaphysical characterization of the self-being of man (Cf. SZ, paragraphs 63 and 64)" (WM, 16).

When we consult these paragraphs of *Sein und Zeit* for their treatment of the self-being of man, we find Heidegger criticizing Kant for making the *Ich* a *res cogitans* as *"eine Form"* that accompanies (*begleitet*) and subjoins (*anhängt*) its empirical intuitions. "The concept of subject characterizes the selfhood of the *Ich* not *qua* self, but rather as the selfhood and permanence of what is already an entity (*Vorhandenes*)," says Heidegger in criticism of Kant (SZ, 230). And Heidegger asks: "Why was it that Kant could not exploit his genuine phenomenological start with the *Ich Denke* but had to fall back instead on the subject, that is on the substantial" (SZ, 320-21).

In *Kants These über das Sein*, Heidegger explains Kant's relapse into the substantial with unambiguous clarity. There Heidegger shows that Kant's fundamental reflex analysis of the subject in terms of the formal and material conditions of experience was derived from the traditional metaphysics of possibility and actuality:

> With the elucidation of possible being (*Möglichseins*) as positing (*Position*), the relation to the formal conditions of experience came into play, and thereby the concept of Form. With the elucidation of actual being (*Wirklichseins*) the material conditions of experience came to expression, and thereby the concept of Matter — With the clarification and grounding of the distinction of possibility and actuality, it came about that the positing of the actual issued from the pure concept of the possible, out of the external as opposed to the internal of the subjective condition of the subject (KT, 30-31).

And in conclusion Heidegger tries to

> show roughly how tradition speaks in Kant's exposition of *Sein* as positing. Already in Kant's early work, *Beweisgrund*, we gather that the elucidation of *Sein* ensues with respect to *Dasein* because the theme of the study is the proof of the *Dasein* of God. Instead of *Dasein* the language of metaphysics also speaks of "existence." It suffices to mull over the word to recognize in the term *sistereSetzen* the connexion with *ponere* and positing. *Existentia* is the *actus, quo res sistitur, ponitur extra statum possibilitatis.* (Cf. Heidegger, *Nietzsche*, 1961, Vol. II, p. 417 ff.) (KT, 32).

Let me now draw the facts together. In the *Einleitung* to *Was Ist Metaphysik?* Heidegger tells us that the first road out of metaphysics into the existential nature of man is to be found in the analysis of the self-being of man contained in *Sein und Zeit*, paragraphs 63 and 64. These paragraphs of *Sein und Zeit* contain a step backward out of Kant's relapse into the substantial *res cogitans* after having started with a phenomenological *Ich Denke. Kants These über das Sein* explains that Kant's relapse into the substantial *res cogitans* resulted from Kant's speaking concerning the subject with his experience out of the traditional metaphysics of *possibilitas* and *actus*. Hence, according to Heidegger, the first road out of metaphysics into the existential nature of man is through a step backward out of the act-potency concept of man as subject with his experience.

This resumé permits me to justify an assumption that I made at the outset of this paper. On the basis of my own analysis I said that an act-potency philosophy need not include a doctrine of substance. But the reader could doubt that Heidegger would accept this position. Now we have clear evidence that Heidegger does accept it. For Heidegger does not charge Kant with falling back in the doctrine that the *Ich* is a substance. Quite on the contrary, Heidegger merely charges Kant with deriving the *Ich* from the *Vorhandenen* and thereby making it into a *res cogitans* which is *"zum Substantiale zurückfallen."* The substantial and a substance are not the same thing, though he says in the *Einleitung* of *Was Ist Metaphysik?*, that they are at bottom (*im Grunde*) the same thing. *Kants These über das Sein* shows this *Grund* to be the act-potency traditional metaphysics. But Heidegger expressly says in this cited passage of *Sein und Zeit* that Kant's analysis saw the impossibility of "reduction (*Rückführung*) of the *Ich* to a substance" (SZ, 319-20). In *Kants These über das Sein* Heidegger reduces Kant's doctrine of the subject to act-potency metaphysics without ever mentioning substance. In *Nietzsche*, vol. II, Heidegger tells us that act and potency first appeared in the times of the Roman Empire when the experience of *Sein* passed from the *ergon* of the Greeks: *"zum opus des operari, zum factum des facere, zum actus des agere"* (N, II, 412). And in his whole explanation of this first historical appearance of act-potency for the next several pages Heidegger shows that *"actus* is *causalitas*. It can and should only place the thing outside its cause as the caused, the effect" (N, II, 419). Existence is counter-distinguished against possibility but the notion of substance is not expressly raised. Heidegger seems in these matters to be following Suarez whom he quotes. The "possibility" is considered only from the point of view of *actus*, of being *extra causas*; and so consequently the intrinsic condition of the effect, its being composed of substance and accident as act and potency never comes to Heidegger's consideration. Hence it is clear that Heidegger thinks of act and potency without necessarily implying a doctrine of substance.

Now let me show how rejection of the act-potency suppositions still retained by Kant has as philosophical consequent a world something like that of the late Heidegger. Heidegger "stepped back out of metaphysics" by rejecting two act-potency suppositions that Kant had retained in his philosophy of the *Ich Denke*. On the one hand, Heidegger rejected the act-potency distinction between form and matter of experience; and on the other hand, he denied the act-potency distinction of faculties of intellect, will, sense, and imagination.

The denial of the act-potency distinction between form and matter of experience enabled him to remove the notion of a subject plus his experience as constituting a thing (*a tertium quid*) distinct from the Kantian thing-in-itself. Had Heidegger limited himself to such a critique of Kant, he would merely have ratified the Aristotelian tradition that act and potency do not apply to the union of knower and known or to that of lover and beloved. For Aristotelians, act-potency composition precisely explained what united composite parts of a complex individual as distinct from every other individual: whereas cognitive and appetitive union with other things precisely enabled the individual to exist as a non-individual. Cognitive and appetitive union thus constituted for the Aristotelians a partial escape from act-potency individualization of beings.

But Heidegger did not limit himself to removing act and potency from the terrain forbidden it by Aristotelian tradition. The validity of act-potency itself had become questionable and he determined to "step back from it." But Kant's retention of faculties of understanding, sense, will and imagination were a clear case of retaining act-potency component parts of an integral individual. Heidegger accordingly removed these act-potency components along with the body-soul distinction implied in distinguishing bodily senses from immaterial faculties of intellect and will (PW, 66-67 and *passim*.).

Now the removal of distinction between the faculties removes distinction between the objects of the faculties in the *Seienden*. Hence intelligible aspects are no longer distinct from imaginary and emotional aspects of *Seienden*. For, traditionally, the intelligible aspect of *Seienden* claimed to be the objective aspect as distinct from the subjective emotional and imaginary aspects. Therefore, by removing the distinction between intellect and sense, Heidegger removed truth as *adequatio intellectus et rei*, and thereby removed the distinction between the objective and subjective aspects of *Seienden*. A good look at a *Seiendes* as understood by the late Heidegger will convince anyone that the rejection of truth as *adequatio* has serious consequences for what now constitutes a "thing." In *"Das Ding"* the thing is integrated from four meaning factors: earth, sky, mortal man and the divine (VA, 176-77). Plainly such a *Seiendes* (incidentally, it was a jug) is integrated independently of any distinction of objective and subjective factors. Such *Seienden* are idiosyncratically typical of a given epoch of human history, each epoch experiencing the *Seienden* in its own unique way according to the total meaning of its world. Thus Heidegger has replaced the *animal rationale* of Western history by *Dasein*. And *Dasein* is a purely historical being. Just how and whether *Dasein* is an individual is no longer a problem for Heidegger just as little as any question arises about other *Seienden* except as included in the becoming of a meaningful historical world (*Sein*); for *Sein* and *Dasein* are the same. The *Differenz* that distinguishes different historical epochs of *Dasein* now rightfully assumes central importance in Heidegger's phenomenology.

Heidegger has stepped out of act-potency metaphysics to which belong man as *animal rationale* and *veritas* as *conformitas*. But he does not deny that something *Richtiges* can be said about *animal rationale* (PW, 66) or that the declaration of physics be *richtig* (VA, 168); and this *richtig* is plainly *veritas* as *conformitas* (WW, 8). And Heidegger sees the all but insurpassable "*Groteske*" in the view that his efforts seek to destroy metaphysics (SF, 36). Thus it seems that his thought should not be interpreted as an all-embracing account of well-founded thought. Types of thought remain that Heidegger's way of thought does not fully explain. Rather Heidegger seems to have spent a lifetime thinking on the origin (*Wesen*) of representational thought as found in the categories of act-potency relations of the tradition of the Thomists, Scotists and Hegel (SZ, 3, 38). Not only does Heidegger place *Sein und Zeit* in this perspective: "*Phenomenologische Wahrheit (Entschlossenheit von Sein) ist veritas transcendentalis*" (SZ, 38); but he refers back to this passage with approval in *Brief über den "Humanismus"* (PW, 83).

Now I can place the question of this paper. For the late Heidegger no act-potency structure of *Existenz* is possible, since it is experienced by stepping out of the act-potency relation of the subject to its experience. *Existenz* is *Inständigkeit in und aus Das Sein;* and hence is *Dasein* whereby *Existenz* "*steht das Dasein aus*" (PW, 71); and accordingly, *Existenz* as the 'essence' of man and *Sein* are the same. Hence, plainly to say the least, *Dasein* can have no act-potency structure. But Heidegger arrives at *Existenz* as standing *in und aus Das Sein* and as the same as *Sein* precisely because the *Ich Denke* as act-potency subject of its experience characterizes the self-being of man as a *Vorhandenes* (SZ, 319). Now eminent Heideggerian scholars like Biemel and Richardson have seen the ontic-ontological structure of *Dasein* in *Sein und Zeit* as distinct inseparable dimensions. And distinct inseparable dimensions are a characteristic act-potency structure. Now I can place my question. *Does the late Heidegger omit the ontic-ontological structure of Dasein because it characterizes Existenz as a Vorhandenes?*

Part Two

Marjorie Grene contrasts the Heidegger of *Sein und Zeit* with the later Heidegger in the following words: "The analysis of Being-in-a-world (as in *Sein und Zeit*) had shape and direction; beside it the search for Being itself is 'verschwommen': formless and blurred" (the later Heidegger).[11] No student of Heidegger can disagree with this global impression. What remains an open question is whether this change is a degeneration to be deplored or a purification to be lauded. In *Über den "Humanismus"* Heidegger says that the most difficult thing in philosophy consists "not in being immersed in exceptionally profound thought or in constructing complex concepts, but rather lies concealed in the step backward that permits thought to enter into an experiential questioning and to let drop the accustomed opinions of philosophy."[12] Hence it behooves us, in considering the variations of the later Heidegger, to notice what he let drop. For no doubt his later thought let drop elements that gave more determinate shape to his earlier thought.

Über den "Humanismus" contains a long passage in which Heidegger drops the distinction between the *possible* and the *actual* because, he says, such a distinction derives from the distinction of act and potency: he describes the undifferentiated reality thus uncovered as historical destiny. (After having on the previous page ridiculed the procedure of those who would try to estimate the nature and power of the fish from its ability to live outside its watery element on dry land, Heidegger goes on to speak of the nature and

[11] Marjorie Grene, *Heidegger* (London: Bowes & Bowes, 1957), pp. 124-25.

[12] "Allein das Schwierige besteht nicht darin, einem besonderen Tiefsinn nachzuhängen und verwickelte Begriffe zu bilden, sondern es verbirgt sich in dem Schritt-zurück, der das Denken in ein erfahrendes Fragen eingehen und gewohnte Meinen der Philosophie fallen lässt" (PW, 91).

power of thought as derived from the element in which it is found: Being.)

Names like 'Logic', 'Ethics', 'Physics' arise first when original thinking is on the decline. During their golden age the Greeks did their thinking without such rubrics. They did not even dub their thought 'Philosophy.' Thought goes into decline when it withdraws from its element. The element is that whence thought is enabled to be thought. The element is properly speaking the enabling factor: the faculty. It takes an interest in thought and brings it thus to have an essence. Simply speaking, thought is the thought of Being. The genitive case here bespeaks something two-fold. Thought is 'of Being' insofar as thought eventuates from Being, belongs to Being. Secondly, thought is thought 'of Being' insofar as thought, belonging to Being, listens to Being. Inasmuch as thought is listening-belonging to Being, it is what it is according to its essential origin. Thought is — this means: Being has always taken a fateful interest in it. To have an interest in a thing or a person for what they really are means to love them, to like them. Such liking considered in the primordial instance signifies: confer the essence. Such liking is the proper essence of a faculty, that cannot only let this or that be accomplished but can let something derive from its origin so as to let it be at all. The faculty of liking is that thanks to which something is properly able to be. This faculty is the *possible* in the proper sense: that whose essence lies in liking. From out of such liking, Being enables thought to be. The former renders the latter possible. Being as the faculty of liking is the possible. Being as the element is the silent power of the faculty of liking, that is of the possible. Our words *possible* and *possibility*, under the domination of 'Logic' and 'Metaphysics' have certainly come to be thought only as distinct from *actuality*; that is to say they have come to be thought only in terms of a particular — metaphysical — interpretation of Being as *actus* and *potentia*. And this distinction has become identified with *existentia* and *essentia*. When I speak of the silent power of the *possible*, I do not mean the *possible* of a merely conceptual *possibil-*

itas, nor do I mean *potentia* of an *actus* of *existentia*. Rather I mean Being itself as having a liking for thought and for the essence of man; and that means that Being has power over thought's relation to Being. To have power over something here signifies: to conserve it in its essence, to retain it in its element.[13]

What strikes the reader of this passage at first sight is Heidegger's studied effort to reverse the customary philosophical usage of

[13] "Auch die Namen wie 'Logik', 'Ethik', 'Physik', kommen erst auf, sobald das ursprüngliche Denken zu Ende geht. Die Griechen haben in ihrer grossen Zeit ohne solche Titel gedacht. Nicht einmal 'Philosophie' nannten sie das Denken. Dieses geht zu Ende, wenn es aus seinem Element weicht. Das Element ist das, aus dem her das Denken vermag, ein Denken zu sein. Das Element ist das eigentlich Vermögende: das Vermögend. Es nimmt sich des Denkens an und bringt es so in dessen Wesen. Das Denken schlicht gesagt ist das Denken des Seins. Der Genitiv sagt ein Zweifaches. Das Denken ist des Seins, insofern das Denken, vom Sein ereignet, dem Sein gehört. Das Denken ist zugleich Denken des Seins, insofern das Denken dem Sein gehörend, auf das Sein hört. Als das hörend dem Sein gehörend, ist das Denken, was es nach seiner Wesensherkunft ist. Das Denken ist — dies sagt: das Sein hat sich je geschicklich seines Wesens angenommen. Sich einer 'Sache' oder einer 'Person' in ihrem Wesen annehmen, das heisst: sie lieben: sie mögen. Dieses Mögen bedeutet, ursprünglicher gedacht: das Wesen schenken. Solches Mögen ist das eigenliche Wesen des Vermögens, das nicht nur dieses oder jenes leisten, sondern etwas in seiner Her-Kunft 'wesen', das heisst sein lassen kann. Das Vermögen des Mögens ist es, 'kraft' dessen etwas eigentlich zu sein vermag. Dieses Vermögen ist das eigentlich 'Mögliche'; jenes, dessen Wesen im Mögen beruht. Aus diesem Mögen vermag das Sein das Denken. Jenes ermöglicht dieses. Das Sein als Vermögend-Mögende ist das 'Mög-liche'. Das Sein als das Element ist die 'stille Kraft' des Mögenden Vermögens, das heisst, des Möglichen. Unsere Wörter 'möglich' und 'Möglichkeit' werden freilich unter der Herrschaft der 'Logik' und 'Metaphysik' nur gedacht im Unterschied zu 'Wirklichkeit', das heisst aus einer bestimmten-der metaphysichen-Interpretation des Seins als actus und potentia, welche Unterscheidung identifiziert wird mit der von existentia und essentia. Wenn ich von der 'stillen Kraft des Möglichen' spreche, meine ich nicht das possible einer nur vorgestellten possibilitas, nicht die potentia, als essentia eines actus der existentia, sondern das Sein selbst, das mögend über das Denken und so über das Wesen des Menschen und das heisst über dessen Bezug zum Sein vermag. Etwas vermögen bedeutet hier: es in seinem Wesen wahren, in seinem Element einbehalten" (PW, 56-58). Further on in the *Über den "Humanismus,"* Heidegger more expressly explains this "fateful interest" of *Sein in Dasein:* "als der Ek-sistierende steht der Mensch das Dasein aus, indem er das Da als die Lichtung des Seins in die 'Sorge' nimmt. Das Dasein selbst aber ist als das 'geworfene'. Es west im Wurf des Seins als des schickend Geschicklichen" (PW, 71). This I translate: "Inasmuch as he is the existing one, man endures *Dasein* by taking under 'care' the *Da* as the clearing of Being. For its part, the *Dasein* properly is that which is 'thrown'. It comes to presence through Being's throwing in the manner of a destining fateful one."

the terms *essence* and *faculty*. According to traditional act-potency analysis, faculty is an accident of the agent, in this case it would be an accident of man, who is the thinker. But Heidegger uses the term faculty (*Vermögen*) deliberately to signify Being inasmuch as Being "has always taken a fateful interest in" thought. Thus Heidegger deliberately removes from the significance of *faculty* or *power* any act-potency analysis in terms of accident *in* a substance. But he does not thereby lose all meaning of necessity from the significance of *faculty*: for the notion of necessity is still carried by the "fateful interest" of Being in thought. But necessity and fact now appear as indistinct from each other under the form of historical destiny.

Moreover, essence is also ripped away from its traditional meaning in act-potency philosophy as necessary substantial potency respecting existence as its contingent substantial act. Essence becomes for Heidegger a mere derivative of historical fate as liking man. The essence of man is thought without any reference to a world of substances composed of act-potency components but rather with reference to the history of Being that destines by liking.

Heidegger's removal of the distinction between the possible and the actual is motivated by the fact that this distinction is based on the distinction between act and potency. And the distinction of act and potency, he declares in the above passage, is but a particular interpretation of Being. In other words, the historical destiny of *Sein's* liking for man has built a particular act-potency home for a particular historical epoch of *Dasein*.

Once Heidegger had thought back behind the distinction of the actual and the possible, it was inevitable that he should remove from his consideration the distinction between the ontological and the ontic. For the distinction between the ontological and the ontic can be shown to be an application of the distinction between the possible and the actual.

Yet it is scarcely credible to me that Heidegger should have been forced to eliminate the distinction between the ontic and the ontological. For, in my opinion, close study of *Sein und Zeit* shows that the scaffold of the book's overall argument rests ultimately on this distinction. Yet, on consideration, it perhaps is not so incredible that a man like Heidegger should discard the foundations of an *argument*, so long as the *basic experience* that underlay the argument remained intact. And Heidegger's basic experience of the historicity of man is not in question. But it must be shown that the overall argument of *Sein und Zeit* ultimately rested on the distinction between the ontic and the ontological, and that he was forced to abandon that distinction.

It is clear the overall argument of *Sein und Zeit* hoped to show that the meaning of *Sein* is time. I say "hoped to show" for it must be recalled that *Sein und Zeit* is not a completed work.[14] And so the book does not conclude that the meaning of *Sein is time*. But the book does end with the question: "Does a way lead from original time to the meaning of *Sein*?"[15] But though the book did not conclude that the meaning of *Sein* is original time, Heidegger intended that it so conclude. For original time is the time of authentic *Dasein*.[16] And authentic *Dasein* is hypothesized as giving the authentic meaning of *Sein*.[17]

The steps leading to the final question about the link between primordial time and the meaning of *Sein* can be condensed thus:

1. The meaning of *Sein* must be taken from how it enters *Dasein*: Thus Heidegger writes: questioning the meaning of *Sein* . . . questions *Sein* itself as it enters into the comprehensibility of *Dasein*."[18]

2. Only authentic *Dasein* is a whole capable of answering the fundamental ontological question of Being: "One thing has become unmistakable: *our existential analysis of Dasein up to now cannot lay claim to being primordial.* Inauthentic *Dasein* alone, and precisely as not-a-whole, filled up its entire purview. If the interpretation of the *Sein* of *Dasein* as foundation of the fundamental ontological question is to become primordial, then it must have brought to light *Sein* of *Dasein* in its authenticity and in its wholeness" (Heideggar's italics).[19]

---

[14] Comparison between the projected outline of *Sein und Zeit* at the end of the second introduction and the actual divisions of the book reveals that the outline was completed only up to Part One, 2 (SZ, 39).

[15] Führt ein Weg von der ursprünglichen *Zeit* zum Sinn des *Seins*?" (SZ, 437).

[16] Cf. point number 3 in the outline below.

[17] Cf. point number 2 in the outline below.

[18] "Und wenn wir nach dem Sinn von Sein fragen, dann wird die Untersuchung nicht tiefsinnig und ergrübelt nichts, was hinter dem Sein steht, sondern fragt nach ihm selbst, sofern es in die Verständlichkeit des Daseins hereinsteht" (SZ, 152).

[19] "Eines ist unverkennbar geworden: *die bisherige existenziale Analyse des Daseins kann den Anspruch auf Ursprünglichkeit nicht erheben. In der*

3. Not the time of inauthentic *Dasein*, but the time of authentic *Dasein* is *primordial time*: "Since the 'time' vulgarly attaching to the meaning of *Dasein* is proven not-primordial, but rather to arise out of authentic time, then according to the maxim, *a potiori fit denominatio* we can rightly call *primordial time* the temporality just adduced."[20]

4. *Dasein* is authentic and whole inasmuch as resoluteness anticipates death. "In death *Dasein* must take itself back absolutely. Being constantly convinced of this in an anticipatory way, resoluteness gains a conviction that is both authentic and whole."[21]

5. Resoluteness (*Entschlossenheit*) and anticipation of death (*Vorlaufen*) are distinct but identical. "Resoluteness (*Entschlossenheit*) does not merely have a connection with anticipation (*Vorlaufen*) as with another than itself. It hides authentic being to death (*Sein zum Tode*) in itself as the possible existentiell modality of its own authenticity."[22]

6. This relation of anticipating to resoluteness is that of the ontological to the ontic: "But must not it (the interpretation of the authenticity and wholeness of *Dasein*) justify itself respecting the existentiell possibilities, with which it gives the ontological interpretation ontic grounding?"[23]

So it is clear that the overall argument of the book ultimately

Vorhabe stand immer nur das *uneigentliche* Sein des Daseins und dieses als *unganzes*. Soll die Interpretation des Seins des Daseins als Fundament der Ausarbeitung der ontologischen Grundfrage ursprünglich werden, dann muss sie das Sein des Daseins zuvor in seiner möglichen *Eigentlichkeit* und Ganzheit existenzial ans Licht gebracht haben" (SZ, 233).

[20] "Wenn daher die der Verständigkeit des Daseins zugängliche 'Zeit' als *nicht* ursprünglich und vielmehr entsprungend aus der eigentlichen Zeitlichkeit nachgewiessen wird, dann rechtfertigt sich gemäss dem Satze, *a potiori fit denominatio*, die Bennenung der jetzt freigelegten Zeitlichkeit als *ursprüngliche Zeit*" (SZ, 329).

[21] "In seinem Tod muss sich das Dasein schlecthin 'zurücknehmen'. Dessen ständig gewiss, *das heisst vorlaufend, gewinnt die* Entschlossenheit ihre eigentliche und ganze Gewissheit" (SZ, 308).

[22] "Die Entscholossenheit 'hat' nicht lediglich einen Zusammenhang mit dem Vorlaufen als einem anderen ihrer selbst. *Sie birgt das eigentlich* Sein zum Tode in sich als die mögliche existenzielle Modalität ihrer eigenen Eigentlichkeit" (SZ, 305).

[23] "Aber muss sie sich nicht selbst rechtfertigen hinsichlich der existenziellen Möglichkeiten, mit denen sie der ontologischen Interpretation den ontischen Boden gibt?" (SZ, 312). Cf. item 5 in this series. Resoluteness and anticipating as distinct but identical are conceived as act-potency.

rested on the distinction between the ontic and the ontological. This only makes it more necessary to show that Heidegger in fact abandoned this distinction. And it would greatly help if I could show that this abandonment was required by his deepest insight.

Now, in *Gelassenheit*, Heidegger declares that neither the relation of *Sein* to *Dasein* nor the relation of *Sein* to the *Seienden* can be thought of either as ontic or as ontological. The text is in the form of a dialogue between a teacher, who represents Heidegger, and a scientist and a scholar. Since the scientist and the scholar in this passage merely put in scholarly language what has already been said by the teacher, what they say should be attributed to Heidegger himself. In this text, *region* and *regioning* (*Gegnet, Vergegnis*) are terms for *Sein; Release* (*Gelassenheit*) names *Dasein's* thought as waiting on the opening of *Sein*.

"Scholar: According to your exposition, the relation of the region to release is neither a causal relationship nor the horizonal transcendental relation. In short and more generally stated, this amounts to saying: the relation of region to release can be thought of neither as ontic nor as ontological, if it can be called a relation at all . . . .

Teacher: but rather merely as regioning.

Scientist: But also likewise then, the relation between region and thing is neither a causal one nor the transcendental-horizonal relationship, and consequently is likewise neither ontic nor ontological."[24]

This text is not ambiguous in rejecting analysis in terms of the distinction of the ontic and the ontological. But the rejection is not sufficiently motivated relative to the fundamental importance that the distinction played in *Sein und Zeit*. This motivation, however, can be traced back to Heidegger's rejection of the distinction between actuality and possibility as an interpretation of Being ade-

---

[24] "Nach Ihrer Darlegung ist die Beziehung der Gegnet zur Gelassenheit weder ein kausaler Wirkungszusammenhang, noch das horizontal-transzendentale Verhältnis. Um es noch kürzer und allgemeiner zu sagen: Die Beziehung zwischen Gegnet und Gelassenheit, falls sie überhaupt noch eine Beziehung ist, kann weder als ontische noch als ontologische gedacht werden. . . . L. sondern nur als die Vergegnis. F. Insgleichen ist nur aber auch die Beziehung zwischen Gegnet und Ding weder ein kausaler Wirkungszusammenhang noch das transzendental-horizontale Verhältnis, mithin weder ontisch noch ontologisch" (G, 55).

quate to express the historicity of *Dasein*: which rejection was so clearly expressed in the above passage from *Über den "Humanismus."* Let us consider the following passage of *Kant und das Problem der Metaphysik* in order to see that the early Heidegger was deriving the ontic-ontological distinction from the traditional metaphysical distinction between the actual and the possible.

'Possible' experience can be understood in distinction from the actual experience. But in 'the possibility of experience' the possible experience poses no more problem than does the actual experience. Rather both together raise a question relative to what possible experience renders possible. Hence, possibility of experience means what renders finite experience possible; and finite experience is experience that is not necessary, but rather is contingent actual experience. This 'possibility' that renders contingent experience radically possible is the possibilitas of traditional metaphysics, and signifies the same thing as *essentia* or *realitas*. 'Real definitions are taken from the essence of things, from the first ground of possibility.' Kant's *Logikvorlesung*, #106, note 2, loc. cit., Vol. VIII (of Kant's Works), p. 447: cf. also, *Critique of Pure Reason*, B 302, A 596, B 624). 'Possibility of experience' accordingly means primarily: the unique totality of that which renders finite experience possible. 'The possibility of experience is thus that which gives objective reality to all our a priori knowledge' (*Kritik Der Reinen Vernunft*, A 156, B 195). Possibility of experience accordingly signifies the same as transcendence. Circumscribed in its essential totality, this latter (transcendence) means: to determine 'the conditions of the possibility of experience.'[25]

[25] " 'Mögliche' Erfahrung kann gemeint sein im Unterschied von wirklicher. Aber in der 'Möglichkeit der Erfahrung' ist die 'mögliche' Erfahrung so wenig Problem wie die wirkliche, sondern sie beide hinsichtlich dessen was sie im vorhinein ermöglicht. Möglichkeit der Erfahrung heisst daher das eine endliche, d.h. nicht notwendige, sondern möglicherweise wirkliche Erfahrung Ermöglichende. Diese 'Möglichkeit', die das 'möglicherweise' allererst ermöglicht, ist die possibilitas der überlieferten Metaphysik und gleichbedeutend mit essentia oder realitas. 'Real-Definitionen sind hergenommen aus dem Wesen der Sache, dem ersten Grund der Möglichkeit'." (Logikvorlesung §106, Anm. 2, a.a.O. VIII, S. 447; vgl. auch B 302 Anm., A 596, B 624, Anm.)

" 'Möglichkeit der Erfahrung' heisst demnach primär: die einige Ganzheit dessen, was endliche Erkenntnis im Wesen ermöglicht. 'Die Möglichkeit der

In this passage, Heidegger is explaining Kant. But let us ask ourselves whether the analysis in *Sein und Zeit* reflects these Kantian notions which Heidegger's just cited exposition traces back to the distinction of the actual and the possible of traditional metaphysics. The above analysis links the unique totality of the possibility of experience as ground of contingent real experience to the traditional metaphysical distinction between the possible and the actual. Let us then frame the question: According to *Sein und Zeit*, is the ontological possibility of experience as a whole *the ground* of ontic contingent experience? In *Sein und Zeit* only authentic *Dasein* can be a whole, so our question must concern Heidegger's analysis of authentic *Dasein*.

The culmination of *Sein und Zeit* is the discovery that only the wholeness of authentic *Dasein* in its future, having-been and present ecstacies can be the ground of historicity (*Geschichtlichkeit*). Now "historicity" is nothing but contingent experience: for it is *fate* to be enacted within a given historical tradition. Hence historicity-fate is ontic contingent experience. Our question can now be sharpened to stand: does *Sein und Zeit* make the unique totality of possible experience found in authentic *Dasein* the ontological condition of the possibility and the ground of ontic historicity-fate? Heidegger writes:

> Fate demands . . . as condition of its possibility the being structure of care, that is, of temporality. Only in care . . . can it (*Dasein*) exist in the mode of fate, that is, only then can it be historical in the ground of its existence . . . Only a being equi-primordially futural and having-been can . . . presently be 'for his time.'[26]

And Heidegger writes on the next page: "Authentic being toward

---

Erfahrung ist also das, was allen unseren Erkenntnissen a priori objective Realität gibt' (A 156, B 195). Möglichkeit der Erfahrung ist demnach gleichbedeutend mit Transzendenz. Diese in ihrer vollen Wesensganzheit umschreiben, heisst: 'die Bedingungen der Möglichkeit der Erfahrung' bestimmen" (KM, 109-10).

[26] "Schicksal . . . verlangt als ontologische Bedingung seiner Möglichkeit die Seinsverfassung der Sorge, das heisst die Zeitlichkeit. Nur . . . wie in der Sorge kann es im Modus des Schicksals existieren, das heisst im Grunde seiner Existenz geschichtlich sein . . . nur Seiendes das als zukünftiges gleichursprünglich gewesen ist, kann . . . augenblicklich sein für 'seine Zeit' " (SZ, 385).

death, that is finitude of temporality, is the hidden ground of the historicity of *Dasein*."²⁷

Hence, the answer is: the unique totality of possible experience found in authentic *Dasein* is stated by Heidegger to be the ontological condition of the possibility and the ground of the historicity of *Dasein*. And the historicity of *Dasein* is plainly ontic, since it springs from an "existentielle Versteh-en" (SZ, 383).

However, before concluding that the ontic-ontological distinction had to be discarded because it covertly hid the actual-possible distinction of traditional metaphysics, we must be sure that these terms in *Sein und Zeit* directly vitiate the basic experience that Heidegger is explicating. Could not "ontological", "possibility of experience" and "ground" be interpreted as harmless traditional phrases that do not determine the course of the argument?

Heidegger's basic experience consisted in stepping back out of Kant's act-potency conception of the subject respecting its experience, as we have already seen. For Kant thus characterized the self-being of man as a *Vorhandenes* (SZ, 319). Hence, Heidegger's basic experience would be betrayed if the wholeness of authentic *Dasein* were founded on an analysis drawn from the *Vorhandenen*.

But Heidegger clearly shows at the outset of Part II of *Sein und Zeit* that the method of this part is taken from *Seienden* other than *Dasein*, i.e., from the *Vorhandenen*. Indeed, Heidegger half perceives the difficulty. For the method immediately raises for him the problem of method taken from interpretation (*Interpretation*) of any kind of *Seiendes*. Yet Heidegger says explicitly that we must proceed from what belongs to any interpretation (*Jede Auslegung*, SZ, 232). The method of *Jede Auslegung* demands a primordial ontological *Interpretation* that gets the thematic *Seiende* as a whole. Heidegger is troubled as to whether the method of *Jede Auslegung* fits the particular *Seinsart* of the particular *Seiende* that forms the theme of his *Auslegung*: "A primordial ontological interpretation (*Interpretation*) ... must make expressly sure that it has brought the whole of the *Seiende* taken as theme (*thematischen Seiendes*) into its purview."²⁸ And Heidegger writes on the next

²⁷ "*Das eigentliche Sein zum Tode, das heisst die Endlichkeit der Zeitlichkeit, ist der verborgene Grund der Geschichtlichkeit des Daseins.*"
²⁸ "Eine ursprüngliche ontologische Interpretation ... muss sich ausdrücklich dessen versichern, ob sie das *Ganze* des thematischen Seienden in die Vorhabe gebracht hat" (SZ, 232).

page: "It is indeed questionable whether it is attainable and whether a primordial ontological interpretation (*Interpretation*) of *Dasein* must not shatter on the kind of being (*Seinsart*) taken as theme."[29]

Hence, it is not mere traditional phraseology that leads *Sein und Zeit* to analyse *Dasein* in the ontic-ontological categories of traditional act-potency metaphysics. The very method that leads to it is derived from *Seienden* of any *Seinsart*, i.e., *Vorhandenen* and then applied to *Dasein*, that particular *Seinsart* counterdistinguished against the generality of *Seinsart*.

Hence, the method goes against the fundamental experience that lay in the step back from characterizing the self-being of man as a *Vorhandenes*. Consequently, the ontic-ontological analysis is a betrayal of Heidegger's fundamental experience and had to be omitted from his later work. Heidegger seems to allude to this weakness of *Sein und Zeit* when he alludes to its incongruous intention (*ungemässe Absicht*) respecting science and research (PW, 110).

Part Three — Conclusion

Once Heidegger is forced to abandon the ontic-ontological (act-potency) structure of *Dasein*, authentic *Dasein* only exists as cast (*Wurf*) of *Sein* which, as Father Richardson says, is the thinker; but that thinker can only think the various fated meanings of *Sein*. So also *Sein* according its various incompatible meanings, Spiritualism, Materialism, etc. (WM, 7) is but a *Geschick* of the *Differenz*. *Existenz* is thus "freed" from any root outside of the fated meanings of *Sein*. Moreover, the *Seienden* also are "freed" from any root outside historical meaning. For a *Seiendes* is but that to which the evolving world meaning draws near. Thus, the *Differenz*, out of which all *Geschicke des Seins* hide more than they reveal of the meaning of *Seienden*, remains the inscrutable mystery underlying historical *Existenz, Seienden* and *Sein*.

Moreover, our modern Western conception of man as *animal rationale* or person, and consequently our Western ethics built on rational principles implying as it does *veritas* as *conformitas*, and our sciences also implying as they do *veritas* as *conformitas*, in sum

[29] " . . . es wird sogar fraglich, ob sie überhaupt erreichbar ist und ob nicht eine ursprüngliche ontologische Interpretation des Daseins scheitern muss — an der Seinsart des thematischen Seienden selbst" (SZ, 233).

the whole root meaning of the world to modern Western man, *all this* the late Heidegger reduces to a *Geschick* of the inscrutable *Differenz* out of which emerged the fundamental act-potency meaning that lends its color to the *Existenz* of modern Western man (PW, 73). In brief, the whole meaning of modern Western *Existenz* is exposed as rooted in a historical fate emerging from the unknowable mystery of the *Differenz*.

I understand Heidegger's work as a prolonged study of the origins of thought prior to the categories of act and potency, and thus understood, his work is continuous with the tradition of the Thomists, Scotists and Hegel.[30] For Heidegger moved into *Existenz* by stepping back out of act-potency metaphysics. Concerning a return back step out of Heidegger's *Existenz* into an act-potency philosophy or into any philosophy having roots outside of historical meaning, Heidegger has nothing to say except that one can say something *"richtig"* outside his experience of *"Wahrheit."* Those who accept Heidegger's back step out of act-potency, but who are not willing to remain in a purely historical meaning to man and his world, bear the whole burden of the return back step.

[30] Heidegger placed *Sein und Zeit* in the context of *veritas transcendentalis* in the tradition of the Thomists, Scotists and Hegel (SZ, 3, 38). And in *Über den "Humanismus"* he refers back to this perspective with approval (PW, 83). These traditions apparently so diverse do in fact agree:
1. In placing original intelligibility in the noting of being and in qualities or properties identical with being.
2. In placing act-potency and the categories of substance-accident and causality as more determinate notions posterior to these notions of original intelligibility.
For the *Thomistic tradition* cf. St. Thomas, *De Veritate*, Qu. I, art. 1, and John of St. Thomas, *Cursus Philosophicus*, Tomus II (Turin, 1933), pp. 24-27. For *Scotus*, cf. *Opera Omnia* (Vatican City: Typis polyglottis, 1956), Tomus IV, Ordinatio I, Distinctio 8, qu. 3, pp. 205-207; and Allan B. Wolters, O.F.M., *The Transcendentals and Their Function in the Metaphysics of Duns Scotus* (Washington: Catholic University Press, 1946), pp. 4-12 and 58-78. For *Hegel*, consider the lengthy dialectic that separates the empty notion of being and the determinations of quality from the notions of act-potency, substance-accident and causality (paragraphs 84-158 of the third edition of the Encyclopedia). Being and the other determinations of quality are roughly the scholastic transcendentals, since they are defined as identical with being. This voluminous and arduous dialectic is conceived by Hegel as a search for the concrete.

Towards the Movement of Reversal:
Science, Technology, and
the Language of Homecoming

John Sallis

Part One — A Vapor and a Fallacy:
The Wonder of Recall

This essay addresses itself to the last two questions posed by Heidegger in his letter.[1] Heidegger asks:

(1) What does the discussion of the question of Being and of the epochs of the mittence of Being (*Seinsgeschick*) accomplish as regards the interpretation of the present age of technology?

(2) In what relation does the thinking of the question of Being stand to modern science, which is distinguished by the absolute priority of method over against its possible objects?

Our first effort must be directed towards understanding what is asked in the questions.

These two questions ask about the relation of the thinking of the question of Being to science and technology. It is significant that Heidegger raises these questions only after a series of other questions about the question of Being and about the thinking of the question of Being with regard to its limits in *Sein und Zeit* and its relation to the tradition. What is proposed in Heidegger's last two questions is the task, not simply of interrogating, much less of evaluating,

---

[1] See the letter from Heidegger contained in this volume.

science and technology, but rather that of thinking through their relation to the thinking of the question of Being.

Heidegger refers to "the interpretation of the present age of technology." We are to understand that the present age is the age of technology, that technology — and with it, modern science — is what gives to the present age its decisive stamp. Thus, Heidegger asks that we meditate the relation of the thinking of the question of Being to the present age.

He asks that we "work out" the questions. To work out a question means neither to rush headlong into an answer that leaves the questioning behind once and for all nor simply to interrogate the question independently of the questioning in which it arises. To work out a question requires that we enter into that questioning from which the question issues and in which it is at issue.[2] In the present case that questioning is just the thinking of the question of Being. Thus, Heidegger asks us to enter into the questioning whose question is the question of Being and to do so in such a manner as to elucidate in this questioning how this questioning stands in its relation to science and technology. Heidegger is posing questions not *about* the thinking of the question of Being but *of* this thinking. Heidegger's questions do not ask that we relate the question of Being to other issues as though there were not already within the questioning whose question is the question of Being an inherent connection with these other issues. Heidegger's questions ask nothing more than the question of Being. His questions invite us to enter into this thinking of the question of Being. His questions offer a "contribution," not by asking new questions — Heidegger asks always only one question — but rather by giving directives for gaining access to and moving within the sphere of that essential thinking which thrives on its "limitation to one thought" (**ED**, 7).

---

[2] Heidegger writes in reference to the question, *"Was heisst Denken?"*: "The answer to the question, 'Was heisst Denken?' is indeed a saying, but not an assertion which could be fixed in a statement with which we could put the question aside as settled. The answer to the question, 'Was heisst Denken?' is indeed a speaking, but it speaks from out of a corresponding. It follows the call and holds the questioned in its question-worthiness. When we follow the call, we do not free ourselves from the questioned. The question cannot be settled, now or ever. If we go to encounter what is here questioned, the calling, the question becomes only more question-worthy. When we are questioning from out of this question-worthiness, we are thinking. Thinking itself is a way. We respond to the way only by remaining underway" (**WD**, 163-64). "What remains in thinking is the way" (**US**, 99).

We need to enter into the thinking of the question of Being in such a way as to be able thereby to come to speak of the relation of this thinking to the present age, in such a way as to be capable of undertaking within the medium of this thinking "the interpretation of the present age of technology." We enter into the thinking of the question of Being when we succeed in asking the question in such fashion as to hear what the question in its being asked already bespeaks. We ask the question in order to gain entry into the sphere of essential thinking; but "entry into" is simultaneously "entry from out of" and in such a way that the "from out of" is necessarily carried over into the entry. Hence, we enter into the sphere of essential thinking, that is, we succeed in genuinely posing the question of Being, only from out of that sphere in which we have already been granted a stand. That sphere in which we already find ourselves cast into a stand at the very inception of our asking is none other than the present age of technology. The present age does not first become an issue only after we have succeeded in working out the question of Being, but is rather already at issue in the very raising of the question. We ask the question, "What is the meaning of Being?" Our asking is a speaking. The question is articulated in our words. But our words are ours only insofar as they are the words of a language in which we are already at home, a language in which a way of articulation is already handed over to us before we ever come to ask the question of Being, a language which, in turn, has its essential connection to the stand in which historical man finds himself cast. The very language handed over to us as the pre-condition for asking any question conceals within itself an essential connection between the question of Being and the stand of the questioning within the present age of technology.

What is more worthy of thought, more thought-provoking, than the fact that we ask the question of Being from out of our stand in the present age of technology — the age for which Being has long since come to be regarded as "a vapor and a fallacy" (EM, 27) — the age in which "it appears as though there were no such thing as Being" (SF, 34)? Heidegger's questions provide a directive in that they direct us back into the "presupposition" of the questioning, and this is what is required of thinking — that it go "directly towards" its presupposition and get "involved in it" (WD, 162). How is it that in the midst of the forgottenness of Being we are called to ask the question of Being?[3] How are we to let our thinking get involved in the present age of technology in its character as the presupposition of the thinking of the question of Being?

In 1955 Heidegger delivered in his hometown of Messkirch a memorial address, later published as the first part of *Gelassenheit*. The address begins by speaking of the homeland (*Heimat*) and of the endowment for which the thinker is indebted to it. In the course of the address Heidegger asks: "Does not the flourishing of any genuine work depend upon its rootedness in the soil of a homeland?" He answers by quoting the words of the German poet, Johann Peter Hebel: "We are plants which — whether we like to admit it to ourselves or not — must with our roots rise out of the earth in order to bloom in the ether and to bear fruit" (G, 16). We are plants sustained by our rootedness. Man has need of roots and of rootedness in an element appropriate to his nature, in an element capable of sustaining him in what he is. It is precisely thus that the highest danger in which contemporary man is caught up is, for Heidegger, expressed in the fact that "the rootedness of man is threatened today at its core" (G, 18).

These words are difficult to hear attentively. Instead, we hear in them only another expression of despair over the deterioration of modern Western culture; we hear only a critique of Twentieth-Century life and culture of the sort that has by now become so commonplace as to be monotonous. Perhaps too we hear in them only the dream of a traditionalist who, confronted with the void into which contemporary man has been cast, takes flight into the security of a naively romanticized tradition. Today we are weary of mere negation of our age and suspicious, if not cynical, towards those who flee into tradition. But Heidegger neither "wastes his time in the mere negation of his age," nor does he engage in a flight to tradition which, in his words, "is powerless, taken by itself, for anything except blindness and delusion over against the historical moment" (HW, 88).

The rootedness of man is threatened today at its core. What is the character of this threat and what is its source? Heidegger says: "The loss of rootedness is caused not merely by external circum-

---

[3] Meno asked: "And how will you inquire, Socrates, into that which you do not know? What will you put forth as the subject of inquiry?" There is the highest irony in Socrates' dismissal of the question as a mere "tiresome dispute." See Plato, *Meno*, 80 d-e.

stance and fortune, nor does it stem only from the negligence and the superficiality of man's way of life. The loss of rootedness arises from the spirit of the age into which all of us were born" (G, 18). The threat to man's rootedness has its source in the spirit of the present age; the present age — the age of technology — is of such a character that within it a threat is posed to man's rootedness. This threatening character of the present age provides us with a means of access by which our thinking can get involved in the present age in its character as the "presupposition" of the thinking of the question of Being. But this can become evident only when we think through the character of the threat.

Man's rootedness is today threatened, and this threat takes its most extreme form precisely when it conceals itself in such a way as to appear in the guise of a liberating of man. His rootedness is most severely threatened in the wake of the appearance that man is freed from his rootedness in order that he might be freed unto himself. Man comes to take upon himself the task of establishing his rootedness and is given to believe that he receives sustenance from his rootedness only insofar as he, first of all, sustains it. He becomes master of his roots in such fashion that his being supported by his roots, his returning to a nearness to the sustaining source, to the origin (cf. HD, 23), depends upon his having already, in advance, instituted that origin. For contemporary man home-coming is made to require home-creation; he takes up his abode only in what he has, first of all, constructed.[4] What is decisive, then, is not just that today roots are lacking but, more essentially, that this lack conceals itself. Rootlessness is such as to conceal itself beneath the assumption by man of the task of providing himself with his rootedness. What is at issue in Heidegger's thinking is, thus, not an *establishing* of a new rootedness for modern man, for this would be to take up precisely that effort in which modern man's rootless-ness is consummated, that is, concealed. What is at issue is not that a new rootedness be *established* but rather that it be *granted* (G, 23). What is required is that man's being always already root-ed — "whether we like to admit it to ourselves or not" — come into view, that the supporting ground of his pretention to be self-ground-ing somehow reveal itself in such a way that in his response to it

---

[4] Cf. my essay, "Nietzsche's Homecoming," *Man and World, II* (1969), pp, 108-116.

man can come to be sustained by a sustaining source of which he takes himself to be neither the creator nor the master.

The rootedness of man is today threatened. Our age is one in which the sustaining source is withdrawn from us and withdrawn in the most extreme way, namely, in such a fashion that it conceals its very withdrawal beneath the semblance of being itself rooted in subjectivity.[5] The source conceals its own concealment. What is the source? The tradition has given it many names (cf. ZS, 28, 60; N, II, 399 ff.), all of which say as little to us today as does the name by which Heidegger called it from the beginning of his way. The sustaining source is Being, and Being is for us today "a vapor and a fallacy" now that the sustaining source has come to appear only as something posited by man. Human subjectivity has come to show itself as the ground of ground (SG, 149), as a subjectivity which establishes in advance the ground in reference to which it is determined what is. Things are only insofar as they show themselves through a conforming to what is prescribed by subjectivity, and it becomes impossible to "permit things to be the measure-giving reality." The threat to man's rootedness simultaneously threatens to annihilate things as things (VA, 168). Man, uprooted from the sustaining source, is no longer at home among things.

The threat to man's rootedness unfolds in the form of man's claim to a self-grounding. This claim is what constitutes the core of modern metaphysics (FD, 75 ff.), and, thus, the granting of rootedness to man requires a recovery (*Verwindung*) from metaphysics. Modern metaphysics — and, with it, this claim — achieves its highest domination in technology, which, in turn, sustains an essential relationship with modern science. If the sustaining but concealed source of this claim is to reveal itself — and this is what is at issue in the granting of a new rootedness to man — then it is required that technology, metaphysics, and science be experienced precisely as escaping the attempt to render them subject themselves to that claim which constitutes their core. It is necessary that the claim to self-grounding reveal itself as violating just that which it claims, that the essence of technology, metaphysics, and science show itself as irreducible to something posited by subjectivity — as, rather, withdrawing from man in such decisive fashion as to escape neces-

---

[5] ". . . the peculiar unchaining of the demand for the supplying of ground (by subjectivity) threatens all homeness (*Heimische*) of man and robs him of every ground and basis for a rootedness. . . ." (SG, 60).

sarily every effort on the part of man to bring it into his grasp.

The granting of rootedness to man is prepared through the disclosure beneath man's claim to a self-grounding of a sustaining source which, first of all, claims man — of a sustaining source which, in placing its claim upon man so as to set him on the way of claiming a self-grounding, simultaneously withdraws from man, conceals itself. But this disclosure is not the result of the activity of a subject, for what is to be disclosed is characterized precisely by its incessant withdrawal from the grasp of subjectivity. How then does there arrive that reversal *from* the forgottenness for which Being is only "a vapor and a fallacy" *to* the granting to man of a rootedness in the sustaining source? We must try to understand that the arrival of this reversal, this "reversal in Being" (TK, 44), is inherently linked to the consummation of the forgottenness of Being in modern metaphysics and science and especially in technology. We can understand this only if we enter into the movement of the reversal.

Heidegger's questions about the relation of the thinking of the question of Being to science and technology thus ask not only that we enter into the thinking of the question of Being in accordance with a certain directive but also that in this entry we make use of the understanding that all genuine entry into the thinking of the question of Being is an engagement in the movement of reversal.[6] Our task is to engage in the movement of reversal in the sphere of modern science, of modern metaphysics, and finally of technology.

Part Two — Modern Science: The Mathematical Project

Our intention is to engage in the movement of reversal within the sphere of modern science. Reversal, however, is not something simply to be executed by a subject, and, hence, it is not a matter of undertaking a reversal in the sense of proposing a rejection or negative evaluation of science. Heidegger speaks not against the sciences "but for them, for clarity concerning their essence" (WD, 49). Heidegger does not seek to give an *evaluation* of science, for to understand his task as one of evaluating, to conceive it in reference to the concept of value, would be to remain totally under the

---

[6] Cf. VA, 184. Note especially Heidegger's insistence that "even in the initial steps of the question of Being in *Sein und Zeit* thought is called upon to undergo a change whose movement cor-responds with the reversal." Heidegger's "Preface" to William J. Richardson, *Heidegger: Through Phenomenology to Thought* (The Hague: Martinus Nijhoff, 1963), p. xix.

domination of the essence of the modern scientific project (cf. HW, 93-94; EM, 151-52) — hence, to remain oblivious to this essence and to what is at issue in the movement of reversal. Heidegger is in search of clarity regarding the essence of science. How are we to understand the character of this search and, in particular, its connection with the movement of reversal? Heidegger writes that "a fog still surrounds the essence of modern science" — and, he adds, this fog "is not produced by man at all" (WD, 49). We shall attempt to understand, first, what distinguishes modern science — what its "essence" is — second, how it is that this "essence" is enshrouded by a fog not of man's making, and, finally, what this fact prescribes as regards the connection between a search directed towards essence and an engagement in the movement of reversal.

Modern science is commonly described as mathematical — in contrast to ancient and medieval science. Modern science, it is held, in distinguished by the fact that it employs mathematics, and this use of mathematics is what is taken as determining its essential character. This view is correct. Modern science is, indeed, distinguished by the fact that it is mathematical. However, modern science is able, according to Heidegger, to "proceed mathematically only because it is in a deeper sense already mathematical" (HW, 71), and it is this more fundamental sense of mathematical that must be recovered if we are to arrive at clarity regarding the essence of modern science.

Heidegger pursues the recovery of this deeper sense of mathematical by means of a meditation on the meaning of the Greek words *mathēsis, ta mathēmata*.[7] The mathematical signified to the Greeks that about things which we already know, which we do not first come to know from things themselves, but which we already bring to these things (FD, 53-59): "*ta mathēmata* means for the Greeks that which man knows prior to his observation of beings and

[7] In this meditation on these decisive words of the Greek language Heidegger does not busy himself simply with the transformation of word-meanings (VA, 212). Nor is his decision to pursue his inquiry through a meditation on certain words an arbitrary one. On the contrary, it has its roots in the way in which the question of language enters into the domain of the thinking of the question of Being. Just prior to a similar linguistic meditation in *Einführung in die Metaphysik* Heidegger remarks: ". . . the question of *Being* will involve us deeply in the question of *language*. It is more than an outward accident that now, as we prepare to set forth, in all its implications, the fact of the evaporation of Being, we find ourselves compelled to take linguistic considerations as our starting point" (EM, 39).

his acquaintance with things" (HW, 71-72). It was only because numbers are those things most obviously known beforehand, most obviously known prior to our acquaintance with things — it was only because numbers are the most apparent of the mathematicals that subsequently the name "mathematical" came to take on its narrower meaning (HW, 72; FD, 58). Modern science is thus distinguished as mathematical, not because it makes use of numbers, but because it is based in the deeper sense of mathematical as pertaining to that which is known of things independently of things, in advance of our experience of them. What is entailed in saying that modern science is mathematical in this more fundamental sense?

Something can be known about things prior to our experience of them only if what is so known is instituted, is put into things, by us. As Kant said, "We can know *a priori* of things only what we ourselves put into them."[8] The mathematical is that pertaining to things which has its source not in things but in the proposing activity of a subject. It is something which the subject proposes to itself as a projection in advance definitive of what things are to be taken to be. It is a project which "skips over the things" in such a way as to open up a domain wherein things can show themselves; it is a projection of the thingness of things. This project, as projecting in advance "that which things are taken as," is axiomatic, is "of such a kind as to set things upon their foundation in advance" inasmuch as they are able to make their appearance only within the already projected blueprint or ground-plan of nature as such (FD, 71).

It is because the projection of a definite ground-plan forms the basis of modern science that method comes to have "decisive priority" (VA, 58). The ground-plan, the mathematical project, as an axiomatic pre-determining of the basic constitution of things, in effect prescribes the manner in which those things are to be investigated. It is only within the compass of the pre-determining project that scientific questioning is able in advance to propose conditions which constrain nature to yield up answers, and such a posing of questions to nature is, as Kant recognized, what is meant by experiment in modern science. How things are to be interrogated scientifically is determined by the mathematical project independently of things themselves, and it is thus that Heidegger in his letter refers

[8] Kant, *Kritik der reinen Vernunft*, B xviii.

to the fact that modern science "is distinguished by the absolute priority of method over against its possible objects." Finally, just as this project determines the meaning of experiment in modern science, so likewise with the mathematical character of modern science in the narrow sense of its making use of mathematics. Because the project posits a homogeneity of all bodies as regards space, time, and relative motion, it dictates in advance that the essential way of determining things, as the spatio-temporal determination of the motion of mass-points, is that of homogeneous measure, which is to say numerical measure, which is to say mathematics in the narrow sense (FD, 71-72).

It has already been stressed that Heidegger's interrogation of science is not to be understood as proceeding independently of the thinking of the question of Being but that, rather, it is integral to that thinking. How, then, is the determination of the character of modern science in terms of the mathematical project to be viewed in its inherent connection with this thinking? How is the aim of this interrogation of science to be so understood as to bring to light its connection with the thinking of the question of Being? In *Die Frage nach dem Ding* Heidegger writes: "*We want neither to replace the sciences nor to reform them.* Nevertheless, we want to participate in the preparation of a decision; the decision: Is science the measure of knowledge, or is there a knowledge in which the ground and limit of science and thus its genuine effectiveness are determined?" (FD, 8). Heidegger's interrogation of modern science in which it is understood in terms of the mathematical project already prepares this decision. Modern science proceeds only on the basis of the already established ground-plan. As science, it presupposes, subjects itself to, the mathematical project — which is to say that, as science, it is incapable of interrogating its fundamental character: the essence of science "remains inaccessible" to the sciences (WD, 57); for example, "Physics can as physics make no assertions about physics. . . . Physics itself is not a possible object of a physical experiment."[9] This, in turn, entails that science is not "the measure of knowledge" at least in that it is not the measure of itself. What then about "a knowledge in which the ground and limit of science

---

[9] VA, 65. This is, of course, not to say that a scientist cannot interrogate science but only that when he does so (as in the cases of Bohr and Heisenberg) he "thinks in a thoroughly philosophical way" — outside the project which defines the domain of his science (FD, 51).

. . . are determined"? Presumably this is the knowledge which Heidegger seeks in his interrogation of science. But in what sense does
the discussion of the mathematical project ground science and
establish its limits?

It is possible to distinguish three successively more fundamental
senses of the grounding and delimiting of science that is underway
in Heidegger's work. First of all, science needs to be delimited with
respect to the range within which its characteristic objectification
has its rights. Modern science proceeds always on the basis of the
already projected ground-plan which prescribes in advance what can
be encountered and how it is to be encountered within the framework of scientific investigation. Modern science places upon things
the demand that they conform to the pre-established ground-plan,
and whatever might happen not to be so conformable could quite
simply not enter the domain of what is scientifically accessible:
"Science always meets up only with that which *its* kind of representation has from the outset permitted as a possible object for it" (VA,
168). But if this is so, then "scientific representation can on its side
never decide whether nature through its objectivity does not rather
withdraw" (VA, 63) — whether nature in its essence does not remain hidden away in that which is inaccessible to scientific objectification. Science, it seems, can at most only encounter — in the
course of its attack, its challenging of things to show themselves
within its proposed horizon — something like a "counter-attack" on
the part of the things grasped in scientific representation, as we find
in the work of Heisenberg (SF, 22). But if the rights and limits of
scientific objectification are to be established, it is required that the
threat of withdrawal somehow be thematized, that the range of
extension of the mathematical project be determined.

This cannot be accomplished within the compass of the mathematical project. Is it then the task of thinking, of the fundamental
ontology undertaken in *Sein und Zeit*, to interrogate the range of
extension of the mathematical project in the various regions engaged and articulated by it? But Heidegger clearly distinguishes
in *Sein und Zeit* between such "regional ontologies" and the
fundamental ontology which is his concern and which is already
required as the pre-condition of progress in the tasks
of "inquiring into the ways in which each particular area is
basically constituted" (SZ, 9). Fundamental ontology has, indeed,
to interrogate the mathematical project, but it undertakes this task

— thereby preparing for an establishing of the limits of science — precisely by seeking to uncover the ground of the project. This is the second sense in which Heidegger is engaged in a delimiting and grounding of science, and this second level expresses just the task which proves to be the pre-condition for the accomplishment of what is proposed at the first level of interrogation. By common opinion, science is an activity of man, and, in particular, the projection of the ground-plan of nature is something which man accomplishes. The ground of the projection — hence, presumably, that in terms of which its possibilities can be delimited — is to be found by an inquiry into man as the one through whom the project is first instituted. The task is, as Heidegger sketches it in *Sein und Zeit*, that of "asking which of those conditions implied in Dasein's state of Being are existentially necessary for the possibility of Dasein's existing in the way of scientific research" (SZ, 357). What are the conditions that are required in order for Dasein to exist "in the way of scientific research"? What is required, first of all, is that Dasein possess the resources for projecting the ground-plan of nature with which science begins and for binding itself to it. But what are the "conditions implied in Dasein's state of Being" that allow it to originate the mathematical project?

Are these conditions intelligible through subjectivity? Is it possible to exhibit subjectivity as the sufficient ground of the mathematical projection? Does the project (*Entwurf*) find its ground in Dasein or, on the contrary, is it the case that Dasein is such as to be able to engage in such a projecting only in that "*Es west im Wurf des Seins* . . ." (PW, 71)? Only if, through the question of the conditions which allow Dasein to project a ground-plan, we are carried "beyond" Dasein in such fashion that science ceases to be regarded as a mere human creation (VA, 57) — only if we are able to transform this question into a questioning regarding what must be granted to Dasein — only then do we come to the third and most fundamental level of Heidegger's interrogation of modern science, the level at which the questioning of science first appears as integral to the thinking of the question of Being. What is required — having already moved, in the first two stages, from the question of limits to the question of ground — is that, finally, we move to the question of the limit of ground. Only thereby could we understand that the "fog [which] still surrounds the essence of modern science . . . is not produced by man at all." What is called for is an engagement in the movement of reversal. How is this call to be answered?

To the extent that the thingness of things, their Being, appears to have its ground in subjectivity, Being as the source which grants sustenance to man remains "a vapor and a fallacy" and shows itself only as nothing (SF, 38). "We must," says Heidegger, "prepare ourselves to experience in the nothing the vastness of that which gives every being the warrent to be. That is Being itself" (WM, 46). But this is just the movement of reversal.

Part Three — Metaphysics and Language

The exhortation that we prepare to experience Being in nothing occurs near the end of the *Nachwort* to *Was Ist Metaphysik?* It is an articulation of the end from which the lecture *Was Ist Metaphysik?* and the question which gives it its name are to be thought through (WM, 23). The question, "What is Metaphysics?", the interrogation of metaphysics, needs to be taken up in the medium of the movement of reversal.

We want to regard metaphysics as it unfolds in an inherent connection with the mathematical project. This unfolding is that in which what already eventuates (*ereignet*) in that project first comes to be firmly and primordially established. This unfolding is the explicit execution of that movement which our interrogation of modern science has already come upon, namely the movement from the mathematical project back into the subject as its ground. Does the interrogation of modern metaphysics as executing this movement grant us entry into the movement of reversal?

What is decisive in the origination of modern metaphysics is "that man becomes a subject" (HW, 81). Furthermore, when man becomes a subject, things simultaneously become objects (HW, 85). We must try to understand how this decisive change, which initiates modern metaphysics, comes about — this change which, according to Heidegger, constitutes a change in the essence of man as such (HW, 81). How does this change happen? What are its roots?

The clue is found in the word. Prior to Descartes (and even in Descartes' own discourse) the word "subject" ("*subjectum*," "*hupokeimenon*") designated not a certain kind of beings over against others (objects) — much less was it a designation of man. Rather, it signified every being as "something of itself lying before, which at the same time lies at the ground of its stable properties and

changing conditions" (HW, 98). What happens in the origination
of modern metaphysics is that a particular kind of being moves to
the center, becomes that which "of itself lies before" (i.e., subject)
in a pre-eminent sense, specifically in the sense of lying before not
only its own "stable properties and changing conditions" but all
other beings as such: "Man becomes the center to which beings as
such are related" (HW, 81).

What is the source of this transformation? According to Heidegger,
it "arises from the demand of man for a *fundamentum abso-
lutum inconcussum veritatis* (for a self-supporting, unshakeable
ground of truth in the sense of certainty)" (HW, 98). Man moves
to the center because, in the wake of the demand for a ground of
certainty, of the certainty of representation, he stands out as that
subjectum "which already lies before in all representing . . ." in the
sense of persisting indubitably throughout all representation (N,
II, 432). The transformation in which man becomes a subject has
its origin in the demand for a ground of certainty. But a ground of
certainty is just that through which one is able by himself to certify
to himself the truth of his representations, i.e., their conformity to
what is represented through them. The demand for a ground of
certainty is, in effect, the demand for a grounding by the self to
the self; it is the demand for a self-grounding.

This demand for a self-grounding determines the unfolding of
the Cartesian *Cogito*. It appears even more clearly in Leibniz'
formulation of the principle of sufficient reason, for this principle
not only asserts that every being necessarily has a sufficient reason
(ground) but as *principium reddendae rationis sufficientis* expresses precisely the demand for the deliverance of ground for every
being (SG, 53-54, 64). With this principle the demand for the
deliverance of ground is, in effect, shoved between man and things
in such a way that something is admitted as being only if it can be
brought forth in its groundedness, which, in turn, is determined in
its connection with subjectivity (SG, 47-48). Beings become objects; Being becomes objectivity and comes to be established in relation to the representational activity of a subject (SG, 99). Reason
as ground of objectivity becomes with Kant the ground of all
grounding (SG, 149), and thereby the way is prepared for the fulfillment of the demand for self-grounding in the Absolute of German
Idealism (cf. HW, 121-24).

Where, in turn, are we to discover the origin of this demand?

How does it come to have its all-obliging force? Heidegger writes: "The demand arises from that liberation of man in which he frees himself from the bonds of the Christian truth of revelation and church doctrine to a legislation posed to himself for himself" (HW, 99). In a degree this demand for certainty is already operative in the middle ages through the fact that revelation and the institution of the church are regarded precisely as guaranteeing, as providing the certification for those truths most important to man (cf. N, II, 425-26). But the force of the demand is felt only when man's bond with what previously supplied such certification is broken. Man then comes to legislate — to certify — "to himself for himself." What is transformed is man's freedom, his way of being bound to something binding. Man comes under the demand for *self-grounding,* the demand that that to which man is bound be itself established by man. That to which man is bound, that through which he receives his rootedness, i.e., the sustaining source, comes to find its origin in man himself. Man becomes its master in being freed unto himself, and this is why Heidegger insists that there is here a change in the essence of man as such. Home-coming becomes home-creation from out of the return to self.

The issue of the reversal is whether thereby the source is genuinely set back upon subjectivity or whether its being drawn into subjectivity is just its most extreme concealment, a concealment which conceals itself. It is between these two terms that the reversal moves. Do the roots of modern metaphysics as they have come to light offer us, finally, an entry into this movement?

We need to look more closely at the way in which modern metaphysics at its beginning assumes its distinctive character in relation to modern science. This character is expressed, for example, in an image which Descartes used in writing to Picot: "Thus the whole of philosophy is like a tree: the roots are metaphysics, the trunk is physics, and the branches that issue from the trunk are all the other sciences. . . ."[10] What specifically is involved when metaphysics comes to serve as the roots of the tree whose trunk is physics? How is metaphysics understood when it is supposed that it is to sustain the mathematical project?

The mathematical project, we have seen, is axiomatic. It determines things in advance by proposing a ground-plan of nature

---

[10] Quoted by Heidegger, WM, 7.

as such, a ground-plan within the compass of which things are con-strained to present themselves. This ground-plan is — as becomes evident in Kant — a system of principles that defines the objectivity of objects; it is thus that philosophy to the degree that it is the presentation of objectivity as such in its essential articulation comes to understand itself through the idea of system (HW, 93).

What about this system of principles that articulates the ground-plan? For science the ground-plan and, hence, the principles that explicitly articulate it are always already presupposed. But in the wake of the demand for certainty these principles cannot remain simply presupposed, simply taken over uncritically. Rather, it is required that they be exhibited in their truth — that they be certified as true. In that they fail to be self-certifying, it is necessary that they be certified from out of certain fundamental principles. Thus, metaphysics turns its attention to certain fundamental principles in order thereby to be able to serve as the roots of the tree whose trunk is physics.

These fundamental principles, the regress to which is for the sake of certifying the entire system of principles, can be genuinely fundamental only if they are such as to ground all other principles and such as to be themselves self-certifying. The principles that make up the system involve a proposing of objectivity by the sub-ject. Thus, a proposing lies at the root of the system of principles. If it were possible to discover principles inherent in proposing as such, then such principles — provided they were self-certifying — could serve as the fundamental, grounding principles. Fundamen-tal principles are, thus, to be discovered by examining what belongs to any proposing as such (FD, 80). But what belongs indubitably to every proposing as such is the "I propose" : "In the essence of proposing lies the proposition: I propose" (FD, 81). The first fundamental principle is the *Cogito*, the I-principle. Yet, this is not the only fundamental principle discoverable through inherence in proposing as such. Any proposing is an assignment of something to something. Proposing as assertion issuing in a proposition says something about something, assigns a predicate to a subject. What is said in the predicate cannot, however, speak against (contradict) the subject, and, hence, every proposing stands under the demand for avoiding contradiction, i.e., under the principle of non-contra-diction. Finally, all principles, as proposed, have their source, not in things, but rather in the subject, in the subject understood as reason (*ratio*): these principles are, thus, reasons. Furthermore, they are sufficient in that they fully determine the object in its objectivity — hence, the third fundamental principle, the principle of sufficient reason (FD, 82-83).

Does the origination of these fundamental principles offer a means of entry into the movement of reversal? Does this origination, in other words, point back to a source which, sustaining throughout its extent the demand for self-grounding, thereby renders this demand self-violating? Is the demand at the root of modern metaphysics itself rooted in a more primordial demand of which man is not the instituting subject but to which he is, on the contrary, subjected? It is through the fundamental principles that the demand for self-grounding is understood and fulfilled to the limits of its possibility. What is needed is that a sustaining source become manifest beneath the origination of these principles — a source already granted in such fashion as to sustain this origination.

The fundamental principles, we have seen, are discovered within the essence of proposing as such, and the operative interpretation of proposing is, in turn, guided throughout by an understanding of proposition. The origination of the fundamental principles takes place, in other words, within the compass of an already granted understanding of language as such. The primary features of this understanding are already evident in the way in which the fundamental principles flow from the essence of proposing as such. The principle of non-contradiction, arising from the fact that every proposing — every proposition — is an assignment of something to something, has at its roots an understanding of language as assertion (cf. SZ, 153 ff.). The origination of the I-principle points back to an interpretation of proposing, ultimately of language, as quite simply an activity not only carried out, but, in fact, decisively originated, by a subject. The manner in which the third principle, that of sufficient reason, comes to light, is perhaps the most revealing case of all, for it refers back to an interpretation of proposing according to which what is proposed, what is assigned to things, has its source in the subject rather than in the things to which it is proposed. Beneath the movement of self-grounding that distinguishes modern metaphysics there is already operative, already granted an understanding of language as an activity which is not essentially guided by things but which could rather, in effect, be performed by a "worldless subject."

Again the terms of reversal are evident. Is our speaking an activity interior to subjectivity, or is it sustained by a source inherently withdrawing from the self-grounding aspiration of subjectivity? Is subjectivity the ground of speech or is its being so taken rather precisely the highest concealment of what primordially nourishes our speech? The question is again, as previously in the case of science, that of a movement from ground to the limit of ground. The disclosure of the issue of language at the roots of metaphysical self-grounding brings us, however, nearer to the movement of reversal, for language resists, in a way that the mathematical projection does not, being supported in its entire compass by a ground in subjectivity. One does not propose his own language to himself but rather has always already taken it over, has it as something handed down, delivered over, when he comes to speak.[11] One always operates already within a language which he has not originated but in which he is, rather, already moving (WD, 169). Language decisively points beyond the confines of self-grounding subjectivity so as to confront us with the necessity of the question of the limit of ground. The manner in which the limitation of subjectivity with regard to language, i.e., in which the character of language as "handed down," "delivered over," is disclosed comes to determine the possibility of reversal. Is this handing down of language, this delivering over that constitutes tradition, to be understood in the final analysis through the transcendence from individual to absolute subjectivity so as to become a delivering by a subject to itself? Is transcendence capable of vitiating, in the end, every limitation of subjectivity? Or can the character of language as handed down be experienced as a genuine limitation of subjectivity, as decisively pointing beyond subjectivity to that under which and from which subjectivity receives its limitation? In both cases the speech of the individual man is less than totally autonomous and to that extent is response. The question — again the question of reversal — is whether that which calls upon us to speak is understood as an ultimately transparent, self-revealing, absolute subjectivity or whether it is experienced as *decisively and essentially withdrawing*

[11] This is philosophically what is most at issue in the discussions — largely in the context of contemporary logic and mathematics — of the limitation of formalism. See, for example, Mikel Dufrenne, *Language and Philosophy*, trans. by Henry B. Veatch (Bloomington: Indiana University Press, 1963), pp. 57 ff. Also US, 263.

— as withholding itself even to the extent of concealing its own withdrawal. The second alternative, in which the movement of reversal is engaged, is an experience of the character of being handed down *as* mittence of Being (*Seinsgeschick*). But this expression, "mittence of Being," is no self-grounding answer regarding how — on what ground — something like language is handed over. Rather the expression remains a question (SG, 109), that is, the discussion of the mittence of Being and of the epochs of the mittence of Being — this word "epoch" designating not certain stretches of time or periods of history but rather precisely the self-withholding character of Being (ZS, 30) — this discussion is a discourse which perseveres in that questioning which demands that we remain always with it, that questioning which is capable of asking the identical questions, "What calls upon us to speak?" and "What calls upon us to think?"

Heidegger says that "the question as to the essence of Being dies off if it does not surrender the language of metaphysics" (SF, 26). What is required by the thinking of the reversal is not, however, merely the substitution of a new language for the traditional language. What is required is no substitution at all in the sense of an activity in which we, assuming mastery over language, extricating ourselves from our rootedness in it, would so shape it as to render it appropriate to the task of thought. Rather we must surrender the language of metaphysics by recovering from the metaphysics of language.[12] What the thinking of the reversal requires is "a transformed relationship to the essence of language" (SF, 25).

Part Four — Technology and Reversal

The thinking of the reversal requires a transformation of our relationship to the essence of language in which we can come to ask the question "What calls upon us to speak?" and to hear what is bespoken in the question. This transformation comes about from out of an already assumed relationship to language which, in turn,

---

[12] Heidegger writes: "Under the domination of the modern metaphysics of subjectivity language almost incessantly falls out of its element" (PW, 60). The extent to which thinking can stay with the language of metaphysics provided it recovers from the metaphysics of language is indicated by the manner in which Heidegger introduces the movement into the reversal by a seemingly innocuous shift of emphasis in the traditional statement of the principle of sufficient reason (SG, 95).

is bound up in the stand granted to us in "the present age of technology." In what way does the movement of reversal announce
itself through this stand?

This stand, rooted in modern metaphysics, is nourished by an
understanding of the essence of language which remained unthought in the origination of modern metaphysics. The mathematical project and the regress to its self-grounding ground in subjectivity are supported from their beginning by an already granted
relationship to language which remains, however, largely concealed
beneath the unfolding of modern philosophy and science. It is thus
highly significant that in the present age of technology not only is a
demand placed upon language (as, indeed, was already the case at
least as early as Leibniz) but this demand is carried through in the
most thoroughgoing fashion — the demand, namely, that language
be brought totally within the framework definitive of modern metaphysics and science. Language comes now to be regarded as "an
instrument for mastery over beings" (PW, 60). In order to become
an instrument it must itself, however, first have been subjected to
man's mastery; man is able to master beings by means of language
only because he has, first of all, mastered language itself. Language,
in other words, comes to be regarded as an instrument which ideally
should be instituted by subjectivity in such radical independence
of things as to permit it to be retained completely under human
control — as an instrument which, like the mathematical project,
has its ground in the instituting activity of the subject and which
prescribes to things in advance how they are to be spoken about —
as an instrument which is, therefore, to be proposed and investigated primarily with regard to its formal features. Symbolic logic
becomes the rightful heir of modern metaphysics (cf. VA, 234; US,
160).

Language, itself subjected to man's mastery, becomes an instrument for the mastery of beings not only in the field of praxis but,
even more fundamentally, in science and in philosophy itself, where
beings now come always to be encountered "with explanations and
proofs" (PW, 60). Philosophical thinking itself comes under the
sway of the demand placed upon language but precisely in such
fashion that the transformation of philosophical thought that was
already secretly at issue in the origination of modern metaphysics
can now come explicitly to light — though, of course, it need not,
in fact, cannot, to the extent that we persist in confronting philoso-

phical thinking only with the demand for "explanations and proofs."
Likewise, the thoroughgoing subjection of language to the framework of modern metaphysics and science serves precisely to bring
into the open the way of understanding language which previously
lay concealed beneath the unfolding of modern thought. In effect,
the metaphysical framework, sustained from its beginning by an
understanding of the essence of language, has in the present age of
technology turned back upon its own roots so as to draw them into
its sphere of dominion. The question of reversal is whether these
roots, in being brought to light, direct us back to a rootedness in an
element which essentially withdraws from being brought under the
metaphysical framework.

The technologizing of language poses — perhaps in the most
decisive way — the question of reversal. We need to understand
more thoroughly what is at issue in the technologizing of language,
what, more generally, is at stake in the essence of technology as
such. We need to bring into the open the connection — already at
work from the beginning — between the thinking of the question
of Being, which is the thinking of reversal, and the present age of
technology in order that we might understand how it is that "The
question of Being, properly understood, appears as the question
regarding the essence of technology and its relation to the man of
today . . . ."[13]

Heidegger's essay "*Die Frage nach der Technik*" reveals in the
very manner of its composition the peculiar character of the thinking
of the reversal in its connection with the issue of language. The
essay is neither a description of the situation of our time (as a
situation shaped by technology) nor a historical inquiry into the
development of technology through the application of modern natural science. Nor is it an attempt to reach a decision regarding how
the destructive potential of technology could be brought under control so as to place technology securely in the service of man. On all
these matters the essay remains profoundly ambiguous — and not
only on these matters. The essay in its entirety engages in a peculiar
back-and-forth movement within a domain of radical ambiguity,
because it is a speaking engaged precisely in the movement of reversal. It does not describe or explain — much less offer proofs for
— the reversal, for to do so would be to remain oblivious to just

[13] Heidegger's letter in *Heidegger and the Quest for Truth*, ed. by Manfred
S. Frings (Chicago: Quadrangle Books, 1968), p. 20.

what is called for by the reversal. The essay is not about technology; what is at issue is *the question* regarding technology, which question is just the question of Being, the asking of which is the movement of reversal. But also the essay is not *about* the reversal but is rather itself *an engagement in the movement of reversal*. The essay is a movement of reversal from what Heidegger terms the instrumental-anthropological interpretation of the essence of technology to the interpretation of the essence of technology as what Heidegger calls *Ge-stell*. It is a speaking in which is carried through — in the medium of a speaking-corresponding — the reversal from technology understood as an activity of man and a means at his disposal to the essence of technology as a way of uncovering in which man is caught up, that is, already pre-disposed. This reversal must remain ambiguous in that its accomplishment remains beyond the possibilities of our thought and action — in that it is a "reversal in Being" (TK, 44) to which our speaking is called to respond.

The movement of reversal at work in the essay *"Die Frage nach der Technik"* can be articulated in terms of five constituents each of which is itself a peculiar movement of reversal and all of which belong essentially together.

(1) The essay addresses itself to the present age, to the task of providing, as Heidegger says in his letter, an "interpretation of the present age of technology." A discussion of the present age presumably gives an analysis of our situation by bringing to light in their interconnection the various dominant features of the age: the crisis in art, the dominance of the concepts of culture and value, the godlessness of the age, the pervasive effects of science and technology (cf. HW, 69-70). To the extent that the age is regarded as one of decline, as nihilistic, such discussion becomes an "enumeration of symptoms" — an enumeration which can be extended almost indefinitely to include even the more minute segments of modern life. But, says Heidegger, "These analyses of the situation do not notice that they operate only in the sense and according to the way of a technological dismemberment and so yield to the technical consciousness its historical-technical representation of occurring (*Geschehen*)" (TK, 46). Such analyses remain wholly caught up in the spirit of technology not just because they proceed analytically by an enumeration but, more fundamentally, because in order to proceed in this manner they must already have implicity come to regard the present age as something in reference to which it is a matter of

obtaining something like a view, a *Weltbild*, a goal which is not even formulable outside the compass of modern metaphysics (HW, 85). These analyses implicity lay claim to setting the present age at a distance in order to address it and to describe its features while remaining wholly oblivious to the rootedness of such addressing and describing in the present age. They thrive on the typically technological claim of avoiding being in any essential regard engaged in and compromised by that to which they address themselves, while, in fact, this claim is precisely that by which they are hopelessly compromised. What is called for is a movement into an addressing of the present age which understands itself as an addressing from out of the present age, an addressing which understands itself as having already been granted its stand, as having already itself been addressed.

(2) According to the usual opinion, technology comes about when man applies to practice the results of modern natural science. This opinion is correct; for technology things appear only as subject "to the attacks of calculative thought" (G, 20), and such attacks indeed take as their instrument the already operative mathematical project definitive of modern science. Modern science is the precursor of technology, technology the application of the results of modern science. But this opinion, however correct, remains entirely oblivious to the fundamental issue (VA, 29). First of all, the relationship between science and technology involves a reciprocity which is ignored by the common conception of technology as the application of modern science. Modern science in its character as experimental is bound to technology through the fact that it is precisely the developments within technology which circumscribe the range of possible experimentation open to modern science. Without a technology capable of fabricating such apparatuses as the cyclotron, there would be no atomic physics. Thus, Heidegger insists that technology "should not be misinterpreted . . . as a mere application of modern mathematical natural science to practice" (HW, 69) — at least inasmuch as technology as applying modern science is, in turn, applied to modern science in an essentially determining way. To the common opinion that technology involves the application of modern science, Heidegger adds that "modern science is grounded in the essence of technology" (WD, 155).

But does Heidegger want only to add to the determination of technology by modern science a converse determination of science by technology? That this is not the fundamental issue is indicated already in the fact that Heidegger speaks not of technology but of the *essence* of technology (cf. VA, 13). He says, for instance: "Modern physical theory of nature is what prepares the way not first for technology but rather for the essence of modern technology" (VA, 29). Again, he refers to "the exciting fact that today's sciences belong in the realm of the essence of modern technology and nowhere else" (WD, 49). The essence which comes to its fulfillment in technology is just that essence which, without coming expressly to light, already holds sway in modern physics from its beginning (VA, 29). It is not, then, a matter of noting that there happens to be a mutual influence exercised between science and technology but rather of uncovering the common essence which rules in both — an essence which, in turn, is identical with the essence of modern metaphysics (HW, 69). What is decisive in this uncovering is that this common essence reveals itself as decisively withdrawing from all grounding in human thought and action — that, as Heidegger says, "the essence of technology is itself nothing technological (WD, 155), nothing capable of being posed through man's disposing activity. The second movement of reversal traces the path from the interpretation of technology as the application of modern science through the recognition of the reciprocal connection of science and technology to the experience of their self-withdrawing common essence.

(3) Technology is commonly regarded in terms of the relation of means to end, that is, as an arsenal of means by which man is able to achieve certain already posited goals. Such achievement requires that things be brought forth and fabricated in strict accordance with these goals which, in turn, requires that the process in which things are brought forth and fabricated be held securely under man's control. Hence, man needs to gain mastery over natural energies in order to direct them to a shaping of things in accordance with his goals. What is, thus, at issue in technology as means is a way of letting things come forth, a way of bringing them forth — as Heidegger says, a way of uncovering (*Entbergen*) (VA, 14-20). In order to understand the essence of technology we must examine the distinctive kind of uncovering that is operative in technology.

The uncovering that characterizes technology is distinguished (for example, from the uncovering operative in manual crafts or in the fine arts) by the fact that it is a provoking (*Herausfordern*):

"The uncovering which holds sway in modern technology is a provoking, which places on nature the demand to deliver energy, which as such can be exploited and accumulated" (VA, 22). Nature comes to appear as a vast store of energy subject to man's domination. It is posed in the sense of being provoked to supply energy to be accumulated, transformed, distributed, and commuted — such that each instance of provoking is itself geared into a complex system which, in turn, is sketched out in advance and held securely under man's control. The hydroelectric dam provokes the river to turn the turbines that yield up electrical power, which can be accumulated and distributed, transformed so as to supply man's need for heating and lighting, directed so as to drive the machines of a factory in which things are fabricated or in which a further source of energy can be unlocked and placed at man's disposal. What is uncovered in that posing which provokes comes to have its distinctive kind of stand (*Stelle*). It comes to be a fund, a stock — what Heidegger calls *Bestand*. And it is dis-posed (*bestellt*) to its stand (*Stelle*) in order to be dis-posable (*bestellbar*) for a further disposing (*Bestellen*) (VA, 24).

We find ourselves always already engaged in this kind of provoking uncovering that is determinative of technology. Is it, then, a result of human decision that things today get uncovered in this fashion? Is this uncovering such as to have its sufficient condition constituted in the thought and action of man so that man is himself the answer to the question "What calls man into this way of uncovering?" Does the call originate from man himself or, on the contrary, is the fact that the call gets so taken — that we, in effect, do not hear the call — just the highest concealment of that which, in calling us onto a path of uncovering, withholds itself from us? This is the question of reversal.

(4) The instrumental interpretation of technology (as means) is already an anthropological interpretation, an interpretation of technology as an activity of man. Obviously, it is man who carries out that provoking through which things are uncovered as *Bestand*. But on what ground does man take up this way of uncovering? Heidegger writes: "Only insofar as man on his part is already provoked to exploit natural energies can this dis-posing uncovering take place" (VA, 25). We find ourselves already provoked, already cast into an uncovering which provokes; we do not ourselves, first of all, institute through our decision this way of uncovering but

rather find it as always already taken up, handed over to us. The issue is the same that we encountered in the case of language. Is this "being handed over" to be understood ultimately as a "handing over to itself" on the part of an ultimately self-transparent absolute subject? Or, on the contrary, is it to be understood in such wise that that from which such a way of uncovering is handed over is thought as decisively withdrawing, as withholding itself? In the latter case man would be called forth into a way of uncovering on which the call and its source would remain in essential respects concealed.

Man, engaged in uncovering in the way of provoking, only corresponds to a call, an appeal which directs him onto this way. This appeal which provokes man to dis-pose (*bestellen*) things as *Bestand* Heidegger terms *Ge-stell* (VA, 27). The essence of technology rests in *Ge-stell* (VA, 31). It is this appeal which brings man on a way of uncovering, which sends (*schickt*) him on this way. That sending through which man, in turn, is sent upon, granted, a way of uncovering is just what Heidegger calls mittence (*Geschick*): "The essence of modern technology rests in *Ge-stell*. The latter belongs in the mittence of uncoveredness (*Geschick der Entbergung*)" (VA, 33). The interpretation of the present age of technology requires that the essence of technology be understood as mittence of Being (*Seinsgeschick*) — that the present "epoch" of technology be interpreted through the epoch of the mittence of Being, i.e., through the self-withholding, the decisive withdrawal, of Being (cf. ZS, 30). Most fundamentally, it is the epochal character of Being which is at issue in the reversal.[14]

The third and fourth movements within the essay on the essence of technology are engaged on the path leading from the instrumental-anthropological interpretation of technology to an understanding of technology as a way of uncovering on which man is sent by the self-withholding mittence of Being.

(5) It is an understatement to say that today technology is a matter of the gravest concern — that however much technology may continue to provide us with benefits, these benefits are progressively

---

[14] The decisiveness of the relation of the thinking of the reversal to the thought of German Idealism is here apparent. Elsewhere Heidegger writes: "Where the last vestige of the concealment of Being disappears, namely in the absolute self-knowing of the absolute spirit in the metaphysics of German Idealism, the uncovering of beings with regard to their Being, i.e., metaphysics, is fulfilled and philosophy is at its end" (SG, 114). Cf. SG, 145-46.

being more acutely overshadowed by the threats which technology poses. We try to articulate what is at issue in the threats posed. We speak of the disproportionality between our technical progress and our moral and political progress, and we describe what is called for by the threats posed by technology as a matter of subduing technology, of establishing our domination, our sovereignty over it in connection with an appropriate moral constitution (WD, 155), as a matter of becoming master of technology rather than allowing ourselves to be mastered by it. However, in so articulating what is called for on our part in the confrontation with technology we remain totally caught up precisely in the essence of technology. Our proposing to master technology, just as technology in its characteristic way of uncovering proposes to master things so as to force them to deliver up energy, is perhaps even the surest way of failing to come to any decision regarding technology. Already in this articulation we understand technology only instrumentally, and we apprehend the problem of technology only as a technical problem, only as a problem of gaining sufficient control — hence sufficient means — over the means which technology has already placed in our hands to assure that the latter means are not diverted into the achieving of goals contrary to those proper to man. These goals, in turn, are understood in the final analysis as values — a concept which remains hopelessly ensnared in the common essence of technology and modern metaphysics and science (HW, 93-94).

But suppose that the essence of technology is not such as to be mastered by the human subject; suppose that it is precisely such as to escape from every such attempt at mastery. Then what is called for on our part by technology and the threat which it poses is not to be understood as an attempt at mastery, for in this case every such attempt would be futile. Should not this question at least be raised before we confidently set about confronting technology in the effort to master it? Heidegger writes:

> For we must first of all respond to the essence of technology in order afterwards to ask whether and how man might become its master. And this question may prove to be senseless, because the essence of technology stems from the presence of what is present, i.e., from the Being of beings, which man never masters, which he at best can serve (WD, 142).

The fifth constituent in the movement of reversal has to do with the issue of responding to the threats posed by technology. It begins with an understanding of the appropriate response as one of moral mastery and directs this back into the question of the essence of technology thought through the epochal mittence of Being.

The movement of reversal is not a movement of inference; of proof, or of argumentation. The thinking of the reversal does not confront the issue of reversal "with explanations and proofs" (PW, 60). The essay *"Die Frage nach der Technik"* does not establish the necessity of the reversal. Rather, as Heidegger wrote in a letter to a young student who inquired about the source from which the thinking of Being receives its direction, "This thinking can never prove itself like mathematical knowledge" (VA, 185) — not, however, because it is something inferior as compared with the exact sciences but rather because such thinking can attend to — be drawn along by — what, in calling upon us to think, simultaneously withdraws from us only if it relinquishes the metaphysical demand for self-grounding, self-certification, only if, as Heidegger says, it "already has renounced . . . the claim to a binding doctrine or a valid cultural achievement or a deed of the spirit." In this thinking, he continues,

> All depends on the very way-ward step backwards into meditative thinking which attends to the ominous reversal of the forgottenness of Being into the mittence of Being. The step backwards out of the representational thinking of metaphysics does not discard this thinking but rather opens up the distance to the call of the truth of Being in which distance the corresponding stands and goes. . . . Here everything is the way of the testing, hearkening corresponding. The way is always in danger of becoming way-ward. To go this way demands practice in the going (VA, 184-85).

Part Five — Thinking as Homecoming

It has already been observed that Heidegger's essay, *"Die Frage nach der Technik,"* moves in a medium of radical ambiguity and, in fact, must so move granted the character of the thinking which is there underway. Even at the level of common opinion technology already confronts us with a profound ambiguity, which we, at first, articulate in terms of the duality of benefits provided and threats posed by technology. Heidegger's essay, in effect, takes up this ambiguity inherent in technology and carries it over to the level proper to the thinking of the reversal (VA, 41).

The mittence which holds sway as *Ge-stell* so as to constitute the essence of technology is entited by Heidegger "the highest danger" (VA, 34). There are three respects in which its character as the highest danger is manifest.

First, there is contained in it the imminent possibility that man may come to take the measure of all things only in relation to an uncovering which provokes and that thereby he will close off in decisive fashion every other possibility of uncovering (VA, 33). If, as we have seen, science can never decide whether or not nature perhaps withdraws from the scientific mode of uncovering so as to hide itself away in those corners which remain outside the circle of the mathematical project, it is at least equally the case that, as long as we remain within the way of uncovering constitutive of technology, we not only can reach no such decision but furthermore remain oblivious to the issue of this decision and to the possibility of a different mode of uncovering which might, in connection with such a deciding, offer a more essentially primordial presence to things. It is thus that *Ge-stell* endangers our relationship to things.

Second, *Ge-stell* represents the highest danger by the fact that it poses a threat to man's own relation to himself to the extent that provoking-uncovering gets taken as the standard by which is measured not only things but man himself. This danger is thematized by Heidegger in *Einführung in die Metaphysik* as the contemporary misinterpretation of spirit. In the wake of the essence of technology spirit gets reinterpreted as intelligence, as "mere cleverness in examining and calculating given things and the possibility of changing them and complementing them to make new things." This mere cleverness, "subject to the possibility of organization," subject to the provoking disposal constitutive of technology, becomes, in turn, a mere tool to be manipulated in the service of something else and is finally reduced to the status of a mere superstructure (EM, 35-36).

Thus, on the one hand, man is brought to the point where he himself is taken only as *Bestand*. On the other hand, however, to the extent that he is brought to take himself as the one through whom whatever is dis-posed as *Bestand* is so dis-posed, he "gives himself airs of being master of the earth" in such fashion that, as Heidegger remarks with an allusion to Heisenberg, it comes eventually to appear as though "man encounters everywhere only himself." Yet it is precisely in this situation that "man nowhere encounters himself in truth, i.e., in his own essence" (VA, 34-35); for he encounters himself only as subject *of*, never as subject *to*, the call under which he stands. This is the third, the encompassing danger inherent in the essence of technology. The way of uncovering which provokes and which determines technology is precisely that way of uncovering which most radically conceals its own character as an uncovering into which man is sent. It is that way of uncovering which in its correlative claims — already prepared in the origination of modern metaphysics and science — to mastery and to radical autonomy most decisively conceals man's rootedness in a source through which he is cast into this way of uncovering. *Ge-stell* is the highest danger in this fundamental respect in that it threatens most radically to deny man's entrance into a domain in which can be heard the call which, withdrawing from man, sends him on his way. The forgottenness of Being reaches here its highest point.

But in the midst of the highest forgottenness of Being it is given to the thinker to say that "it is fitting that we should raise anew *the question of the meaning of Being*" (SZ, 1). It is given to him to say, "This question has today fallen into forgottenness" (SZ, 2), and, hence, already to be drawn along in essential cor-respondence into the movement of reversal from forgottenness of Being to a thinking which lets itself be bound to Being through the questioning to which belongs the question, "What calls upon us to think and to speak?" The question of the meaning of Being is asked and what is bespoken in the asking can be heard; *and* we stand in the midst of the highest forgottenness of Being, in the present age of technology. The fundamental ambiguity is expressed at the level proper to the thinking of the reversal in the words of Hölderlin:

> Wo aber Gefahr ist, wächst
> Das Rettende auch.[15]

We have spoken of the threat which the essence of technology poses to language and of the fact that this very threat contains the possibility of directing us back into the relation to language which remained unthought in the origination of modern thought, the pos-

[15] Quoted by Heidegger in *"Die Frage nach der Technik"* (VA, 36, 43) and in the essay *"Die Kehre"* (TK, 41).

sibility of retrieving what lies unthought in the past as just what draws us forward in the effort of thought. Heidegger writes:

> The oldest of the old comes into our thinking
> from behind us yet in front of us (ED, 19).

We have seen, too, that the essence of technology threatens equally our relationship with things. It threatens, as Heidegger says, to annihilate things as things and decisively blocks our access to an uncovering in which things could be permitted to be "the measure-giving reality" (VA, 168). Yet it is precisely in the response to technology, in the effort at thinking back into its self-concealing essence, that the question of a renewal of the presence of things as things comes to light.

In the wake of the essence of technology our relation to language and to things stands threatened. These are not, however, two different threats but, in the end, one and the same, for "words and language are not wrappings in which things are packed for the commerce of those who write and speak. It is in the word, in language, that things first come into being and are. Therefore, the misuse of language ... destroys our genuine relation to things" (EM, 11). And this threat has its origin in the fundamental threat posed in the forgottenness of Being: "The *rootedness* of man is threatened today at its core."

Heidegger's work invites us to let ourselves be engaged in the movement of reversal in which may be granted a new rootedness to man. Such thinking, as a willing not-willing (G, 59), remains bound to that strife — which the Greeks, perhaps most of all Plato, knew — the strife between the utmost *hubris* and a self-binding releasement (*Gelassenheit*) into the bindingness of *Moira;* thus "the possibility of going astray is with this thinking the greatest" (VA, 183). This thinking requires that we attend to the call of the sustaining source so as to come to speak the language of homecoming:

> We may dare the step back out of philosophy into the
> thinking of Being as soon as we are at home in the source
> of thinking (ED, 19).

Prolegomena to "Time and Being": Truth and Time

Andre´ Schuwer

Part One — Introduction

"Time and Being" immediately evokes in the mind of every Heidegger-scholar *Being and Time*. "Time and Being" is a work of the later Heidegger and *Being and Time* is the work of the early Heidegger. Does this way of speaking of an early Heidegger (*Being and Time*) and a later Heidegger ("Time and Being") not suggest a change in the thinking of Heidegger? Does it not raise the problem or question of its continuity? Could it not be that there occurred in the later Heidegger a more or less radical departure from the position Heidegger took in his early work *Being and Time*? We might very well suppose so if we listen to what Heidegger himself says about the three ways open to the thinker:

> . . . one which thinking must go before all other ways; one to which thinking must also pay heed as it proceeds; and one which remains impassable to thinking. . . . The way of thinking is of such a kind that this crossroads [of way, no way, and wrong way] can never be crossed by a once-for-all decision and choice of way, and the way can never be put behind as once-for-all behind us. The crossroads accompanies us on the way, every moment (WD, 108).

In the last paragraph of *Being and Time* Heidegger qualified his

philosophic endeavor as the search for "a way of casting light
on the fundamental question of ontology" (SZ, 437) and asserted
that "this is a way one must go." Already at the end of the Introduction it is indicated that the way proposed with the project of *Being
and Time* entails the change from "Being and Time" to "Time and
Being." In this connection commentators distinguish between a
thinking which evolves while remaining within the transcendental
horizon of subjectivity[1] and a thinking of a "way of thought . . .
that abandons subjectivity" (PW, 72). In the *Letter on Humanism*
Heidegger asserts in reference to the third section of the first division of *Being and Time* (namely "Time and Being"): "Here the
whole thing is re-versed."[2] From this time on *Die Kehre*, the reversal, entered on the philosophical scene and gave birth to
"groundless and endless prattle."[3]

Whatever might be argued in favor of a more or less radical
change, we ought, first of all, to observe that Heidegger does not
interpret his so-called "later" works as a radical departure from the
earlier position articulated in *Being and Time*. This is clear in
Heidegger's response to a question posed to him by Richardson.
Heidegger was asked: "Granted *that* a 'reversal' has come-to-pass
in your thinking, how has it come to pass? In other words, how are
(we) to think this coming-to-pass itself?" To this question he answered: "The 'coming-to-pass' of the reversal which you ask about
'is' Be-ing [*Seyn*] as such. It can only be thought *out of* the reversal. There is no special kind of coming-to-pass that is proper to
this (process). Rather, the reversal between Being and Time, between Time and Being, is determined by the way Being is granted,
Time is granted. I tried to say a word about this 'is granted' ['*Es
gibt*'] in the lecture 'Time and Being' . . . on January 30, 1962."[4]

Secondly, we should note that Heidegger agrees that there has
been a change in his thinking. In the preface to Richardson's book
he writes: "The thinking of the reversal *is* a change in my thought.
But this change is not a consequence of altering the standpoint,
much less of abandoning the fundamental issue, of *Being and Time*.
The thinking of the reversal results from the fact that I stayed with

[1] ". . . eine Wesensbestimmung des Menschen aus der Subjectivität . . ."
(WM, 12).
[2] "Hier kehrt sich das Ganze um" (PW, 72).
[3] Heidegger's "Preface" to William J. Richardson, *Heidegger: Through
Phenomenology to Thought* (The Hague: Martinus Nijhoff, 1963), p. xviii.
[4] *Ibid.*, pp. xvi, xx.

the matter-for-thought (of) 'Being and Time,' sc. by inquiring into that perspective which already in *Being and Time* was designated as 'Time and Being.'" He insists that "even in the initial steps of the Being-question in *Being and Time* thought is called upon to undergo a change whose movement cor-responds with the re-versal."[5] He says: "One need only observe the simple fact that in *Being and Time* the problem is set up outside the sphere of sub-jectivism — that the entire anthropological problematic is kept at a distance, that *the normative issue* is emphatically and solely the experience of Da-sein *with a constant eye* to the Being-question — for it to become strikingly clear that the 'Being' into which *Being and Time* inquired can not long remain something that the human subjects posits."[6]

Thirdly, let us underline what Heidegger himself has said of "Time and Being," the proposed third section of *Being and Time*. He writes: "This section was suppressed because the thinking failed the language adequate to this re-versal and did not succeed through the aid of the language of meta-physics" (PW, 72). When asked by Professor Tezuka of Tokyo University why he did not publish this third section he answers: "How should be named what is only searched for" (US, 110). As a matter of fact the later thinking of Heidegger comes to concentrate more and more explicitly on lan-guage. The fact that Heidegger almost suddenly appears seriously engaged in interpreting poetry (and was Nietzsche not considered a — somewhat be-wildering — poet rather than a thinker likely to find his place in the history of philosophy?) has also been referred to as one of the reasons why it is permissible to speak of a consid-erable change in Heidegger's outlook and standpoint compared with the atmosphere of highly scholarly articulations of *Being and Time*. In *Unterwegs zur Sprache* Heidegger even asserts that he has abandoned a former standpoint: "*Ich habe eine früheren Stand-punkt verlassen*" (US, 98). He adds, however, that he did not aban-don his standpoint in order to substitute another standpoint for it "but rather because the former standpoint was only an abode along a way. . . . And ways of thinking conceal within themselves the mystery that we can travel forward and backward along them, that even the way backward first leads us forward."[7]

---

[5] *Ibid.*, pp. xvi-xviii.
[6] *Ibid.*, p. xviii (Italics mine).
[7] "sondern weil auch der vormalige Standort nur ein Aufenthalt war in

Fourthly, we need to call attention to the fact that for Heidegger "all words which give utterance to the intrinsically manifold matter of 'Being and Time' (like reversal, forgottenness and mittence) are always *ambiguous.*"[8] For Heidegger the distinction between various periods in his thought, the talk about the reversal as some kind of operation which took place *in* his *Fragendes Denken,* the distinction between the texts that are anterior and the texts which are posterior to the reversal — as if the reversal were some kind of event determined chronologically — are not very *ad rem,* not to say it in less euphemistic terms. Heidegger writes: *"The reversal is in play within the matter itself. Neither did I invent it nor does it affect merely my thought.* Up to now I know of no attempt to reflect on this matter and analyze it critically."[9] For Heidegger "The reversal *is* above all *not an operation of interrogative thought*; it is inherent in the very matter designated by the headings: 'Being and Time,' 'Time and Being.' For this reason, the passage cited from the 'Letter on Humanism' reads: 'Here the whole is reversed.' 'The Whole': this means the matter [involved] in 'Being and Time,' 'Time and Being.' "[10] And in his little essay entitled *"Die Kehre"* Heidegger even asserts that "Perhaps we stand already in the shadow cast by the arrival of *this* reversal. When and how it fatefully eventuates no one knows."[11] So for Heidegger we are dwelling in a shadow which the coming reversal casts already upon us, and we do not know when it will come to pass.

Fifthly, we observe that in his preface to "Time and Being" Heidegger writes that he wants to say something about his endeavours to think "Being" without *das Seiende* (. . . *Sein ohne das Seiende zu denken*); that he wants to think "Being" without regard to a *Be-gründung,* a foundation of Being in and through beings. And he declares that such an attempt seems necessary in order to bring into view the meaning of what "is" around the global village (to use an expression of McLuhan) and to bring that into view in

einem Unterwegs . . . . Und Denkwege bergen in sich das Geheimnisvolle, dass wir sie vorwärts und rückwärts gehen können, dass sogar der Weg zurück uns erst vorwärts führt." (US, 98-99).

[8] Richardson, *Heidegger,* xxiii. (Italics mine).

[9] *Ibid.,* p. xviii.

[10] *Ibid.* (Italics mine).

[11] "Vielleicht stehen wir bereits im vorausgeworfenen Schatten der Ankunft *dieser* Kehre. Wann und wie sie sich geschicklich ereignet, weiss niemand" (TK, 40-41).

its own-ness. In *Was heisst Denken?* Heidegger writes that "most thought provoking in our thought-provoking time is that we are still not thinking"; this assertion implies for Heidegger " . . . *ein Urteil über das gegenwärtige Zeitalter* . . . ." He adds: "What is decisive about such judgments, however, is not that they evaluate everything negatively *but that they evaluate at all.* . . . They determine the value, so to speak the price range into which the age belongs . . ." (WD, 14. Italics mine.). It is well-known how expandedly Heidegger judges in his work the age we live in, how harsh his accusation is of modern society, how violent — I risk to say — his opposition is to modernity.[12] So we see that on the one hand Heidegger rejects any kind of *Be-gründung* of "Being" in and through *das Seiende;* such an undertaking — I presume — being only motivated by the question why being is and by the question: "by what is being caused?"[13] On the other hand, it seems clear that Heidegger, in his essay "Time and Being" is in search of some kind of *Grund* in order to *achieve* a thinking which *has already* brought into view *"was heute rund um den Erdball ist"* (ZS, 14).

We can say then that the reversal is "in play within the matter itself"; within that which calls on us to think. That which calls on us to think, Heidegger writes in his lecture "Time and Being", has a binding and obliging force under the condition that we are responsive to this call: *"eine Verbindlichkeit die jedes Denken bindet, gesetzt dass es sich dem Geheiss des zu Denkenden fügt"* (ZS, 61). Heidegger is referring here to his book *Was heisst Denken?* Following this hint which Heidegger gives in his lecture "Time and Being," our paper is an attempt to say something about the reversal as "in play within the matter itself", within the matter of thought (ZS, 38). In the lecture "Time and Being" Heidegger writes that his lecture aims at only one thing: "to bring in view Being as *Ereignis.*"[14] Our attempt to say something about the reversal as in play within the matter of thought will concentrate on *Ereignis,* since it is *Ereignis* which is the *Sache des Denkens, Ereignis* which "grants Time, which grants Being."

[12] Cf. Jean-Michel Palmier, *Les Ecrits politiques de Heidegger* (Paris: L'Herne, 1969).

[13] Heidegger writes: "Today we want to know only why Being is" (WD, 167).

[14] "Allein geht nicht auch die einzige Absicht dieses Vortrags dahin, das Sein selbst als das Ereignis in den Blich zu bringen?" (ZS, 60).

We would like to conclude this introduction with the verse of Martin Heidegger from *Aus der Erfahrung des Denkens* (ED, 5):

> *Weg und Waage,*
> *Steg und Sage*
> *finden sich in einen Gang.*
> *Geh und trage*
> *Fehl und Frage*
> *deinen einen Pfad entlang.*

Part Two — Was Heisst Denken?

We want to speak of the "reversal" as "in play within the matter itself," the "matter" which calls upon us to think and in thinking to be who we are. The question "*Was heisst Denken?*" is a question *asked* in a fourfold way. It asks: (1) What is designated by the word "thinking"? What does the word "thinking" signify? (2) What does the prevailing theory of thought, namely logic, understand thinking to be? When, in logic, one speaks of thinking, what is meant thereby? (3) What are the prerequisites that we need in order to perform thinking rightly? What is needed for us to accomplish thinking with essential rightness? (4) What is it that calls on us to think?

Heidegger remarks in *Was heisst Denken?* that "we can not rehearse these differences too often" (WD, 160). Following this advice we will attempt to "rehearse these differences" by articulating the characteristics which, in our opinion, Heidegger attributes to his question "*Was heisst Denken?*"

1. The question "*Was heisst Denken?*" is *asked* in a fourfold way. In saying this we want to emphasize that these four questions, in spite of their highly significant differences, *are but one question.*[15]

2. If the question "Was heisst Denken?" is asked in a fourfold way and if, therefore, we have to say that these four questions are but one question, then we need to know where their unity stems from? The unity of these four questions in their significant differences stems, Heidegger tells us, from the fourth question: "What is it that calls on us to think?" The fourth question develops and explicates itself in such a way that it calls forth the other three.

3. This fourth question, "What is it that calls on us to think?," is the decisive question because "it sets the standard. For this fourth question itself asks for the standard by which our nature, as a think-

---

[15] "These four questions . . . are nonetheless *one* question" (WD, 160).

ing nature, is to be measured" (WD, 160). Recall in this connection the first chapter of Heidegger's *Introduction to Metaphysics,* which every student who wants to come to an initial understanding of the significance of the philosophy of Heidegger ought to read again and again. Heidegger says in this first chapter: "Philosophy always remains a knowledge which not only cannot be adjusted to a given epoch but on the contrary imposes its standards upon its epoch" (EM, 6).

4. We have seen up to now that the fourth question, "What is it that calls on us to think?," is the decisive question because it sets the standard. In setting the standard it calls forth the other three questions unifying them into *one* question: "*Was heisst Denken?*" Yet we have to say that the three other questions do not relate in the same significant way to the fourth question. There are here degrees of significance. Heidegger says that "the third manner of asking is closest to the fourth" (WD, 160). This third question which "inquires about us [which] asks us what resources we must tap in order to be capable of thinking [is] the most difficult of all to answer." There is, Heidegger says, "only one way" to answer the question "*Was heisst Denken?*" in its third form. And Heidegger tells us that if we do not discover here the answer, "all talk and listening is in vain. And," he continues, "in that case I would urge you to burn your lecture notes, however precise they may be . . . and the sooner the better" (WD, 160). This might at first sight be a disturbing remark. Are these remarks we have just mentioned not suggesting — at least in some way — that the question "*Was heisst Denken?*" aims to establish an answer by which the question can be disposed of in a conclusive way (to use in a modified way Heidegger's own words from the summary of the fourth lecture of the second part)? Is Heidegger not contradicting here what he wrote so impressively in the Postscript to *What is Metaphysics?*: "All questions that do justice to the subject are themselves *bridges* to their own answering. Essential answers are always but the last step in our questioning. The last step, however, cannot be taken without the long series of first and next steps. The essential answer gathers its motive power from the inwardness (*Inständigkeit*) of the asking and is only the beginning of a responsibility *where the asking arises with renewed originality.* Hence, even the most genuine question is never stilled by the answer found" (WM, 44, Italics mine.). In spite of the most peremptory way in which Heidegger says that we can-

not burn our lecture notes quickly enough if we do not discover the "only" (*nota bene*) answer to the question "*Was heisst Denken?*" in its third form, Heidegger makes it quite clear that in trying to answer the question "What is it that calls on us to think?" in its fourfold structure "we stand at the beginning of a long road whose full extent we can hardly envisage" (WD, 160). In answering the question with us Heidegger asserts: "The way is long. We dare take only a few steps. If all goes well, they will take us to the foothills of thought" (WD, 48). It is clear then that Heidegger does not want to suggest that he already possesses a ready-made answer, which once and for all renders any questioning needless. Heidegger is "underway", he is aware of the "cross-roads" accompanying him on his "*hodos*" but also in that he is in his thinking nearer to the matter of thought, his "*hodos*" becomes more and more significant: "The nearer we come to the matter, the more significant the way becomes. If, therefore, the style of the following presentation is one in which we speak repeatedly about the way, then therein the matter comes into consideration. The discussions of the way are no mere reflections about method."[16] Heidegger is aware that he is in his thinking more and more "*bewёgend.*"[17] So we can repeat that each of the first three questions is related to the fourth according to a different significance. The fourth question asks: "What is it that calls on us to think?" The third question which inquires about us and which asks us what resources we must tap in order to be capable of thinking is closest to the fourth. It is the most difficult of all to answer and there is only one answer, but Heidegger is more and more in *Be-wёgung*.

5. This question is *a radical question*. In order to understand the radicality of the question it is necessary to observe, however, that the radicality which is at stake here is not that expressed in the ideal of presuppositionlessness. In lecture four of Part II of *Was heisst Denken?* Heidegger looks back on the way he has gone

---

[16] "Je näher wir der Sache kommen, um so be-deutender wird der Weg. Wenn daher im Stil der folgenden Darlegungen öfter vom Weg die Rede ist, dann kommt darin die Sache zur Sprache. Die Erörterungen des Weges sind keine blossen Überlegungen über die Methode . . ." (SG, 94).

[17] Einen Weg bahnen, z. B. durch verschneites Feld, heisst heute noch in der alemannisch — schwäbischen Mundart *wёgen*. Dieses transitiv gebrauchte Zeitwort besagt: einen Weg bilden, bildend ihn bereit halten. Be-wёgen (Be-wёgung) heisst, so gedacht, nicht mehr: etwas nur auf einem schon vorhandenen weg hin-und herschaffen, sondern: den Weg zu . . . allererst erbringen und so der Weg sein" (US, 261).

thus far and suggests that it might appear as though the question *"Was heisst Denken?"* were a question "of the kind to which modern philosophy liked to lay claim as it went looking for the most radical question — the question without presuppositions — which was to lay the unshakable foundations of the entire edifice of the system of philosophy for all future ages" (WD, 161-62). Heidegger refers here to the *inconcussum fundamentum* of Descartes with all the impact it has had up to the efforts of Husserl to build philosophy as a *"Strenge Wissenschaft"*, as rigorous science. Heidegger, however, insists that "the question '*Was heisst Denken?*' is not without presuppositions. Far from it, *it is going directly toward what would here be called presupposition and becomes involved in it.*"[18] Our question does not invite us to think *about* what thinking is, our question inquires about us, asking what our resources must be in order that we be capable of thinking. We are drawn into the substance of the inquiry *in order to be what we are* — in order that we not "remain blind to the mission and destiny of our nature" (WD, 103). In answering the question "What is it that calls on us to think?" we are drawn towards our center, towards our source, towards our *ground*. In the book *Was heisst Denken?* Heidegger is not concerned with a definition of thinking — thinking about what thinking is — but with a definition of man who is defined with reference to a "source", and it is therefore that we can ask about *our resources* that can render us capable of thinking. This is the third question which is closest to the fourth one and for which there is — according to Heidegger's assertion — but one answer. If we have now to assess more precisely in what way we have to conceive the radicality of the question, we have to go back to all the characteristics that we have already mentioned. The question *"Was heisst Denken?"* is, first of all, radical in that it has a four-fold structure; this means that the question *must be asked* in a four-fold way. And the fourth way is the *radix* which calls forth the other three questions, unifying them into one question. The question is furthermore radical in that the third question which is an integral part of the question in its structural unity admits only one answer. The question is thirdly radical in that it is a decisive question because *it sets standards*. And the question sets standards because in our endeavours to go on the way towards the answer we have to be involved

---

[18] WD, 162 (Italics mine).

in what is always already presupposed in the very questioning as that from out of which thinking itself originates as its *radix*.

6. The question is in the most authentic sense of the word an *actual question*. We have to speak here of the actuality of the question or — if you like — the relevance of our question to the time in which we live. How are we to articulate this actuality here. It is clear to any careful reader of the first three lectures that the asking of the question *"Was heisst Denken?"* calls us who ask the question into question. Heidegger refers to the fact that we live today in an industrial society with a highly developed technology which threatens to condemn us to reshaping the person to fit the demands of technology. On the basis of the standard appraisals of the present age one could add to this *ad nauseam*. Heidegger suggests clearly that the question, *"Was heisst Denken?"* is addressed "to the man of today" — to us men of today, "of a 'today' that has lasted since long ago and will still last for a long time, so long that no calendar can give its measure" (WD, 7). We have to understand the actuality of the question very precisely. Heidegger certainly does not want to be wholly concerned with the present and the immediate future; much less does he want to be involved in fads and sensations of the moment. We are not asked to be perpetually on the *qui vive* for the newest and the latest. Neither does he want in his philosophy to cling to the past for its own sake with nostalgia and exaggerated romantic attachment. These alternatives are for Heidegger false alternatives because they are not exclusive alternatives. One could perhaps say that Heidegger somehow wants to be — rather than a "now" or a "then-person" — an "always-person" who in his philosophy wants to transcend both the frantic cult of the new and the feeble cult of the old. In his *Introduction to Metaphysics* Heidegger writes: "All essential philosophical questioning is necessarily untimely. And this is so either because philosophy is always projected far in advance of its time, or because it connects the present with its antecedent, with what initially was" (EM, 6).

In light of these characteristics that Heidegger attributes to the question *"Was heisst Denken?"* we can now understand that this question is *unique*. Its uniqueness derives from its multiple characteristics which only together make the question what it really is. The question is structural, hierarchical, decisive (because it sets standards), dogmatic, radical, and relevant (although not in a total compliance with the *Zeitgeist*).

Part Three — Ereignis
1. *Primordial and Preludial* Ereignis

At the end of "Time and Being" Heidegger writes that the thought expressed therein will be acknowledged in its binding character by all those who are on the way to cor-respond to what calls on us to think (ZS, 66). Heidegger says: "Insofar as we are at all, we are already in a relatedness to what gives food for thought as far as we are men of "today, i.e. [in] an industrial society."[19] In the modern technological world there occurs a constellation of Being and man which Heidegger tries to think by means of the ontological term, *"Gestell"*, "pro-posal."[20] He writes in *Identität und Differenz* that "What we experience, through the modern technological world, in the pro-posal, as the constellation of Being and Man, is a prelude (*ein Vor-spiel*) of what *Ereignis* is" (ID, 32). In the same text he writes: "We may discern a first flash, an urgent flash, of *Ereignis* in the pro-posal. This makes up the essence of the modern technological world. In the pro-posal we discern a mutual belonging of man and Being, wherein the letting-belong first determines the kind of togetherness and its unity" (ID, 31). The pro-posal designates "the growing emergence of man on the stage of his own representation."[21] This emergence is described by Heidegger as the claim (*Anspruch*) to master the essent as a whole in technology, in provocative and exacting technology for which *nothing* will be safeguarded and which penetrates beings as a whole.

Let us consider some of the passages in Heidegger's works where he dwells upon the all-encompassing penetration of the technological spirit as the domination of planning and calculating subjectivity in all areas of life. He says, for example, of this spirit that it "comprises all areas of the essent, objectified nature, planned and calculated culture, fabricated politics and the super-construed ideals" (VA, 80). To consider another instance, in the eighth lecture of Part I of *Was heisst Denken?* he tries to indicate what kind of Being (meaning of Being) prevails in the so-called modern age "which is

---

[19] Heidegger's letter in *Heidegger and the Quest for Truth*, ed. by Manfred S. Frings (Chicago: Quadrangle Books, 1968), p. 18.

[20] This translation retains the same root "stell" ("pose") as well as the meaning of "pro" in "pro-vocation" in the sense of calling-forth.

[21] Paul Ricoeur, "The Critique of Subjectivity and Cogito in the Philosophy of Heidegger," *Heidegger and the Quest for Truth*, ed. by Manfred S. Frings, p. 69.

not ending now but only just beginning, since the Being that pre-vails in it is only now unfolding into the predestined totality of beings" (WD, 31). Here Heidegger quotes Nietzsche: "We have invented happiness and we blink." And he continues: "We shall see to it from every angle, with the aid of our sociology, psychology and psycho-therapy and by some other means besides, that all men are soon placed in identical conditions of identical happiness in the identical way, and that the identity of the welfare of all men is secured" (WD, 31). In *"Der Satz der Identität"* Heidegger writes: "Let us finally be done with representing technology only technolog-ically, i.e. in terms of man and his machines. Let up pay heed to the claim under which, in our age stands not only man but all beings, nature and history, in respect to their Being. What claim do we mean? Our entire existence everywhere finds itself pro-voked, now lightly or playfully, now urgently, now hounded, now pushed to plan and to calculate everything" (ID, 26-27). In the lecture "Time and Being" Heidegger writes: "Now that modern technology has established its development and dominion over the whole earth, it is not therefore that Sputnicks and all kind of space-junk are circling around our globe but Being as presencing (*Anwesen*) in the sense of calculable fund (*berechenbarer Bestand*) puts its claims uni-formly upon all inhabitants of the earth" (ZS, 26).

So we have to say that Heidegger distinguishes between pri-mordial *Ereignis* and a prelude to *Ereignis*. And we suggest that *Gestell* is a prelude to *Ereignis* because the "Being" that prevails in the *"unbedingte Besinnungslosigkeit"* of our industrial global society unfolds itself into the totality of beings and affects our entire existence everywhere. The springing forth of this clear duality be-tween Being and beings is for Heidegger what is most worthy of questioning.

2. Ereignis *Absolutely Sui-Generic*

"Ereignis" as "a guide-word in the service of thinking" (ID, 29) is according to Heidegger not translatable.[22] Heidegger writes: "It lets itself be translated just as little as the Greek guide-word *Logos* and the Chinese *Tao*. Here the word 'Ereignis' no longer means what we ordinarily designate as just some happening, an occurrence" (ID, 29). In "Time and Being" Heidegger writes: "What has been

[22] n'en déplaise Mr. Zygmunt Adamczewski's masterful efforts to attempt an English translation in close collaboration with Heidegger it seems.

said allows us, in a certain way even makes it necessary, to say how *Ereignis* is not to be thought. We can no longer represent that which is named with the name *"Ereignis"* under the guidance of the usual word-meaning; for this understands *"Ereignis"* in the sense of occurrence or happening — not from out of befitting as the extending and sending which lights up and preserves."[23] The English translations "event" or "occurrence" are wrong translations since they seem to overlook that (first of all) the word is used as a *Singulare tantum:* "What it designates occurs only in the singular, nay, not even any longer numerically, but uniquely" (ID, 29). Heidegger writes furthermore in "Time and Being", commenting on *Ereignis*: "Formerly philosophy thought Being from beings as *idea*, as *actualitas*, as well, and now — one may think — [Heidegger thinks Being] as *Ereignis*."[24] But Heidegger rejects such an interpretation of Being as *Ereignis*: "Thus understood, *Ereignis* would mean a modified interpretation of Being which, if it is gone through rightly, would represent a continuation of metaphysics" (ZS, 60). One may not ask: What is *Ereignis*? One must rather refrain from such un-essential questioning (ZS, 58), because it cannot be said of *Ereignis* that it *is* or that *there is Ereignis* (ZS, 66). It is the ultimate *Apriori*,[25] the source (ZS, 66) from which all that *is* flows and springs forth. You can not derive the source from the stream. *"Ereignis"* does not designate another meaning of Being; rather it holds together all meaning of Being (*to on legetai pollakoos!*) and encompasses them all as *Identität*, and identity which comprises all "differences" as its meditation. Heidegger asks: "What has '*Ereignis*' to do with identity? Answer: Nothing. On the contrary identity has everything to do with *Ereignis*." This identity designates the mutual belonging of man and Being (ID, 30-31). Thus, *"Der Mensch gehört in das Ereignis"* (ZS, 64).

---

[23] "Das jetzt Gesagte erlaubt, nötigt sogar in gewisser Weise, zu sagen, wie das Ereignis nicht zu denken ist. Wir können das mit dem Namen 'das Ereignis' Genannte nicht mehr am Leitfaden der geläufigen Wortbedeutung vorstellen; denn sie versteht 'Ereignis' im Sinne von Vorkommnis und Geschehnis — nicht aus dem Eignen als dem lichtend verwahrenden Reichen und Schicken" (ZS, 58).

[24] ZS, 60. Cf. also ZS, 32, where Heidegger mentions idea, koinonia, energeia, Position, absoluter Begriff, Wille zur Macht.

[25] Heidegger speaks of "the task of laying bare that *Apriori* which must be visible before the question of 'what man is' can be discussed philosophically" (SZ, 45).

3. *The Thinking of* Ereignis *as Preparational Thinking*

The Heideggerean guide-word for thinking is a guide-word for a thinking which is not foundational but which is "preparational" as he himself writes in a very recent text. He writes in "La fin de la philosophie et la tâche de la pensée": "The task of this thinking which uses '*Ereignis*' as a guide-word is very modest; it has the character of a preparation and not at all of a foundation. It suffices this kind of thinking to pro-voke the awakening of an availability of man for an outstanding and essential human possibility of which the contour remains obscure and of which the forthcoming remains unsure ..." (FP, 182). We can get some insight into the kind of preparation Heidegger has in mind if we try to become aware of the fullness of meaning — Ricoeur would say the *"plentitude de sens"* — of this wonderful guide-word of thinking, "*Ereignis*." I give here one of the best texts I know where Heidegger in his unsurpassable way brings much of the wealth of its meanings together: "The *belonging*-together of man and Being in the manner of reciprocal provoking brings disconcertingly near to us that and how man is appropriated to Being while Being lays claim to the essence of man. In the pro-posal there holds sway a strange appropriating and laying claim. It is a matter simply of experiencing this befitting in which man and Being are delivered over to one another, i.e. of entering into that which we call *Ereignis*."[26]

4. Ereignis *and Time*

We have said in our Introduction that Heidegger wants to think Being without regard to a *"Be-gründung"* a foundation of Being in

---

[26] "Das Zusammen*gehören* von Mensch und Sein in der Weise der wechselseitigen Herausforderung bringt uns bestürzend näher, dass und wie der Mensch dem Sein vereignet, das Sein aber dem Menschenwesen zugeeignet ist. Im Ge-stell waltet ein seltsames Vereignen und Zueignen. Es gilt, dieses Eignen, worin Mensch und Sein einander ge-eignet sind, schlicht zu erfahren, d.h. einzukehren in das, was wir das *Ereignis* nennen" (ID, 28). Note that in translation the important connections between *Ereignis, Zueignen, Vereignen,* and *Eignen* are not retained.

We may remark here that there are in the home of Heidegger's brother in Messkirch several of the most important writings of Heidegger's *Nachlass.* There is, among others, a rather voluminous text on *"Ereignis"* which carries the title *"Beiträge zur Philosophie"* and which Heidegger keeps back from publication, according to Heidegger himself in a conversation which this author had with him on July 12, 1968, at his home in Freiburg.

and through beings and that he thinks that such an attempt is necessary in order to bring into view the meaning of what *"is"* around the "global village." Now we have to ask: what does Heidegger mean by "What is today"? Is Heidegger one of the now-generation? Because of the importance and immense difficulty of this topic, *"Ereignis* and time," we shall proceed very cautiously and remain close to Heidegger's own words. Let us begin by citing several passages from Heidegger's writings which speak to this issue.

(1) In *Der Satz vom Grund* Heidegger writes: "What is, is not what is actual, what is 'in,' neither what is now . . . What is, is what emerges out of a past in the sense of what has been and which as such awaits us, comes towards us . . . . This which comes towards us out of a past and which is underway already for a long time is the unconditional claim of the principle of ground in the form of complete rationality."[27]

(2) In the essay *"Überwindung der Metaphysik"* Heidegger speaks of metaphysics as something past and observes that the "pastness" of metaphysics "does not exclude but rather includes that it just now starts its unconditional domination amidst beings. But in its being 'past' as it unfolds itself now in the present it also comes to its end. This coming to its end has an endurance which is longer that the history of metaphysics" (VA, 71). Furthermore, he says, "Metaphysics in its coming to its end is the very foundation of the planetary mode of thinking, provides the frame-work of an organization of the earth which will presumably last very long. . . . This organization does not need philosophy any more because it is its very foundation" (VA, 83).

(3) In the essay *"Die Erinnerung in die Metaphysik"* with which he concludes his two-volume work *Nietzsche* Heidegger writes: "The originary occurs prior to everything that will come to pass; it, therefore, always already awaits historical man — it is, therefore, always ahead of historical man in a pure awaiting him; it does not pass away, is never something belonging to a mere past. We therefore do not find the originary in stepping-backward to

---

[27] "Was 'ist,' das ist nämlich nicht das Aktuelle und nicht das Gegenwärtige. Was 'ist,' ist das aus dem Gewesen und als dieses Ankommende. Dieses Ankommende, längst schon unterwegs, ist der unbedingte Anspruch des Satzes vom Grund in der Gestalt der vollständigen Rationalität" (SG, 138).

a historically ascertainable past but in a remembrance . . . of the mittent character of Being."[28]

(4) In *"Wer ist Nietzsches Zarathustra?"* Heidegger addresses himself to the question whether the inquiry beyond Nietzsche's thinking can be a continuation of his thought or must be a *"Schritt zurück,"* a step backward. He answers that "It remains to be considered whether this step backward signifies only a retreat to an historically ascertainable past which one would wish to revive (for instance, Goethe's world), or whether the 'step backward' points to a past whose origin still awaits remembrance in order to become a beginning which breaks upon the dawn" (VA, 107).

(5) In *"Wissenschaft und Besinnung"* he writes: "What has been thought and poetized in the dawn of the ancient Greek culture is today still present; it is a past-present, so present that its *"Wesen,"* which is still veiled to it, is ahead of us and awaits us and most of all there where we do not expect it: in the domination of modern technology" (VA, 47).

(6) Finally, in *Unterwegs zur Sprache* Heidegger writes: *"Das Gleich-Zeitige der Zeit sind: die Gewesenheit, die Anwesenheit und die Gegen-Wart, die uns entgegenwartet und sonst die Zukunft heisst"* (US, 213). The con-temporaneity of the temporal ecstases are the past, the unfolding of the past in the present, and what is still ahead of us, what awaits us because of this unfolding of the past. This passage is especially important for our interpretation of the text "Time and Being."

What do these texts, which can hardly be discussed to the extent they deserve, tell us at least with regard to "Time and Being"? There is a con-temporalizing of the three temporal ecstases, a mutual porrecting, extending, of these ecstases in which the three dimensions of time are mutually implicated in some kind of reciprocity. This reciprocity must be further determined. We might perhaps say, with reference to *Being and Time* (SZ, 479) that for Heidegger, both in "Time and Being" and in *Being and Time,* the "now is not pregnant with the not-yet-now." It is the no-more-now of a past which is a past-present which is pregnant with a future that consti-

---

[28] "Das Anfängliche ereignet sich allem Kommenden voraus und kommt deshalb, obzwar verhüllt, als das reine Kommen auf den geschichtlichen Menschen zu. Es vergeht nie, ist nie ein Vergangenes. Das Anfängliche finden wir deshalb auch nie in der historischen Rückwendung zum Vergangenen, sondern nur im Andenken, das zumal an das wesende (das Ge-wesende) denkt und an die geschickte Wahrheit des Seins" (N, II, 481).

tutes the *Gegenwart*, the present. Present, or pre-sence arises from a future, a *Gegenwart* in the sense of *entgegen-kommen*, which has its roots in a past — *ein Gewesenes*. This is what we have understood when Heidegger writes in "Time and Being" that he endeavours to determine *"das Eigene der Zeit aus dem Hinblick auf die Gegenwart im Sinne der Anwesenheit"* (ZS, 36). *Anwesen*, presencing is a presence that emerges or arises from something that is ahead of us *because* it has its roots in a past which as *"Ge-wesen"* still endures. *"Anwesen,"* understood in this way, is granted by *Ereignis*.

But we have to distinguish *two modes of Anwesen*. In "Time and Being" Heidegger writes that *"nicht jedes Anwesen ist notwendig Gegenwart"* (ZS, 42). In order to understand this we have to be aware of the important declaration of Heidegger in *Was heisst Denken?*: *"Entzug ist Ereignis"* (WD, 5). In "Time and Being" Heidegger speaks of this *"Entzug,"* this withdrawl, in several places (ZS, 46, 48). About the withdrawal in question here Heidegger says some very important things in *Was heisst Denken?* In *Ereignis* as primordial a withdrawal occurs "a withdrawal which may concern and claim man more essentially than anything present that strikes and touches him. Being struck by actuality is what we like to regard as constitutive of the actuality of the actual. However in being struck by what is actual, man may be debarred precisely from what concerns and touches him, in the surely mysterious way of escaping him by its withdrawal. The event (*Ereignis*) of withdrawal could be what is most present to all our present — and so infinitely exceed the actuality of everything actual" (WD, 5). What is important here is that in this withdrawal there occurs the same contemporalizing of the temporal ecstases, the same mutual porrecting of temporal ecstases which we have tried to understand in the term *Anwesen*: there is here an originating incipience which as pastness is still at work, letting spring forth a future out of which a *Gegenwart* can arise. *Ereignis* is withdrawal, or — we have to say — withdrawal is *Ereignis*. Heidegger writes in *Was heisst Denken?*: "What withdraws from us, draws us along by its very withdrawal. . . . We are drawn toward what draws, attracts us by its withdrawal" (WD, 5) and which is — apparently — incomparably *near* to us, *"Die näherende Nähe"* (ZS, 46). What withdraws is that "which calls on us to think in the sense that it originally directs us to thinking and thereby entrusts to us our *own* essential Nature as such —

which is insofar as it thinks" (WD, 152). We would like, following "Time and Being," to characterize the distinction between two modes of *Anwesen* as a distinction between *eigentliche* and *uneigentliche Zeit* (ZS, 48).

5. Ereignis *as Source*

In "Time and Being" Heidegger calls *"Ereignis"* a "source," *ein Quell* (ZS, 66). We have noted already that according to Heidegger one cannot derive the source from the stream. One cannot ask any question regarding what *Ereignis* is. One cannot question *Ereignis*, we might say, as *Singulare tantum*, since the questionable character of everything obvious is disclosed to us by *Ereignis*. Heidegger says that *"Ereignis er-eignet"*; what else can be said (ZS, 66). As such, as *Er-eignen*, we can apply to *Ereignis*, named a source or origin, what Heidegger writes in *Being and Time*: "The ontological origin (source) of Dasein's Being is not inferior to what springs from it, but towers above it in power from the outset; in the field of ontology any 'springing from' is degeneration. If we penetrate to the source ontologically, we do not come to things which are ontically obvious for the common understanding: but the questionable character of everything obvious opens up for us" (SZ, 383). Let us connect with this very profound statement the "definition" Heidegger gives in *Being and Time* — in the Introduction — where he writes that philosophy is an analysis of historical existence which "has made fast the guideline for all philosophical inquiry at the point where it *arises* and to which it *returns*" (SZ, 38). Heidegger writes in *Being and Time* that in the field of ontology any arising, any springing forth is degeneration. The return now, of which Heidegger speaks in his definition can be called a regeneration or — as Heidegger called it in his letter to Manfred Frings — a regress, a step-back. We can characterize this step-back formally in a three-fold way: There is, first, the return or *"Schritt Zurück"* on the noetical level which is the return from calculative thinking to preparational thinking. There is, second, the return on the ontological level from beings to their Being (meaning of Being) and from their Being as preludial *Ereignis* (*un-eigentliche Zeit*) to primordial *Ereignis* as *eigentliche Zeit*. There is finally a return on the historical level which is the return from the philosophy of Hegel and Nietzsche to the original incipience of the pre-Socratics. I should add here that Heidegger does not at all approve of the term "pre-

Socratic" philosophers. He thinks "that it is not just a chronological designation but a downgrading, [for] Plato is considered the greatest thinker." But, although Heidegger thinks it foolish to call Parmenides a pre-Socratic, "equally mistaken is the reverse procedure into which we are easily drawn by any emphatic mention of thinkers such as Parmenides" (WD, 112-13). Heidegger makes the distinction here between the understanding of a thinker by retracing the questioning of a thinker starting from his own thinking and the understanding of a thinker "in his own terms." To wish to understand a thinker in his own terms is and remains impossible — because no thinker and no poet understands himself. On the other hand, the endeavor to "take up a thinker's request and to pursue it *to the core of his thought's problematic* . . . is rare and of all things most difficult."[29] Yet this is what Heidegger means by the return to thinkers like Parmenides and Heraclitus, for whom there was no *Cogito*, "since man did not 'face' world," but rather was "faced *by* the existent and . . . gathered into its presence by self-disclosing."[30] This return is *"Einkehr."* Is this *"Einkehr"* primarily something we have to do? This is the question that we must, finally, consider.

6. *The Thinking of* Ereignis *as* Handlung

In his letter to Manfred Frings Heidegger writes that "The Being-question properly understood appears as the question about the essencing of modern technology and its relation to the men of today, i.e., to an industrial society."[31] And he writes in his letter to Father Richardson that "What is at stake is a transformation in man's Being itself. This transformation is not demanded by new psychological or biological insights . . . . Man here is not the object of any anthropology but . . . comes into question in the genuinely fundamental perspective: man in his relation to Being — sc. in the reversal: *Das Seyn und dessen Wahrheit im Bezug zum Menschen.*"[32] Again, in his letter to Frings he says: "As soon as we become aware of this, however, we have the experience *that thought can no longer,* in terms of the traditional scheme of the distinction between theory and practice, *be relegated to the merely theoretical.* One can experience thought as an original kind of acting (*Handeln*)

[29] WD, 113 (Italics mine).
[30] Ricoeur, "Critique of Subjectivity . . ." *Heidegger and the Quest for Truth*, ed. Frings, p. 68.
[31] Heidegger's letter in *Heidegger and the Quest for Truth*, ed. Frings, p. 19.
[32] Richardson, *Heidegger*, p. xx.

that does not, indeed, aim at any immediate effects, but precisely for that reason surpasses in its very uselessness any type of technical-practical undertaking. In this way it prepares the determinability of the future existence of man."[33] In "Time and Being" Heidegger says that his thinking (*Denken, das Philosophie heisst*) does not provide any "*nutzbare Lebensweisheit.*" At the end of this lecture he writes that the kind of philosophical thinking he advocates should not even endeavour to overcome metaphysics (ZS, 68), and since we know that Heidegger identifies technology with "*vollendende Metaphysik*" (VA, 80) we can conclude that Heidegger wants us not to do anything by means of action to "overcome" technology. In the essay on the overcoming of metaphysics Heidegger writes: "*keine blosse Aktion wird den Weltzustand ändern*" (VA, 98).

Is what Heidegger writes here about a thinking which can no longer be relegated to the merely theoretical basically the same as what Ricoeur writes in the Preface to the first edition of his *History and Truth?* Ricoeur says: "The philosophical way of being present to my time seems to be linked to a capacity for reachieving the remote intentions and the radical cultural presuppositions which underlie ... the civilizing drives of our era. This amounts to saying that one need not be ashamed of being an 'intellectual,' as is Valery's Socrates in *Eupalinos*, doomed to the regret of having made nothing with his hands. I believe in the efficacity of reflection because I believe that man's greatness lies in the dialectic of work and the spoken word. Saying and doing, signifying and making are intermingled to such an extent that it is impossible to set up a lasting and deep opposition between 'theoria' and 'praxis.' The word is my kingdom and I am not ashamed of it." He asserts emphatically: "I categorically refuse to dissociate the elucidation of directive concepts, according to which we are trying to *think* our insertion in history, from the concern for actively intervening in the crisis of our civilization and thereby *giving testimony*, to the force and the efficacity of thought."[34] We do not think that Ricoeur's concern for actively intervening in the crisis of our civilization would find grace in Heidegger's eyes.

[33] Heidegger's letter in *Heidegger and the Quest for Truth*, ed. Frings, p. 19 (Italics mine).
[34] Paul Ricoeur, *History and Truth*, trans. by Charles A. Kelbley (Evanston: Northwestern University Press, 1965), pp. 4-5.

Heidegger's essay *"Die Kehre"* is here most interesting. Heidegger writes: "We think the great essence of man in the fact that it is claimed by the essence of Being, is needed by it to preserve the essence of Being in its truth. Therefore, it is above all necessary that we first consider the *essence* of Being as that which is worthy of thought, that in thinking such we first experience to what extent we are called in such experience first to follow a path and to prepare the way into the previously impassible. We are capable of all of this only if, *before* the question which is seemingly nearest and apparently the sole urgent question, i.e., what should we do, we consider the question, how must we think. For thinking is the authentic practice, provided practice means to give a helping hand to the essence of Being."[35]

It should be mentioned in this regard that Eugen Fink has planned, but has been forced to postpone, a colloquium between Heiddegger and some leading Marxists of the "Praxis-group." The "topic" of the colloquium: *"Die Handlung."*

Heidegger writes at the end of "Time and Being" that he has given up the overcoming of metaphysics. If any overcoming is still wanted, it concerns this kind of thinking that gets involved in the question of what it is that calls on us to think, namely in the presuppositions of the question, "What is it that calls on us to think?," engaging itself into *Ereignis* in order to name it *"aus ihm her und auf es zu"* (ZS, 68). Heidegger can say with Ricoeur: The word is my kingdom. And it is exactly this that the Marxists wanted to discuss with Heidegger.

In the essay *"Die Kehre"* Heidegger writes that *"Die Gefahr ist die Epoche des Seins, wesend als das Gestell"* (TK, 42). In the same text, he says: "In the essence of the danger essences and dwells a favor, namely the favor of the reversal of the forgottenness of Being into the truth of Being." With this reversal which is *"Ereignis"*

---

[35] "Das grosse Wesen des Menschen denken wir dahin, dass es dem Wesen des Seins zugehört, von diesem gebraucht ist, das Wesen des Seins in seine Wahrheit zu wahren. Darum ist das zuerst Nötige dies, dass wir zuvor das *Wesen* des Seins als das Denk-würdige bedenken, dass wir zuvor, solches denkend, erfahren, inwiefern wir geheissen sind, solchem Erfahren erst einen Pfad zu spuren und ihn in das bislang Unwegsame zu bahnen. Dies alles vermögen wir nur, wenn wir *vor* der anscheinend immer nächsten und allein als dringlich erscheinenden Frage: Was sollen wir tun, dies bedenken: *Wie müssen wir denken?* Denn das Denken ist das eigentliche Handeln, wenn Handeln heisst, dem Wesen des Seins an die Hand gehen" (TK, 39-40).

facies terra renovabitur. What we have to do is only to reach for the hand of Being, which is granted to us in *Ereignis* and which will give us — by willing not willing — time for the mystery of life and death, time for the earth in its splendour and expanding release, time for work which will not enslave, and perhaps time for God.

At the end of "Time and Being" Heidegger connects *Ereignis* with *alētheia* (ZS, 66). *Ereignis* grants time, *Ereignis* grants Being; *Ereignis* encompasses as a "whole," as the "*Kukleion sphairos*" of Parmenides all the epochs of man's history. Man cannot objectify *Ereignis*, since he is always "in" it, belonging to it.[36] It is not a "whole" which he, man, comprises, or of which he can get hold. This is not given to finite man. On the contrary, man as finite is involved and "*ge-borgen*" in it; it is open to him in such a way that "*es geht ja alles ueber uns hinweg.*"[37] The *renovatio terrae*, the 'liberation' of man, about which Marcuse writes most strikingly, is never our merit. *Tempus et Esse filiae Veritatis!*

[36] "Wir haben die Anmassung alles Unbedingten hinter uns gelassen" (VA, 179).
[37] Heidegger's own words spoken to me during my "*Gespräch*" with him on July 12, 1968.

Cosmos, Nature and Man
And the Foundations of Psychiatry

Anna-Teresa Tymieniecka

If we throw a glance at the origins of philosophical reflection, we will be tempted to believe that man's attention has been first captivated by the mysteries presented by life on Mother Earth. Marvelling about the cyclic course of seasons regulating the ever-returning life and preceding an unavoidable extinction, its dependence upon climate, winds, clouds, the sun and the moon, man has seen his existence on Earth related to that of other living beings, stars and planets within the scheme of the whole of the universe. Puzzled about the ultimate reasons for his earthly condition as intertwined with that of other beings within this system, man's first philosophical endeavors seem to have been to seek the reasons and laws governing the system of the universe. How intimately he felt himself to be an element of this universe we can guess from the fact that he clad the powers governing it in mythological shapes tailored upon the model of himself. Yet, within the all-encompassing universe, man considered himself only a tiny — even if privileged — segment.

It is only much later that man gradually developed awareness of his distinctive inner self as a particular object of wonder and reflection. In the course of development, however, starting with Heraclitus, Socrates, Plato, continuing through Augustine and

191

Pascal, and culminating in the contemporary philosophy of existence, the human self became emancipated as a distinctive and primordial object of wonder from its primitive bonds with nature. With this turn to an opposite extreme, the answer to the questions concerning the conditions of man's existence among other beings is sought in the nature of the human self. The universe on the one hand and the human self on the other became two central points of philosophical reflection, which like two opposite polarities underlie its organization, dividing among themselves the focus of attention. Until Descartes, there is a continuous line between them along which they assume intermittently different degrees of attraction-value, depending upon whether attention focuses more upon the autonomous laws of nature or upon the distinctive rights of human consciousness. Yet they were both originally comprized within one scheme including all. However, the Cartesian split between mind and body brought about the irreconcilability of human self (or consciousness) and nature. Although the Cartesian dichotomy of mind and body has been rejected in our times through the phenomenologico-existential concept of man, yet on this view the gravitational attraction of the human self is emphasized to such an extreme point that the distinctive rights not only of nature but also of the universal scheme of the All disappear.

This conception draws upon the great progress in human knowledge which occured not only from the time of the Presocratic philosophers and the cosmogonies that gave priority to nature over self, trying to establish a balance between them within the universal scheme of things, but also from the time of Descartes, who abruptly tore it apart. And yet, with the ever-advancing progress of science the question arises whether this new position — that we will show to be extreme — is warranted by what we continue to learn about nature and man. No lasting conception in philosophy can, of course, be expected if it is based directly upon concrete scientific results which incessantly are superseded by new ones. However, what these continually progressing results may contribute is insight into reality which we might gain through them.

Maybe the progress of science and philosophy, instead of an unwarranted priority of consciousness to nature (or its inverse), leads us to a glimpse of a higher vantage point from which the scheme of the All can be illuminated at a level coordinating harmoniously the distinctive status of nature and that of the human self.

What is at stake is the vision of the universe or *cosmos,* which is lost in contemporary philosophical reflection. Could it be regained within the framework of a new approach towards nature and man in its original purity of intuition.

In the present essay, we will attempt to approach such a vantage point, culminating in the elucidation of the notions of *nature* and *cosmos.*

We will start by analysing briefly the notion of cosmos as essential to Heidegger's conception of man's being-in-the-world, with which he overcomes the Cartesian dichotomy of mind and body. This conception, accepted by phenomenologically-inspired psychiatry, will be then subjected to criticism, utilizing the practice of psychiatry as an empirical science, which will open new, larger perspectives for leading towards a novel approach to the problem of nature, man and cosmos.

Part One — The Heraclitean Approach to the Cosmos as the Presupposition of the Conception of Man's Being-in-the-World

A. *Phenomenological Anthropology*

If we want to revise the conceptions of man and nature both in their most advanced philosophical versions and in the perspective of the progress of science, phenomenologically-inspired psychiatry offers an exceptionally instructive field for examination. Psychiatry is indeed the field of science in which phenomenology and the philosophy of existence have found the deepest response and have in various ways contributed not only to the modifications of its methods, but even to the very understanding of its object and task.[1] We may distinguish among psychiatry thus inspired such different approaches as those represented on the one hand by Van den Bergh and Karl Jaspers; Binswanger, v. Gebsattel and Henri Ey on the other, with the original approach of Minkowski standing out from both; yet all of them and their subsequent differentiations and variations seem to refer to the basic conceptions of man and the world which Heidegger originated in *Sein und Zeit.*

The universally accepted attitude towards man's psychic life as simultaneously possessing a specific content irreducible to physio-

---

[1] Cf. by the present writer, *Phenomenology and Science in Contemporary European Thought* (Noonday, 1961).

logical processes yet not encapsulating man in an "interior life" but extending him, on the contrary, into the life-world, has been in its psychiatric resonance most articulately presented by Ludwig Binswanger under the name of "phenomenological anthropology." It is consequently through Binswanger's eyes that we will envisage the relation of man and nature, both in phenomenology and empirical science into which it has been incorporated.

Binswanger sees the contribution of phenomenology to psychiatry as providing philosophical foundation to the latter through several insights which can be grasped as an organized theory ("phenomenological anthropology"). We should point out first, in summarizing his position, that although drawing upon the theoretico-speculative philosophy of Husserl and Heidegger, the philosophical intuitions and theories of these thinkers could have become relevant to psychiatry only when incorporated into a scientific mold of mind. Thus, phenomenological anthropology is meant as a phenomenologico-empirical science. Yet the specifically phenomenological conception of the irreducibility of the content of experience, of man as fundamentally an experiencing being and of his relation to the world, puts it in sharp contradistinction to the theoretico-functional empirical sciences of nature. Indeed, its subject matter is the structures of the specifically human type of being (*Menschseins*). As a philosophical theory of man, it offers to the concrete sciences dealing with man a system of reference for establishing norms of man's functioning and indicating appropriate methods to deal with that which is specifically human.

Although phenomenological anthropology, as an inventory of notions that have pervaded psychiatry, took its starting point from Husserl's categorial perception as revealing at every level of inquiry irreducible *sui generis* phenomena and from his theory of intentionality as bringing together all dimensions of man's manifestation irreducible to physiological processes, Binswanger emphatically maintains that psychiatry has received a "real foundation" for its concrete pursuits in the form of norms for diagnosis and therapeutics only in Heidegger's analytic of *Dasein*.[2]

As a matter of fact, Heidegger's analytic of *Dasein* culminates in

[2] For a detailed discussion of phenomenological anthropology, we refer the reader to our previously mentioned work, *Phenomenology and Science*. In the present essay we will limit ourselves to its most striking features as relevant to the scrutiny of its validity in the psychiatric practice itself that we engage in.

a (in the history of modern philosophy) radically novel idea of man and his world. Man is conceived in his most specifically human aspect, and yet not in sharp opposition to the world as an "inward" being opposed to an "outside" world, but on the contrary, as two correlated if not interchangable notions. The specifically human mode of being (*Dasein*) emerges from the totality of beings through an act of self-transcendence into the world. It is in his expansiveness in the world that his essential modes, *existentialia*, actualize, whereas the world is already the projection of man's potentialities.

Undoubtedly Heidegger's conception of man as being-in-the-world, as an anthropological insight, gave to psychiatry a long sought clue and is, in its various interpretations, almost universally accepted. But Binswanger goes beyond its relevance to diagnosis and therapeutics, claiming that through this new view of man and the world, phenomenological anthropology gave to the science of psychiatry the hitherto lacking philosophical foundation.

It is this latter claim that must be examined by the scrutiny of the psychiatric work itself.

As we know, psychiatry is an empirical science, which in respect to its object of inquiry (man's psychic life) is on the one hand inter-related with biological sciences such as physiology, bio-physiology, anatomy, neurology, pharmacology, etc. and on the other hand, stays in intimate relation to psychoanalysis, which treats man's psyche as a radically autonomous dimension. At its origin, psychiatry inherited the Cartesian dualistic attitude which separates radically mind and body. This attitude has introduced into the heart of psychiatry a line of a radical separation between fields of investigation concerning the organic aspect of man's condition, his well or ill-being belonging to the clinical work, and the therapeutic, insofar as psychoanalysis is concerned exclusively with mental phenomena. Although psychiatry operates by bringing together the somewhat varied results of all these fields of investigation — all of them equally indispensable, their interrelations can be treated only by trial and error, with a seeming lack of a common ground, with both sides of the fence utilizing an internally distorted, torn apart model of man. Each side has been considering only one of the facets as exclusively representing the whole and without having a link with the others.

The crux of the problem is the relation of the biological investigations concerned with the organism as a physiological system, as a nervous system, etc., to the approach of the phenomenologically-inspired psychologists, who followed the need felt as early as Dilthey to treat the psychic manifestations of man as a specific dimension irreducible either to the physical, organic factors or to the natural instincts.

What seems to be at stake is the relation of man to the world. Probing deeper, however, we find that the conceptions of man and of the world both refer in the final analysis to that of *nature*. As we will attempt to show in the course of our subsequent discussion, a conception of man and of the world might well give fundamental points of reference for psychiatric diagnosis and therapeutics and yet fall short of solving problems about nature itself. In that case, it could hardly provide a foundation capable of unifying all the fields of research involved in psychiatric work. Binswanger, however, claims that Heidegger's conception of man as being-in-the-world not only (a) establishes a relation of man and the world such that diagnosis and therapeutics find common norms of man's condition, but also that (b) this idea of man conceived in his basic world allegiance would be also a ground for the unification of the various fields of psychiatry hitherto torn apart; a ground upon which it could map its complete territory without the presence of distorting separations.

No major objection arises concerning the first claim. Indeed, at the level of man's fundamental intentionality, at which phenomenological anthropology places itself, there is no sharp distinction between the specifically psychic and the specifically bodily expression of man. Man, understood primordially as an experiencing being, expresses his innermost life in his life-world which assumes a shape of man's self-projection reflecting most intimately his experiential life. Consequently, in this perspective the world does not appear as alien to man. As far as the world-as-experienced or the life-world is concerned, there is no dualism of mind and body, since both belong to the same experiential scheme of man.

Since the mental state—normal or diseased—finds its essential expression in the ways in which man experiences himself, other beings and the world, the existential structure of man's self-projection into the world gives to psychiatry norms, clues and models for discrimination between the ways in which experiences of the world deviate from the fundamental existential structure of world-projection.

Concerning the second claim, however, where nature comes to the fore, serious doubts arise. Binswanger believes that the conceptions of man as being-in-the-world, and of the world as including also the presence of man among other beings in their common "facticity," expresses also man's essential conditioning by nature. *Dasein*, limited in the realization of his existential virtualities by the constant interplay with other beings and things among which he is "thrown," shows thereby man's existential finitude which indicates man's place in the physical world. According to Binswanger these aspects of the *Dasein* are precisely studied by the biological side of psychiatric research in terms of the organism, body, heredity, climate, milieu, physiology, anatomy, etc. Binswanger concludes that upon the basis of the theory of man's being-in-the-world, which seemingly comprises man in his entirety, the two apparently different horizons of understanding man that come together in the psychiatric research—the horizon of the natural science of the clinical work dealing with the sick man from the point of view of organism, and that same object of research that in psychotherapy is approached as the mentally ill man; that is, from the point of view of the specifically human dimension of the psychic life — would have found a common horizon of understanding comprizing the whole man in all his dimensions. In short, through the conception of man as being-in-the-world, phenomenological anthropology would provide a foundation for both, the biological science of the organism and the psychological inquiry involving the social and cultural aspects of man.

Concerning this claim: it might well be true that at a certain level, the mind-body problem which arises in philosophical speculation because of the constructive abuse of mind may be overcome by Heidegger's idea of man and of the world, and that in returning to lived experience, we find again mind and body interwoven within the same system; it might well be true that on this model, the specific, irreducible status of psyche finds itself established through interworldly relations, such that the world itself, instead of opposing the specifically human element, appears to justify it; finally, it might well be true that this conception constitutes an enormous advance for psychiatric research, in giving it a direct access to what is specifically human and has hitherto appeared as undefinable, unclear, and difficult to approach, and which can be now grasped as expressed in the worldly relations of the individual.

And yet, in our brief account it already appears clear that on this conception, man as well as the world are grasped "as experienced" by man himself.

Having overcome the mind-body dichotomy in this way, we might have opened another more fundamental difficulty. What the analytic of *Dasein* was called to restore was the unalienable rights of the psychic, the mental, and the spiritual within the empirical research which ignored them. It remains to be seen, however, whether with this theory we have reached a final equilibrium between *psyche* and *physis*, or whether only the first of Binswanger's claims has been satisfied, while the second lies at a deeper level of investigation. This approach establishes the distinctive rights of the psyche within the world understood as a system of man's experience, but does it warrant equally the distinctive rights of the *physis*? Binswanger himself puts the finger upon the critical point by saying that the "facticity of man" upon which Binswanger, following Heidegger, establishes the rights of the *physis*, is "the transcendental document of the finitude of man."

Of course, it has been often argued in this connection that there is nothing to worry about beyond the grasp of the human mind, yet it remains to be seen whether man's experiential world understood phenomenologically reaches the borderlines of man's cognition. That is, the question arises *whether the concept of the world covers also that of nature.*

B. *The Heracleitean Approach to the Cosmos*

What we put in doubt with our questions is the universal validity of Heidegger's conception of man as being-in-the-world.

For Heidegger, *Dasein* and the world are two indispensable counterparts of the fundamental structure of the specifically human. Should we understand the type of being that we are ourselves, *Dasein,* as characterized through what we may call "being a subject"? Its fundamental structure consists, according to Heidegger of "transcending," going beyond itself. Heidegger writes: "We call that, *into which (woraufhin) Dasein* as such transcends, the *world,* and determine now the transcendence as being-in-the-world" (WG, 20). The world, explains Heidegger, constitutes then the structure of transcendence, in turn, as belonging to transcendence, the concept of the world is called by Heidegger "transcendental" (WG, 23).

Heidegger acknowledges that Kant first recognized the "transcendental" as the problem of the very possibility of ontology, yet for Kant it meant the possibility of experience, setting its limits and thus opposing the "transcendental" to the "transcendent" which reaches beyond experience. Heidegger, on the contrary, postulates a more "radical" and "universal" concept of transcendence.

What is then the meaning of "transcendental" for Heidegger, and what are its consequences for the understanding of the "world"? The sharp outlines of Heidegger's position are sketched when Heidegger, commenting upon Kant's conception of man and the world, stresses that "world" does not mean for Kant man's cosmic appearance on earth as a species of living beings, but rather the existence of man in the historical unfolding of his interplay with other men. Heidegger's specific view of the world as related to man's existence and its justification brings him back to Heraclitus. Heidegger points out that Heraclitus, in contradistinction to the nature-philosophers of the Presocratic period, distinguishes between *two* worlds which each man has, depending upon the state in which he finds himself: the public world (when he is awake), and the private one (when he is asleep). In line with this interpretation of Heracleitos, Heidegger conceives then of the nature of the world as relational (*bezughaft*): the nature of the world depends then upon the basic ways in which the human being exists. In question is not man's being as a part of nature, where nature is a configuration of all beings and things, but rather the specifically human mode of existence, which Heidegger calls *"Dasein."*

"Transcendental" means then, for Heidegger, not the *condition* of experience by which a borderline would be set between what falls within the human limits and what transcends them, but rather *relativity* upon the specifically human way of existence.[3]

If, as we have elsewhere interpreted Heidegger's theory, we understand by "world" exactly the human world as the complete system of the personal and social world which is intentional in nature and which originates and stretches out through man's experience in its manifold forms: cognition, volition, imagination, concern, etc., it would then seem, indeed, that the world expresses man's specific interiority which man accomplishes precisely in transcending the narrow limits of his physical being into a self-created

[3] Cf. by the present writer, *Phenomenology and Science*, Part III.

universe.[4] It is this understanding of the world that in its final implications, having resolved the encapsulated "interior life" into "the
expression of the world and experience of the presence of others,"[5]
has revolutionized psychiatric practice by giving access to this previously unsoundable "interior" through the observable set of man's
relations to the world which express it. Binswanger, v. Gebsattel,
and more recently H. Ey and others can now establish the "abnor-
mal" symptoms of the mentally ill, in opposition to the "normal"
ones, as a pathological deformation of the system of *meanings* of
the presence of the world and other beings. It seems to have been
universally accepted in psychiatry that "the foremost feature of
man is to exist in relation to a world, towards which he projects
beforehand his own essential potentialities."[6]

But by "world," Heidegger and Binswanger after him mean
more than the "human world" as distinguishable from the "world
of nature" or from the "universe" as an interplanetary system. By
"world" they mean the cosmos.

In point of fact, in establishing his theory of the world, Heidegger posits at the very start the problem of the nature of the cosmos.
Surveying the development of the notion of cosmos in history, Heidegger emphasizes that by "cosmos" Heraclitus meant a) neither
the totality of factually existing beings, b) nor the configuration of
the existing world-order, c) nor being as such, but rather the
"how," the state in which beings are. This "state," however, whether
it is the individualized world of sleep or the unitary world of the
awake, which is to everyone accessible, is for Heidegger not only
(as we have already pointed out) relative to the fundamental way
of man's specific existence. This "how" also *determines Being in
its totality*.

Finally, although the world so conceived embraces *all being*,
Dasein included, yet it belongs specifically to human *Dasein* (WG,
24).

Heraclitus supposedly initiated this turn from the macro-cos-
mic conception of the physical philosophers to the "human heart,
this passionate feeling, acting, and suffering center, in which the

---

[4] *Ibid.*, p. 20.
[5] G. Lauteri-Laura, "Phénoménologie et psychiatrie," *Entretiens Psychiatriques*, vol. 6, 1961.
[6] *Ibid.*, p. 27.

radii of the whole cosmos meet . . . thus opening the eyes of the mortals upon themselves."[7]

Expressing the innermost relation of man to the rest of beings and things, the cosmos is then a notion centered in man. Man's specific modes of existence, expressing his relation to the rest of beings, then become representative of these beings themselves.

But the question arises whether with this approach the problems concerning cosmos — the all of being, which we otherwise "naively" consider as nature, the earth, the interplanetary system, etc. — would not be completely neglected.

Binswanger sees the answer to this question in Heidegger's previously-mentioned analytic of *Dasein*.[8] On the one hand, the world as the structure of transcendence represents the potentialities of the human being to accomplish his specific mode of existence; on the other hand, these very potentialities are, according to Heidegger, limited by *Dasein's* primordial condition of its factual being among other beings, its being "thrown" in the midst of them at an equal footing; a condition from which it arises, frees itself by transcending, and yet through which it is determined and limited.

This level of primordial "facticity" of the human being in its interplay with the totality of the rest represents for Binswanger the "transcendental horizon" for the "naive reality" of nature which natural science treats as a distinctive, strictly physical realm of investigation. In this central position of *Dasein*, which simultaneously transcends "brute nature" and gives meaning to it within the system of the world, Binswanger believes he has found a ground for the reconciliation of the methods and techniques used in psychiatry, which have been traditionally split along the Cartesian mind-body separation line into those of natural science and those of man's psychic dimension.[9]

And yet, in this way, is not the understanding of nature reduced to whatever status the reach of man's existential involvement may grant it? Is it legitimate to extend the type of relations which man entertains with the rest of the beings and things to the relations which these beings and things entertain among themselves?

Beings other than man, living and non-living, are not supposed

---

[7] Jaeger, quoted by Binswanger.

[8] Ludwig Binswanger, *Gesammelte Vortraege und Aufsaetze* (Franke, 1959), p. 270.

[9] *Ibid.*, p. 271.

to follow the scheme of "throwness" reserved for *Dasein*, and yet they seem to have among themselves sets of vitally important relations.

Finally, it remains to be seen whether the core of physical nature could be exhaustively, primordially grasped in the perspective of the question "how?"

Part Two — The Understanding of Nature:
A New Vision Proposed

We propose presently to examine the issue of whether the concrete scientific research involved in the psychiatric praxis legitimizes the claim to universal validity of such a basically man-centered conception of the *cosmos*; that is, whether the "world" as the projection of man's existential potentialities should not be restricted to the "human world," whereas a fresh insight into natural science and man, both as *psyche* and organism, may not yield a new view of nature that will require a revision of the problems concerning *cosmos*, and their reformulation on an entirely different plane.

The questions we propose to treat are : "Can nature as the object of science be *in its entirety* legitimately drawn into the frame of the specifically human horizon of understanding?" or "Can nature be reduced to its meaningfulness for man's existence?" (We should always keep in mind that "existence" means in this context not everyday existence but an intentional phenomenon.)

Biological science dealing with the organism of man approaches man in his particularity as e.g. human organism, animal organism, living body, etc. The question is whether the total dimension of the interconnections and of the interplay of the indefinite number of organisms, of organic and inorganic elements among themselves lies within the reach of man's existential concern, of his *lived experience*.

We will attempt to show that psychiatric work shows "cracks" within the specifically human horizon of man's being-in-the-world. The Heideggerian world cracks at its seams; through its cracks we may follow the intuition of science towards a more adequate view upon nature and cosmos.

As we have already mentioned, the conception of human being as fundamentally world-related and of his world as the expansion of man's innermost potentialities has transformed the understanding and treatment of that strange universe in which the psychotic patients live. The types of deviations in the space-time systems of the patient express distortions in the basic modes of experience. Yet, the disease itself appears not to be restricted to the level of personal experience of the patient. This is clearly to be seen from the fact, that whenever a psychiatrist speaks about the symptoms of illness or about the disgnosis he also speaks always about the organism of the patient. Furthermore, as Honigswals says, diagnostic judgment of medicine, whether concerning bodily or psychic facts, are always judgments of biological purpose or value, referring ultimately to the norms of the "normal" functioning of the organism (e.g., mania is defined as "hyperfunction of the organism," the schizophrenic folly as "symptoms of hindered functioning of the organism, especially of the brain," etc.).

The conception of organism as a mechanism of the human body may well belong to the experientially meaningful world-system, and yet the directions in which the biological treatment of the organism expands further may well point out further regions of the inorganic that cannot, in their particular meaningfulness, be drawn into the human orbit of lived experience, and of which psychiatry cannot yet dispense.

Dr. Ey recently defined psychiatry as a distinct field from neurology on one extreme and from psychoanalysis on the other, yet operating in strict relationships to both. In this connection, neurology is described as having for its object "the totality of affectations that disintegrate the instrumental functions of the nervous system"; psychiatry, on the contrary, as having for its object of research "the totality of affectations that change consciousness or alienate the *persons,*" psychoanalysis is, in turn, distinguished from both as a therapeutic approach towards the psychic life of the person.[10]

As distinctive and autonomous as might be the treatment of human personality as a field of research, it is still, according to Dr. Ey, inseparable from *the complete set of research* belonging to the medical sciences of neuropathology, biopathology, pathological anatomy, physiology, heredity, pharmacology, etc. Through them, it extends into the resarch of bio-chemistry, chemistry and the rest of the biological disciplines.

There are at least three strictly correlated levels of inquiry which psychiatry draws upon which in their most recent development

[10] Dr. H. Ey, "Plan d'organisation du champ de psychiatrie," *Entretiens Psychiatriques*, vol. 12, 1966.

merit attention in this respect. We have here in mind 1) new insight
into the nature of consciousness to be obtained from neurological
studies; 2) revolutionary light thrown upon the relation of personality to the *biological basis of consciousness* and its transformability
in relation to the *complete system of human functioning* by pharmacological experimentation; and finally 3) the "physical basis of consciousness" treated from the point of view of the origin of the
psychic disease.

When we see that in actual practice, human being as the object
of medicine extends into the science of nature, we might wonder
whether any conception of man that flows from the bias of the
specifically psychic nature of man expressed by his personality can
alone lay the foundation for unifying branches of inquiry dealing
not only with psychic life of man, but with *all* nature. We might
also wonder whether a new insight into *nature itself* and into man
is not necessary and cannot possibly be gained from a quick perusal
of the whole territory which we propose to discuss in what follows.

1. Recent neurological research and surgery has penetrated so
deeply into man's vital and psychic operations relating them to the
nervous system and to the physical structure of the brain that the
question arises whether the complete psychic life cannot be reached
directly through neurological avenues and whether, consequently,
psychiatry cannot be completely absorbed by neurology as a
biological discipline.[11]

It would be certainly too hasty to attempt to reduce the specificity of man to nature, and yet the research in this field has given
many astonishing clues towards a considerable progress to be made
in approaching human consciousness. There are in philosophy and
psychology many conceptions of consciousness. The notion of consciousness is, after all, the key to understanding the human *psyche*,
but equally crucial to understanding man's *bios*.

With behaviorism denying the existence of consciousness on the
one extreme, and Freud distinguishing several dimensions (pre-
conscious, conscious, and subconscious) on the other, we can say
that every psychological theory offers its own approach to the phenomena that we speak of as being "conscious." In general, we consider a man to be "conscious" if he recognizes his surroundings and
manifests an understanding of his purposeful activities.[12] Thus, in

[11] Dr. Azima, "Les fondements biologiques de la conscience," *Entretiens
Psychiatriques*, 1951.

general, consciousness expresses both the bodily (and other) operations of man and his psychic awareness, extending over their various degrees, expressing *bios* as well as the soul. While the conscious essence of the soul is obvious, it is much more difficult to disentangle the conscious expression of *bios*. Consequently, a survey of the results obtained in neurology seems particularly appropriate for our purpose.

As is too well known, neurosurgery has related several functions of consciousness to the structure of the brain. Of course, there can be no question of a "locus" of consciousness "in" the brain; neither will a phenomenologically informed psychologist seek a direct interaction of the two. Dr. Azima, upon whose penetrating account we will draw, quotes Aristotle as having pointed out that neither can the body determine the soul to think, nor the soul determine the body towards motion or rest or towards any other way of being (if there be any).

And yet neurosurgery claims to have established experimentally the existence of three "centers of consciousness" in the brain substance! That is, various functions of the nervous system seem to have a physical "location" in particular regions of the brain in the sense that the possibility of their performance seems to depend upon the condition of the corresponding part of the brain substance. In studying centers, three orders of conscious phenomena are being considered: sleeping-waking, intelligence-memory, and the corporeal scheme of the corporeal self. The acuity of the waking condition (the degree of attention) seems to be related to the nervous functioning of the frontal lobe of the brain;[13] the corporeal scheme or the corporeal self seems to be related to the parietal lobe; the temporal lobe seems to be the center of vision and of the automatic activity of consciousness.

It is incontestable that our foundation in the human world, the "lived-world," or our "being-in-the-world" lies as Merleau-Ponty has ingeniously shown, in the consciousness of our body, and yet this consciousness appears to entertain a connection, to be linked with something that is inaccessible in its nature to the evidence of lived experience, it is merely rationally reconstructed from some observations, experiments and sensory data as a functioning mechanism that science calls the "inferior parietal areas of the brain."

[12] Penfield, quoted by Azima.
[13] Azima, p. 58.

In point of fact, lesions of certain parts of this region of the brain seem to cause the *total loss of awareness of certain parts of the body.* The patient whose brain has been affected in this part remains aware of his existence and can communicate this awareness, but has lost completely not only the awareness of a certain specific part of his body, but also the *memory of ever having had it.*[14]

The phenomenologically informed psychologist does not, however, draw the crude conclusion that consciousness is an "effect" of the sectional functioning of the nervous system. Being accustomed to the analytic distinctions and fine nuances of the phenomenological inspiration, he will see such a correlation of events as pointing, on the contrary, to a diversification of levels of the organization of the human functional system. He will argue that consciousness of the body itself, although fundamentally linked to the "incarnation" of the *psyche,* does not present a conscious "image" of the body. In other words, in the total consciousness of the body, the awareness of the specific parts of the body is not explicit. Only on special occasions, when our attention is attracted to a certain part of our body, do we explicitate it in a direct representation as a part of our total consciousness. And yet, although inexplicit in a representation, this consciousness is the conscious root of the *psyche,* the threshold that may still become experientially meaningful to the individual, due to its virtual holding of a latent representation.

This would indicate that the consciousness of the body, itself a fundamental dimension of the *psyche* as the primary level of awareness to which all the higher levels of the mental life refer, itself the last conscious root of the *psyche,* refers in turn to other levels of organization of the human functions as its "functional substratum."

Although we may make the "subliminal" image of our body experientially explicit it seems to be linked to the complete net of organization of the human being which extends to the functioning of the brain, itself a merely rationally reconstructed notion, beyond the evidence of lived experience. And yet, this extension of the function of consciousness can be neither arbitrarily dismissed nor disregarded, nor can we introduce these experimentally reconstructed dimensions of the brain into the framework of man's lived experience, which stays under the jurisdiction of man's existential potentialities. Not only the levels of sensation and

---

[14] L'Hermite, quoted by Azima, p. 60.

kinesthesis, which lie within the reach of intentionality (i.e.: which are intentional), but also the several levels of operations — which we try to show to be non-intentional operations of the nervous system, which extend deep into nature, belong to the same system of functional organization through which we expand not only the human manifestation of being-in-the-world, but concurrently (if not primordially) *establish our being within the scheme of nature*.[15]

Moreover, our "world" in its forms seems itself to be an element involved within the complete system of this organization.[16]

With the neurological experiments relating vision and automatic activity of consciousness and memory to the temporal lobe of the brain, we have moved to the basic functioning of consciousness. With these activities, consciousness is constitutive of the self as well as of its world. In the first case, concerning vision, it seems, that vision is indeed one of the basic constitutive agencies of consciousness. Can the world of those who are born blind be compared to the "normal" world? Second, without the proper functioning of memory and its automatization, the constitutive process (which constructs the self and its world) can not proceed at all.

Both of these functions represent two of the basic agencies through which man as being-in-the-world emerges out of "brute" nature. Yet, science shows that interference with certain parts of the temporal lobe of the brain, which results in the deformation of the functioning of the nervous system, seems to coincide with a distortion or loss of vision and/or memory.

It would seem that the specific mechanisms of consciousness constitutive of the human world are involved with the universal functional organization we have already hinted at.

Finally, neurology seems to reach the culminating point where consciousness appears to meet the very condition of *bios*. Lesions or distortions of the vital bulbar centers are correlated with a rather radical alteration of consciousness accompanied by an "acute

[15] It has been Merleau-Ponty's aim to correct Heidegger and to embrace the complete functional system of man as *psyche* and *bios* under the notion of the "intentional arc." What we show here is that this is not legitimate; we attempt to establish precisely a borderline of intentionality as a conscious phenomenon and to show the impossibility of placing nature under the jurisdiction of the "arc" of *"experience vécu."*

[16] How the different levels of this system of organisation are linked together calls for a special philosophical investigation. A larger framework is necessary to discover their interrelations, which encompass the limits of science itself.

feeling of anxiety that could be considered as the signal of the imminent collapse of the organism."[17] It seems as if, in these centers, consciousness and life meet in their common vital condition. According to medical records, the instant the lesion reaches this part of the brain, most patients instantly die.

After this brief survey of these scientific facts, we must ask what our discussion can contribute to the knowledge of such fundamental notions as consciousness? How can it be evaluated so as to enlarge our perspective upon man and nature?

Phenomenological caution warns us against a naive and uncritical application of the results of empirical science. Yet unless we reject the validity of human cognition as such and fall into total scepticism, we can not deny the pertinence of certain results of experimental research to the inquiry into man and cognition itself, even if we have to take them as mere steps of the ever-advancing science, to be superseded by the next. Indeed, our study may be most fruitful if we pass the results of science through the filter of the critical attitude of the reduction, regaining the core of the inquiry within its proper constitutive region.

Instead of either uncritically interpreting the inter-relationship of the fundamental conscious functions with the nervous system located in the brain monistically by reducing consciousness to a phenomenon of naively conceived nature (as if nature were merely a series of facts), or (in a parallel fashion) viewing both nature and consciousness as two distinctive dimensions but correlated in their function rather like two mechanisms wound up separately but which point towards a coordinated parallel activity, we will avoid arbitrary reductionism and parallelism and adopt the more nuanced pattern adopted also by scientists themselves.

Our survey of the psychologico-neurological research shows, in the scientific context, consciousness as the expression of the *final integration of the human functional system at large.* On the other hand, however, this functional system is interpreted, within the scientific context itself, as being *organized with reference to the patterns of the nervous system and extending over all levels* of man's functioning, which culminates in the psychic life.

The contribution that this view of consciousness, which comes from scientific sources, offers to our philosophical query is twofold:

[17] Cf. Azima, p. 73.

a) It shows the extension of consciousness from the psychic into the physical realm. Thus, there can be no question of a mind-body dichotomy; and this extension is not meant in terms of consciousness, as in the theory of the "arc of consciousness' — not to mention even the theory of being-in-the-world here under direct discussion — but in terms of *parity* between consciousness and *physis*. The physis into which consciousness extends is not itself conscious; it remains inaccessible and cannot be transmuted into direct "lived experience." And yet consciousness is extending into the "brute" nature through reference to the patterns of the nervous system that cannot be thematized. By the same stroke, consciousness reveals its alterity from, and its dependence upon the heterogeneous dimension of nature.

b) We observe concurrently that the borderlines of the psyche in its autonomous self-reliance are limited to the levels where, presented by primordial intentionality (consciousness), human being is being constituted together with his world. Whereas, the same consciousness extends in its vital operations and its basic patterns below that level where this same consciousness, as expression of the biological functioning of man, seeks its patterns, ultimate commitments and regulations in the inner workings of nature.

It seems to appear clearly that man's being-in-the-world, man's ontic potentialities as limited to the *psyche* (intentionality), reaches only certain regions of this complete organization. The lowest level that might be accessible as directly experienceable is the consciousness of the body. Here the sytem of kinesthesis has its threshold. The deeper involvement of the constitutive functions of consciousness in nature from which it draws the very pattern and the regulations of its operations, seems to escape it. And yet the dimension of man's being-in-the-world is a segment of this vast scheme. What is more puzzling than the question of the principles of its integration?

2. However, the bio-physical conception of consciousness discussed so far approaches consciousness from the point of view of its operations alone. Phenomenology, on the other hand, has made a distinction (Ruehmke) between the "content" of the psychic life and its "forms."

By "forms" of psychic life are understood the modalities of conscious operations (e.g.: acceleration or slowdown in the succession of representations; the temporal aspect of development, tensions, etc.). By "content" of the psychic life we should understand what appears most specific, personal, individual, unpredictable in man's existence: *the quality of experience,* as expressing the personality in its relation to other human beings, the self and the world. It is the particular quality of the content of experience, that is, both the texture and expression of the individual's lived-world and of his own being, his "personality," its texture and flavor, that constitute the fabric of man's lived-world within which he has created himself in a particular web of commitments and their evaluations; a fabric which is the background, the loom for his ever advancing current of experience and which becomes transformed perpetually in its flux.

It appears, then, that we have arrived now at the crucial question of our discussion, namely, *whether the content of experience is entirely and autonomously enclosed within the psychic, intentional dimension of consciousness, or whether it is also linked with the biological foundations of consciousness.*

We could suggest that the quality of experience as the texture of the lived-world and of man circumscribes their reach; it seems indeed to contain everything that there might be altogether possible *sub sole.* Whatever the operations and their forms, in which consciousness produces experience and thus the texture of the human, would depend upon, the quality of this texture depends upon man alone. Man should be understood in his specific and primordially creative position, seated above "brute" nature as the giver of form, quality and meaning. It is in this ontically-rooted perogative, attributed to man as a meaning-bestower in Heidegger's conception of the transcending of brute nature into a self-created web of meaning called "the world," that roots Heidegger's notion of man, existence and the world. Man can transcend his physical condition because through his existential virtualities he is capable of elevating himself into a system of meaningful experiences within which he creates his own being and its milieu, the world. But what if this very texture of the existential projection is *not exclusively rooted in the existential virtualities of man expressing a certain structure of intentionality, but shows deeper roots, deeper involvement, deeper allegiances within brute nature itself?*

What is the status of the content of experience in psychiatric work?

The forms of the psychic life have been from a certain time considered by psychiatrists, and by Ruehmke himself, to be suscept-

ible to successful treatment by pharmacological means. Already this
meant an important and long unsuspected insight: that consciousness is linked in the forms of its operations with the organic but
also inorganic system of interactions.

However, the features of the psychic disease concerning the
content of the psychic life (e.g., the personality structure as we
find it in the schizophrenic distortion of the lived-world of the patient) were viewed as inaccessible to pharmaceutic therapeutics. In
fact, the use of pharmaceutic means (e.g., insulin) treatments of
the brain (lobotomy), electroshocks, etc. were seen as mere tem-
porary relief of the marginal symptoms. They seem to have produced some improvement at random points, but no direct action
upon the basic symptoms has been seen, and the disease itself (e.g.,
chronic schizophrenia) has been considered incurable.

The most recent experiments seem, on the contrary, to have
brought a revolutionary change. With it, however, the decisive
question emerges: "What should we say about the 'specifically human,' distinctive and autonomous dimension of the psychic life, if
we discover that our most personal world-view, our most nuanced,
fragile, unforseen and intimate relations to our fellowmen and to
our emotional life in which we forge our inner self and existence,
may be influenced, directed and even re-oriented in correlation to
the effects that bio-chemical factors can exercise upon our brain?"

Effectively, the survey of results obtained in treatments of psychic disease with the newly-invented neuroleptic products indicates
that the improvements obtained will maintain themselves. Most surprising, however, about their effect upon the bio-nervous system of
man is that they seem to reach not only the *forms* of the psychic
life, but its *very content*: it appears, indeed, as if the use of these
means were correlated to transformation in the quintessence of the
psychic life, the personality itself. These facts, according to a psychologist, "pose in a quite new fashion the question of the relation
between the biological treatment and the transformation of the
complete system."[18]

Indeed, the use of neuroleptics in the case of chronic schizophrenia seems at first to diminish the pathological rigidity of the
"super-ego," which, of course, is not a direct action but correlates
with several levels of bio-conscious operations; it is considered to

---

[18] Dr. E. Meurice, "Psychologie et les neuroleptiques," *Entretiens Psychiatriques,* 1962.

correlate subsequently to the simplification of the ways in which the ego performs its functions in approaching the problems confronting it, which appears to stay within the same line of inter-motivations as the increasing of the flexibility.

This relaxation of the ego seems to pave the way to a more efficient approach to reality.

Whether it is assumed (with Bergougnan) that anxiety — as the central feature of the schizophrenic experience pattern — is itself not directly related with this modification, which only dissolves the psychotic defense mechanism, or whether we believe (Winkelman) that the drug affects the anxiety directly, there seems to exist a progressive correlation of the drug treatment by biochemical means to the very content of the experience which expresses most specifically the disease (e.g., with the progress of the treatment, hallucinations decrease in number, and finally disappear). The patient who is sunken into a condition of autism (total self isolation from his surroundings, utter alienation from the world) slowly "revives"; first through a totally new start in his sensory relation to the world; then by acquiring a more flexible mode of self-expression and more fitting concrete experience and intersubjective reality, which facilitate communication. The relaxation of the initial rigidity also allows search after a mode of self-expression adequate to the concrete situation. Through all these modifications, the patient's contact with other men (from whom he has been separated and cut off due to the basic syndrome of his disease) is slowly reestablished. With these developments the previously distracted lived-world of the patient is on the way to reconstruction.

Concurrently, however, with the renewed experience and with the lived-world shaping itself anew in a "normal" pattern, there develops also a new attitude of the patient towards himself, most specifically towards the content of his delirium.

The content of his psychosis is, in point of fact, centered in his delirium and the specific interpretation that the patient gives to it expresses the deformation of the structure of the patient's lived-world, its topsy-turvy organization and peculiar quality. Although the basic schizophrenic scheme may remain, the patient, through the renewal of his sensory experience and of his emotional life, gives to his delirium a new, more "realistic" interpretation that goes along with his reestablishment of a "normal" lived-world and a "normal" self.

In short, through this transformation of the patient's sensory, effective, communicative and finally intellectual functioning, his personality together with his world are transformed and reconstructed. These developments culminate in the emergence of "a new mode of lived experience."[19]

Through the maze of factual experimental data organized tentatively into a net of correlations by the scientist, we may catch a glimpse of reality itself in a way much more acute than before we focused upon the heart of the matters alluded to in the foregoing discussion.

The phenomenon of the reconstruction of the schizophrenic personality appears to us as a process in a multi-leveled unity of intermotivations (or correlations). Starting with the bio-chemical and developing through the bio-neurological and the psychic forms of consciousness, it seems to bear upon this very "substance" or source of the psychic life and texture of the being-in-the-world of man. The rôle of the interpretation of the delirium weaves most intimately the intellectual function into the total scheme as one of the essential factors of experience.

Furthermore, a whole array of functional organizations of man as an organic being, which show the roots of his *bios* to lie in an organic nature, lurks from behind the scientific facts. Of this array, which consists of a diversified variety of functional strata, only a few such organizations seem to have been so far distinguished by science; many are yet to be discovered; still they are, however, not the final answer. Science may in its rational reconstructions only approximate the skeleton of the infinitely complex texture of reality that we find underneath. The "specifically human" level of the "inner life, life of the soul, quality of experience," appears interwoven into a vaster net of operational intermotivations than any conceptually and rationally distinguishable system can ever account for.

Three points have to be extracted from our discussion:

a) The "psycho-physical basis of consciousness," in words of an eminent psychologist,[20] seems to lend the pattern of organization to the lived experience, resulting in the lived-world; this basis of consciousness is linked with the functional system of the brain,

---

[19] *Ibid.*, p. 198.
[20] Dr. H. Ey used this expression in the discussion of Dr. Meurice's lecture, *ibid.*, p. 202.

and through it with the complete array of organic and inorganic functions.

b) And yet it is clear that man transcends "brute nature in a self-projected world in which he finds his existential accomplishment encompassing the whole human horizon, and which does not extend beyond consciousness in its psychic functions (intentional). The conception of man's world, of man's-being-in-the-world does not explicitate nor extend into the complete linkage system in which consciousness appears as merely one set of functions. Even the conception of man's "throwness" into the rest of beings from which he has to lift himself by devising the meaningful world is itself meaningful only with reference to the idea of transcendence and existence itself; it belongs not to nature as such, but to the structure of existence. The question "How does the medication which results in the restructuring of the field of consciousness act upon the pathology of personality?" cannot be answered within its framework.

c) The array of intermotivations which we have discovered does not stop at man's boundaries, not even in such a sense that the "specifically human element" is separable from the total, but rather it goes through man in its overall organization.

And yet, although functionally interlinked, interwoven in this anonymous system of operations stretching far beyond it, the specifically human functional levels retain their specific quality. This irreducible, uninterchangible quality of experience becomes even more emphasized in its autonomous essence while being an object of such a complex and diversified scheme of operations which are necessary to lead to its modification.

3. There is still a deeper insight to be gained through the inquiry into the "biological basis of consciousness" which will corroborate the glimpse so far gained of the vast scheme of operations involving man, his world and *nature in its inner workings*. That is, we intend to approach the issues under discussion from the viewpoint of the *origination* of psychic disease.

Although a psychic disease such as schizophrenia can be determined biologically only in its vaguest features, it seems now to be to a clinician irrefutable that: a) this syndrome carries with it a number of physical anomalies, and b) that the notion of "functional

[21] Dr. H. Azima, "Les problèmes biologiques de la pathogenie et de la schizophrénie, essai d'une synthèse des donnés récentes," *Entretiens Psychiatriques*, 1952, p. 53.

psychosis" without an organic lesion is unthinkable.[21]

Opposing the hitherto accepted view that schizophrenia can result only from the social inadaptation, and drawing upon the evidence of the bio-physiological and neurological studies of schizophrenia, a hypothesis is advanced that the anatomical anomalies accompanying schizophrenia have to be pursued further than does the histological level. In point of fact, these anomalies are correlated with the *deformations of the most intimate infra-cellular life of the body.* This hypothesis brings the origin of the anatomical anomalies into connection — even in the remotest of ways — with the origin of the psychic anomalies; the distortion of the personality and of the world links into the complete system of growth and development of things and beings.

A vast perspective opens when we consider that, on the prevailing scientific view, the cell is the ultimate particle in nature that enjoys a life of its own in which it regulates itself. Furthermore, every organic process within a body — the body is some sort of cell-organization — depends upon the proper functioning of the spontaneous cooperation of cells; but ultimately it depends upon the most intimate life within each of the cells; in particular, it depends upon the adequate regulation of the influx of inorganic substance into the cell, and their appropriate use and reflux.

The organic anomalies accompanying schizophrenia are brought back to an inadaptation of the organism to its surroundings. In examining the causes of this organic inadaptation, Dr. Azima utilizes evidence from cellular study which indicates a correlation of these anomalies with the deformities of the cellular organization, or more specifically, with what he calls the "genetic immaturity" of the cell.[22]

It seems as if we had along these lines found confirmation of a pervasive linkage system which is not only a functional array of operations responsible for the progress and conservation of life, but which also *stands in the perspective of its generation in its distinctive forms and in the type of their cooperation.*

In this vast perspective which opens upon universal generation of forms extending through inorganic and organic nature and culminating in intellectual creativity, it seems to be emphasized a) that the genesis of man's specific psychic life in all its dimensions as expressed through his being-in-the-world might well be unified

[22] *Ibid.,* p. 92.

within one and the same system of universal genesis as the origination of his specific *bios*; b) that in the personal scope of his self and
its world, self-enclosed within his own creation, it constitutes merely
a tiny, fragmentary and rhapsodic segment in the *great scheme of the
workings of nature*; c) these conclusions opened yet more puzzling
questions. "The inner workings of nature," even if there is particular
acuity in their intuition, lurk only vaguely behind this extensive but
fragmentary rational construct of scientific facts. No completion of
its fragments can ever explain the passage from one dimension of
functioning to the other, which, the more carefully scrutinized with
microscopes and instruments, appears more distinct from others in
its increasing complexity. Can scientific scrutiny, sticking to the
concrete facts, ever give us the reason for the selection of such
forms, for the specific links of intermotivation among the various
levels, for the ways of coordinating the *All*?

In our discussion of the psychiatric practices in clinical work
and therapy, we hope to have shown that psychiatry with its various
scientific fields cannot be confined within the borders circumscribed
by the fundamental existential structure of man's being-in-the-
world. On the contrary, scientific research upon which psychiatry
draws clearly shows the narrow framework of the human world to
be in contrast to dimensions that lie beyond man's direct experience.

These dimensions, although not given in primordial experience
but rather rationally reconstructed by science, cannot be disregarded; neither can they be taken as the final answer. There cannot
be a question of "explaining" the specifically human world in its
quality and origin by reference to its biological foundation, or of
seeking such an explanation in the notion of brain, organism, cellular
life, etc. as conditions of man's psychic or existential virtualities.
On the contrary, the closer science comes to these phenomena, the
more they appear original, and their autonomy stronger and more
puzzling. What we have gained from our discussion of the scientific
results is a deeper insight into *the reality lying behind all artifacts
of mind, into the presence of a vast array of functional and genera-
tive organizations which extends over an indefinite number of
heterogeneous levels (only some of them already discovered, others
only intuited), into the great scheme of origination and perdurance
of all things and beings.*

The presence of this array shifts the accent from the distinctive-
ness of *psyche* and *bios* to the questions concerning the rules of

selection, linkage and integration of the whole system of the *inner workings of nature*, and beyond it, upon the great system of the *All*.

Part Three — The Cosmos

"When a man is projected into outer space, when these trans-sidereal spaces are traversed, what do we learn more about the reverberations of the *cosmos* upon the *bios*? And yet, as living matter, we are a part of it."[23]

Attempting to show that psychiatric work itself disqualifies the Heideggerian conception of man as being-in-the-world as a foundation unifying all the sciences taking part in the psychiatric work, we have rejected the Heraclitean identification of the human world which represents man's transcendental dimension with the *cosmos* encompassing the *All*.

What about the cosmos?

In our critical discussion we have won, however, a positive glimpse of reality, which has given us some clues towards a new conception of nature. Will these insights not offer us a lead towards an insight into the *cosmos*, the Great Game of the *All?*

In its approach to things and beings, contemporary science has turned away from the classical "objectifying" point of view, which leads to the questions "How things and beings are?" and "Why are they as they are?" In the perspective of these two questions, nature in its laws presents itself as the correlate of our searching intention, that can be thematized according to the pattern of our cognitive system and appropriated by man as belonging to his horizon. Heidegger investigates the profound virtualities of man through which he constitutes himself and this very perspective.

Contemporary scientists, on the contrary, are suspicious of the constructions of concepts and other artifacts of mind, and want more the mastery of nature than the "truth." Instead of following the line of man' natural wonder about the universe and his intellectual propensity to respond to it with a mind-satisfying picture, the scientist wants to grasp nature as it operates. He attempts to grasp the *inner workings of nature* instead of a picture of "nature," by *entering the game of nature* itself.

[23] Question raised in the French Academy of Science and reported by T. Gillibert in "Génèse, structure et l'origine de l'être, ou de l'auto-génèse en psychopathologie," *Entretiens Psychietripus*, 1961, vol. 10, pp. 11-48.

Recent natural science devised models, matrices and other devices as means of reaching below the categories and forms of thought established throughout the centuries, below the basic thematizing and reconstructing media of our cognitive system, in order to gain access to the functioning of nature manipulative of its elements according to its own rules of operations.

The models and matrices of biological and physical science do not teach us "how" nature is, nor "why" things and beings are as they are, but rather show us nature in its game of functions as generating, modifying, ever advancing in the inacting of a great project involving the *All*.

Even if, in order to express its ways of procedure, it may be necessary to return to the traditional conceptual apparatus, we are reminded that these concepts are relative and that we should focus our attention upon what lies below them.

Since science has in this way radically avoided the imprint that a human evaluation of it in reference to man's direct experience would have given, should it be considered as "dishumanized," and disregarded by philosophy? Or should man, instead learn a great lesson about himself. If by discovering his *true situation within the scheme* of the *All?*

In this larger perspective, there is certainly place for man in all his irreducible specificity; yet his existence, richest and highest in its forms and content of all that there is, creating its own world of meanings, appears — to use Kant's expression — like a tiny island floating upon an unchartable sea.

Only a tiny fraction of the system of *nature in its inner workings* seems to be accessible to existentially concerned man insofar as he experiences it at the boundaries of his specifically human functions. In the perspective of his existential concern, he is bound to miss the rest. He might *enter*, as science and technology show us, into the great game of nature, yet there can be no question of making this game in any sense relative to his own being with its existential pre-eminence over the rest of things and beings. The very fact that he *may* enter it does not seem to depend upon *Dasein* alone; it depends also upon the game, in which he seems to be fundamentally a participant, but merely a marginal partner.

Consequently, the specifically human world, the counterpart of *Dasein*, cannot be a foundation unifying the sciences of man and of nature. The relations between *psyche* and *physis* appears to be much less sharply defined, and much more complex, differentiated, nuanced than has been so far acknowledged in philosophy. Although it is difficult — if even possible — to draw a sharp line of separation between the specifically psychic level of consciousness and its physical basis in nature, the puzzle concerning the conjunction of both of them does not disappear. It only reaches a more concrete and nuanced level.

As for psychiatry: there is no more question of a direct intercourse, in any sense, between *psyche* and *physis*, taken as two "substances," realms or structures. Both of them appear as harmoniously spread out within a vaster functional system of inter-motivations at several levels. If we ask now about the philosophical foundations which unify the various methods used at each of these, we will have to ask after *principles, rules, patterns and laws of the interplay* of these levels, distinctive and autonomous in respect to each other.

We must, however, seek further than the concrete scientific notions, further than the philosophical conception of the *inner workings of nature,* and further than that of the constitutive potentialities of man.

Should we not seek such a foundation pertaining to nature and man in some great scheme comprising *All,* in the sense of *cosmos?*

Yet how shall we understand it? We have discarded with Heidegger the factually existing totality of things and beings; we have discarded as well the factual configuration of the existents, or the world-order, to stand for it. Finally, we have attempted to refute the Heideggerian transcendental conception of the world as a legitimate identification of the *All* comprising the distinctive rights of nature.

In the process of this critical scrutiny we have gotten from science a few glimpses of the reality of nature itself in the vast scheme of its operations, which has led us to revise the notion of it, within a larger framework. Nature, in its inner workings, is also incapable of accounting for the *All.* On the contrary, the spontaneous continuity within the discontinuous system of levels in the process of incessant operations raises more questions than it answers.

If we want to lift ourselves towards the final answers, we must account for the rules of the functional harmony which governs equally generation and progress. We have to find the rules of the integration and coordination of its operations, laws, and the ultimate reasons for the linkage of the autonomous levels participating in this great game. Finally, we have to envisage the question of the primordial selection of its forms and means.

Moving with these questions to the "Architectonic Project" of the *All*, to the scheme of the universal constitution presiding over creation and progress,[24] we will follow the Presocratic claim to account in this conception for both order and origination, and submit to calling such a system of ultimate conditions governing the primeval virtualities the *cosmos*.

[24] For the "Architectonic Project" cf. by the present writer, *Why is There Something Rather Than Nothing*, Royse Von Gorcum, Assen (Holland), 1966.

August, 1966 — June, 1968

Heidegger and the Existential A Priori

John Wild

In this paper I shall be concerned with an aspect of Heidegger's philosophy which has already had a widespread influence on thinkers like Sartre, and Merleau-Ponty especially, as well as many others. I believe that it is of revolutionary significance in the history of Western thought, and that it will have a growing importance in the future, though, of course, I am no prophet. This is his conception of an existential *a priori* which includes a number of fundamental patterns treated separately under the heading of *existentials* in *Sein und Zeit*. Among these are being-in-the-world (*In-der-Welt-sein*), life-space (*die Raumlichkeit des Daseins*), being-with-others (*Mitsein*), care (*Sorge*), dying (*der Tod*), temporality (*Zeitlichkeit*), and several others.

These are not fixed properties, inhering in a human substance. They are ways of existing, stretched out spatially and temporally, and constituting the being (*Sein*) of *Dasein*, which, in a loose sense, we may translate as *human reality*. This being cannot be identified with any of the particular, ontic manifestations, or facts, that may be observed in the life-histories of human individuals or groups. It is prior to these ontic facts, and is found in them as patterns which condition them, and in a Kantian sense, make them possible. Hence it is appropriate to refer to these conditioning patterns as *existentially a priori*.

In this paper, I shall deal with five topics. First I shall present a brief outline of Heidegger's view of the existential *a priori*, attempt-

already familiar with it by a direct knowledge that belongs to our existence. As he says, *"Dasein* is primordially familiar (*ursprüng-lich vertraut*) with this (world), in which it already understands itself" (SZ, 86). This familiarity (*Vertrautheit*), he then says, does not require that the relations which constitute the world as world should be theoretically transparent. "However the possibility of working out an explicit ontological-existential interpretation of these relations is grounded on this direct familiarity with the world (*Weltvertrautheit*), which belongs to *Dasein*, and contributes to its understanding of being (*Seinsverständnis*)."

Thus in his ontological analysis of *Dasein*, Heidegger is claiming not to be constructing an interpretation of his own, but rather to be revealing in an explicit, conceptual manner, patterns of existence (*Existentialien*) with which all men are already implicitly familiar. In my opinion, he has sometimes, though not always, succeeded in shedding more light on these existentially *a priori* structures in *Sein und Zeit*, and as I see it, this is the major phenomenological contribution of his book. It is with this notion of an existential *a priori* that I shall be concerned in this paper.

Heidegger often speaks of the way in which this task of clarify-ing the existential *a priori* has been neglected in the past history of Western ontology, how the existentials, as he calls them, have been confused with categories, and how, as a result of this confusion, man has been misconceived as a thing that is simply there (*Vorhanden*) before the mind. Objective thinking of this kind has now become so dominant that the phenomenological task of focusing these existen-tial patterns has become extremely difficult. In order to get on his way, the phenomenologist must first penetrate through a number of objective interpretations and attitudes, which hide these structures from us and even make them inaccessible.

With these explanations which Heidegger gives, for example, in his discussion of the nature of phenomenology (cf. SZ, 27-38), I find myself in general agreement. But when he begins to develop these difficulties into a general theory of the unauthentic, social condition of *das Man* (oneness), I find serious questions arising in my mind. I do not have time in this paper to argue out these issues in detail. But I shall not be concerned with Heidegger's views con-cerning *Seinsvergessenheit, Verfallenheit,* the status of *das Man* and other cognate theories. I shall not consider these aspects of Heideg-ger's thought. My remarks will be directed rather to his conception

ing to single out its most basic features. Second, I shall compare his view with those of other phenomenological thinkers. Third, I shall point out four respects in which this view resembles traditional versions of the *a priori*, and which justifies our calling them *a priori*. Fourth, I shall contrast it with these traditional conceptions of *a priori* knowledge and indicate what is radically new. Finally, fifth, I shall show three distinctive philosophical tasks to which this conception of the *a priori* leads.

Part One — Heidegger's View of the Existential *A Priori*

A major aim of Heidegger in his now classical text, *Sein und Zeit* is to reveal more clearly and thematically certain patterns of existence (*Existentialien*, existentials) which are already known pre-thematically (*unthematisch*) to all men. He sometimes refers to these patterns of existence (care (*Sorge*), dying (*der Tod*), etc.) as *a priori*, or as "the existential *a priori* of philosophical anthropology" (SZ, 131). A direct familiarity with human existence and its situation in the world is presupposed by ordinary discourse, and, indeed, by the technical discourse of human science, which is a mode of human understanding and, therefore, involves some implicit understanding of man. Hence the term, *a priori*, is appropriate to this sense of his own existence which belongs to the being of man.

Any new enterprise on which men embark is actually based on this prior existential awareness which has already been achieved. Hence on p. 85, Heidegger speaks of the "*perfect* tense *a priori*" as a peculiarly appropriate way of expressing such knowledge, and he constantly makes use of it through the whole text of *Sein und Zeit*. The oriented life-space, in which we live and move, belongs to the very being of *Dasein*. Hence in bringing out its *a priori*, existential character, Heidegger says, "*Dasein* always has space presented to it as already discovered, though not thematically" (SZ, 112). And in speaking of care (*Sorge*) he says "that no sooner has *Dasein* expressed anything about itself to itself, than it has already interpreted itself as care (*cura*), even though it has done so only pre-ontologically" (SZ, 183).

Heidegger writes in a similar way concerning the basic structure of being-in-the-world. It is "an *a priori necessary* structure of *Dasein* . . ."[1] Before we begin to think about it conceptually, we are

[1] "Das In-der-Welt-sein ist zwar eine a priori notwendige Verfassung des Daseins . . ." SZ, 53.

of the existential *a priori*, which, as I think I have shown, plays a basic role in *Sein und Zeit*. My purpose is to single out this conception, to compare and contrast it with similar ideas that are found in other phenomenologically oriented authors, and to make certain further comments on it of my own.

Part Two — The Analysis of *Sein und Zeit* in Relation to Other Investigations of the Pre-predicative (Husserl)

Heidegger was not the first to become interested in the pre-conceptual or pre-thematic knowledge that is presupposed by science and even what we refer to now as *ordinary discourse*. Our interest here is not primarily historical, but we may mention at least two important predecessors who were deeply concerned with such pre-theoretical knowledge, and with one of whom, at least, Heidegger was certainly familiar when he wrote *Sein und Zeit*. This was Husserl who made certain significant references to what he called *pre-predicative knowledge* in *Experience and Judgment* (*Erfahrung und Urteil*) and later in the *Krisis*. Before Husserl, in our own tradition, William James, a phenomenological thinker as many of us are now beginning to see, referred to this as a knowledge by direct acquaintance, and sharply distinguished it from a conceptual *knowledge about*, which presupposes the former. According to him, language is always surrounded by a direct situational awareness which it presupposes. Thus the subject of a sentence, and demonstratives, like *this*, *that*, *Lo*, *voilá* and *look*, involve a pre-predicative knowledge of this kind, without which meaningful language cannot even begin.[2]

There is a sense in which this knowledge is pre-conceptual. But this does not mean that it cannot be conceptually clarified and expressed through verbal communication. In fact, James devoted major portions of his great text to precisely this task, and Merleau-Ponty has followed the same course in his *Phenomenology of Perception*. I believe that it is fair to say that further light has now been shed on some of these *a priori* patterns with which we are all directly familiar in our lived existence. These patterns are first known vaguely by direct acquaintance, to use James' term, or by living them through pre-thematically. What then are these patterns?

[2] Cf. *Principles of Psychology*, I, pp. 222-23.

As we have indicated, we shall make no claim to be giving an exhaustive list. We shall mention only a few of them which have been carefully examined and conceptually formulated by Heidegger and others, and which seem to constitute the *a priori* conditions for wide ranges of particular human phenomena. We shall be concerned, first of all, with several of them dealt with by Heidegger in *Sein und Zeit*: being-in-the-world, the oriented space, quite different from any geometric space, in which we live, move, and maneuver, the active care for persons and things, which is manifested in all the particular projects of individual life and history, the ending or dying of his own death which, as Kierkegaard pointed out, no individual person will ever observe as an object, but which he must face, or reject, in some way, and die for himself, and finally, the ecstatic lived time, with its moving ecstasies of future, past, and present, which, as Heidegger holds, is the most basic pattern, or meaning, of human existence. To these we shall add the lived body (*corps vécu*) and being-with-others, largely neglected in *Sein und Zeit*, but carefully analyzed by Merleau-Ponty and others.

These patterns have been described by different phenomenologists, coming from different national cultures and traditions. In many respects the conclusions at which they have arrived are different. But *in certain important respects*, there are agreements. Thus the analysis of life-space presented by Heidegger in *Sein und Zeit*, is markedly similar to that of Merleau-Ponty in his *Phenomenology of Perception*, and of Bollnow in his more comprehensive recent book on *Mensch und Raum*. One can say that in spite of certain differences, there are no downright contradictions in these diverse analyses. There is sufficient inter-subjective confirmation, I think, to justify the conclusion that the clarification of these patterns is leading to a conception of *a priori* knowledge and structure that is radically new in the history of Western thought.

Part Three — Four Traits of the *A Priori*

They are *a priori* in four respects which agree with traditional notions of the *a priori*, and which justify the use of this term. First of all, these patterns are *a priori* in the sense that they are found universally in all men, and seem to be essentially human. Traditional conceptions have identified this *a priori* with lists of concepts, or categories, and more recently with forms of linguistic syntax. But grave questions can be raised concerning the universality of any of

these. Thus one may well ask whether the Kantian category of substance is really present in certain primitive and non-Indo-European
languages. But can any reasonable doubt be raised concerning the
universality of those pre-linguistic and pre-conceptual patterns
which are found even in the experience of the child? Is there any
known tribe or people, no matter how primitive or advanced, that is
not at least familiar with the regions of the world in which it lives,
with the life-space of this world, its different distances and directions, with social life and its basic modes?

We are not saying, of course, that different tribes and individuals interpret these direct experiences in the same way, or even
that they necessarily have a coherent verbal interpretation. We are
speaking of that knowledge by direct acquaintance which is presupposed by any verbal interpretation. Is there any human individual who has no familiarity with his living body, as he moves and
feels it, who, for example, would not grasp the negative meaning
of a sharp blow on the face? In the light of the evidence to which
we now have access, is it reasonable to deny that a familiarity with
these patterns is universally present in the experience of all men?
In this respect, then, they are worthy candidates for an *empirical a
priori* that is not merely supposed and postulated, but that is actually
found in *human existence* as such.

In the second place, these patterns are *a priori* in that each of
them is presupposed by an indefinite range of particular phenomena
conditioned by it. The prior condition retains its structural identity
and indeterminacy throughout innumerable variations in specific
content. Thus the world-ground, described by Merleau-Ponty and
Heidegger, retains its worldhood even though different things in
the world, different figures, as we may call them, appear on the
ground. And the ecstatic structure of temporality persists as the
different events *in time* come and go. Furthermore, we can truly
say that these persisting field-patterns are presupposed by the varying content, since no thing, or set of things can appear in the
world, unless this world is already there, and, without time itself,
there can be no events in time. As Heidegger points out (SZ, 194-
96), the three-fold pattern of care, as ahead of itself, as already in,
and fallen among, is presupposed by the different forms of wish,
desire, impulse, drive, will, etc., that we experience in our different
projects. These patterns are "earlier than" and preconditions for
vast ranges of particular phenomena.

There is a third feature of traditional theories of the *a priori* which we must now consider. They all maintain that this prior knowledge of ultimate patterns is hidden from the common understanding of men and requires special procedures to be brought into the light. Thus the Platonic forms, which give order and stability to the flux of experience, are revealed only by the arduous processes of Socratic questioning, and the Kantian categories are focused only after an elaborate transcendental deduction. Are the empirical patterns with which we are concerned also hidden in some way, so that the term *a priori* may be naturally applied to them?

With the development of linguistic and conceptual self-consciousness, this is certainly the case. Everything we think falls within the range of the basic concepts that are prevalent at a given time; everything we say, within that of the basic patterns of our language, in a universe of discourse. So the world of sense fades into the background, and is discounted as we have noted, and reduced to "a mere manifold of sense." How can our thought escape from its own structures to reveal the alien patterns of another world? How can language go beyond itself to speak out the unspoken? Hence the marked tendency of modern philosophy to drift into different forms of idealism, the earlier conceptual idealism of the Nineteenth, and the more recent linguistic idealism of the Twentieth Century. Thus the philosophic mind becomes imprisoned in a universe of discourse which becomes more and more self-sufficing and remote from the world of existence, whose patterns are either ignored as obvious and unworthy of disciplined examination, or distorted by one-sided conceptual interpretations. In these ways, they become deeply obscured and hidden by the very logical instruments which, if rightly used, might clarify them and bring them into the light. At the present time, even words, like *experience* and *empiricism,* have become so overly intellectualized and linguistified (if I may use this term) that the struggle to gain an empirical, or phenomenological approach to philosophy, has become extremely arduous.

Finally, we must take note of a fourth trait that is found in traditional versions of the conceptual, or linguistic, *a priori.* That is the logical contraditions, antinomies, and category mistakes which result from their denial or misuse. Is the empirical knowledge by direct acquaintance, which is prior to these, protected by sanctions of an analogous kind? I believe that an affirmative answer to this

question is also justified in the light of relevant evidence. If I conceptually deny the world in which I exist, or assert that I am disem-
bodied, or deathless, this may be mere verbal play. But the knowledge of which I am speaking is not purely verbal and detached. It is
independent of language, and bound up with my existence. Hence
if I seriously come to doubt it, or begin to lose it, and become confused with respect to my life-space, for example, I become mentally ill or socially disturbed. If I really begin to doubt and dis-
trust not some theory, but the world in which I actually exist, and
the *Urdoxa*, as Husserl called it, by which I believe in it, what the
psychiatrists call *my sense of reality* is affected, and I am in need
of clinical care. We can say, therefore, that this existential *a priori*
is protected not merely by logical, but also by existential sanctions.

The meaningful patterns of which we have been speaking and
the knowledge we have by direct acquaintance with them seem to
possess these four marks that have been traditionally attributed to
intellectualist and verbal versions of the *a priori*. This knowledge
seems to be universally present in all men of whatever race, or
tribe, or culture. Second, these patterns condition wide ranges of
particular phenomena, and a hazy knowledge by direct acquaintance with them is presupposed by science, philosophy, and ordinary
discourse. Would any of our lengthy treatises on space, social relations, and time ever have been written, if no one had ever become
familiar with them in his lived existence? Is it not true that what we
have come to know *about* them, through science and philosophy,
presupposes this knowledge by acquaintance that we already have
— *a priori*? Third, this knowledge is concealed from us by the limits
of our languages and universes of discourse, which become tighter
as they become more organized, and by the many difficulties involved in any attempt to conceptualize the pre-conceptual. Fourth,
this knowledge by acquaintance with existence is protected by existential sanctions. These four similarities, I believe, justify us in calling such knowledge *a priori*. But it is radically different from traditional conceptions. So let us now turn to what is new.

Part Four — An Empirical *A Priori*

The most evident difference from traditional conceptions is that
this *a priori* is *perceptual* or *empirical*, rather than intellectualistic
or linguistic. Instead of a chaotic realm of sense experience, presup-
posing intellectualistic and linguistic forms of order, it is now intel-

lectual and linguistic formulations that presuppose a world of perception and feeling, of which we already have *a priori* knowledge by direct acquaintance. This change in the order of priority, which we may call a "turning of the tables," is the most novel feature of this new conception which is emerging from recent phenomenology. But this involves certain other novel features which we may briefly summarize as follows:

Traditional philosophy in the West has tended, throughout its history, to disparage and discount the primordial world of feeling and perception, at different times for different reasons. Thus in classic and medieval times, it was discounted as vague, confused, and ephemeral, in modern times as subjective, and as a mere manifold lacking all order and structure (Kant). But if, as Heidegger holds, there is a pre-thematic *a priori*, this negative attitude towards the world of sense will have to be abandoned. This world may be vague and fleeting, but structures are there. It may include subjective factors, but it is not subjective in the sense that it is included within a mind-container. As Heidegger and others have shown, it stretches out ecstatically in a vast spatiotemporal field, within which all the diverse regions and objects of human experience can be found. In the light of the investigations of recent phenomenology, it can no longer be dismissed as a chaotic "manifold." It is rather an ordered world with distinctive patterns of its own.

This means that the traditional dualism of sense vs. reason, the sensible vs. the intelligible worlds, as they were called, is deprived of empirical support. In reflecting today on Kant's famous statement that concepts without percepts are empty, and percepts without concepts are blind, the phenomenologist can accept its first part. Concepts without any reference to direct experience are certainly empty, and with this aspect of the Kantian criticism he will have a deep sympathy. But the second part he cannot accept without serious qualification. Percepts without concepts may be vague, incommunicable, and even floating. But they are not totally *blind*. Certain structures are vaguely present, and this knowledge by acquaintance can be clarified and rendered communicable by phenomenological description and analysis. Reason does not begin to operate *de novo* in a structureless chaos, as Kant himself recognized in the transcendental aesthetic. But he did not dwell on it long enough. If he had, he would have seen that reason begins to operate in a world that is already structured and provided with implicit

meanings. Hence the traditional dualism is no longer tenable. As de
Waelhens has pointed out in commenting on Husserl and Heidegger: "The general 'categories' of consciousness, intentionality, meaning (*sens*), temporality, retention, protension, and to use Heideggerian terms which must be understood here analogically, understanding (*Verstehen*) and project (*Entwurf*) are already manifest
in perception, and in it they find a first concretion."[3]

If there is an ultimate, empirical *a priori* of this kind, questions
may certainly be raised as to how it is to be revealed and brought
into the light. Certainly not by any purely rational dialectic, like
the Platonic questioning for the pure form, freed from any admix-
ture with the confusing apprehensions of sense, nor by any trans-
scendental deduction of the pure forms or categories. For the ultimate meanings we must return rather to the primordial patterns of
our being-in-the-world, which are already known to us pre-thematically by direct acquaintance. Then by a hermeneutic use of
concepts, working in close cooperation with perception and feeling,
we may hope to clarify these original meanings in the phenomenological way and to bring them into the light. This, I believe, was
Heidegger's procedure in arriving at the insights of *Sein und Zeit*.
And I would suggest that it also applies to his later writings where
he is far more fearful of reducing and distorting the original experience of a thing, a bridge, a pitcher, and a work of art, by some over-
simple intellectual description or construction. Even here, however,
he is still using language to express the original meaning as it is
lived through, not deduced but *found* in our primary experience.

Part Five — A New Empirical Philosophy

Finally, we may note in recent years under the influence of
phenomenology and other similar movements of thought, the development of a new kind of empirical philosophy. Past empiricists have
often shared with the intellectualists and the Kantians an over-
simple conception of the original data of experience. This has
prevented them from glimpsing the structures of the *Lebenswelt*
and the mysteries involved in many everyday phenomena which, as
Heidegger has shown, without careful, empirical reflection so easily
fall under the veils of what we call *the obvious* (*selbstverständ-
lich*). Is this not, at the present time, the most prevalent way in
which the most basic meanings, like being, the life-world, life-

[3] *Phénoménologie et Vérité* (Paris: PUF, 1953), p. 24.

space, the living body, and many others, are hidden from us?

We are already familiar with them by feeling and perception. Hence they are *obvious*, and we do not need to think about them seriously. But it is precisely here, in these *obvious* things, that we face the most difficult questions, once we focus them. With their over-simple views of experience, the traditional empiricists have not delved deeply enought into questions of this kind. So they have not focused the *Lebenswelt*, and have turned their attention primarily to science, and to scientific method. This has led them to foster the widespread prejudice that every fact of any kind falls within the province of some science, and that there is, therefore, no point in developing a truly empirical philosophy which tries to look, to observe, and to learn. All the facts belong to the sciences. So there is nothing left over for philosophy except language and logic.

The new empiricism of our time (James called it a *radical empiricism*) differs from traditional versions in all these respects. James focused the "world of sense," as he called it, in his *Principles of Psychology*, written in 1890. Towards the end of his career in his *Krisis der Europäischen Wissenschaften* Husserl clearly focused it as the *Lebenswelt*, pointed out that it was presupposed by the sciences, and called for its disciplined investigation. So with the aid of these and other authors, many of us in our time have been able to focus this *Lebenswelt*, its vast wealth of implicit meaning, and some of its basic patterns. We have read Heidegger's critical comments on the deceptive term, "obvious," and its synonyms. These have led us to see that the world facts and meanings, to which we refer in this way, are in a sense already known pre-thematically, and that this "knowledge" is vague, confused, and incommunicable.

But these meanings involve factors of ambiguity which make them susceptible to *exact* interpretations, coming from uncritical traditional sources. Such interpretations, however, which now seem obvious to us, as Heidegger has shown, for example, in his *destruction of Western ontology*, are usually over-simple reductions and distortions that fail to do justice to the original meanings. This calls for a disciplined study of these familiar phenomena of the life-world. And so we find whole books devoted to the lived phenomena of *Pain* by Buytendijk,[4] on *Laughter and Tears* by the biologist, Helmut Plessner and many others. Each of these authors is thoroughly

[4] *De la Douleur* (Paris: PUF, 1951).

trained in a single science (physiological psychology and biology). But each of them sees that while scientific methods and results are relevant to the world facts he is studying, they are not sufficient to gain an adequate understanding of them, since these phenomena involve subjective (noetic) as well as objective (noematic) factors, and since they occur in a different world horizon. Similar studies of lived phenomena have been made by philosophers, as by Heidegger in his later works.

But for the most part, philosophers, with their understandable interest in what is ultimately *a priori*, have been more concerned with the basic structures of the *Lebenswelt*, like the existentials of *Sein und Zeit*, and the structure of perception in Merleau-Ponty's *Phenomenology of Perception*. But they, and others, have now made it very clear that these basic patterns, like all the original world facts of the *Lebenswelt*, lie beyond the range of the objective methods of the sciences, and require a different phenomenological approach. There is, therefore, a whole world of facts and meanings, presupposed, as Husserl pointed out, by the sciences, and known either vaguely, or more clearly, in other ways. The empirical philosopher has certain peculiar responsibilities to this prior world in which we exist, face death, and pursue our chosen projects, both as individuals and groups.

As I see it, from the nature of his discipline (philosophy), his responsibilities to this *Lebenswelt* primarily fall into three distinct groups. First, he is concerned with particular world facts, historic facts as we often call them, like the Black Death in the 14th Century, or the origins of science in the 17th, and the elucidation of their meanings. This is a lesser responsibility which he shares with history and the other human disciplines. But the philosopher has always been especially concerned with digging down to the ultimate presuppositions, the underlying patterns which condition all the rest. So he has a special responsibility for clarifying the *a priori* patterns of experience, such as perception, understanding, the living body, time, space, and being-in-the-world. Finally, in the third place, he has another *speculative* responsibility in connection with the meaning of human history, or, as we may say, of human existence in the world.

As an empirical philosopher, he is not interested in speculation as such, with no firm empirical ground. In line with the Kantian critique, he distrusts the appeal to pure reason, or pure logic, as independent grounds apart from experience. Such speculation, and the interminable disputes in which it becomes involved, he finds to be artificial, empty, and verbose. This is the meaning of Heidegger's destruction of Western ontology and his criticisms of Western metaphysics, which have become sharper at the end of his career. There has been too much of this ungrounded system-building in our history. But there is another kind of speculation to which Kant pointed, an empirically grounded speculation, a metaphysics of experience, or of the *Lebenswelt,* as we may call it, which is an inescapable need of life and in which the empirical philosopher will engage in a disciplined way. In fact, Heidegger has himself engaged in it in some of his later thinking about the meaning of being, though he prefers, I think, unwisely, to call it by other names. This is a last and inescapable resonsibility.

Such, then, is the new empirical philosophy which is emerging around us in our time. It recognizes the feeling that men have had, since civilization began, that whenever they started to think, or discourse, with themselves, they were aware of certain things they *already* knew in some strange way, which they were never easily able to express adequately in terms of language and clear concepts. So they began searching for this *a priori* knowledge, and we find Socrates, by his maieutic method, seeking for that *prior* knowledge latent in every man, which lies at the root of all that we ever come to know by conscious discourse and argument. Plato, of course, gave his answer in terms of the changeless ideas, and other similar answers have been worked out throughout our history down to the linguistic idealists of our own time. But empirical thinkers are now trying a new tack.

Perhaps this *a priori* knowledge that we are dimly aware of belongs to another order. Perhaps it comes from sense, and feeling, and the existence with which we are all directly familiar in our lived experience. Perhaps this knowledge does not have to be imagined, or deduced, or postulated, as in Kant. Perhaps it can be *found* if we pay attention to our lived existence as we live it, and then clarified by a special use of language and concepts. The empirical philosopher of our time will be especially concerned with the ultimate *a priori* structures of this prior world. But with the other human disciplines, he will also be interested in the decisive events of this *Lebenswelt,* and with speculation concerning its overall meaning.

Heidegger has accepted all of these three responsibilities. So let me conclude by a brief comment on the way in which he has brought together basic trends of the living thought of our time. One can recognize this without accepting all of his specific theories and interpretations, some of which are open to serious question. As I have indicated, I believe that the point of view of *Sein und Zeit* is overly anthropocentric, and that he sometimes confused special patterns of European culture with *a priori* human existentials. Some of his later studies of concrete phenomena are overly obscure and fanciful. His reading of the history of Western thought is, in my opinion, over-simple, and his speculations concerning the meaning of being are often not only opaque but highly anthropomorphic and dubious.

Nevertheless, in spite of these difficulties, I must recognize him as a living philosopher of the very first rank, whose life-long efforts to dig down to the ultimate roots of our Western thinking, which he finds in the pre-Socratics, have been carried through with extra-ordinary depth of insight and historical erudition. This search for the ultimate *a priori* has led him back to the world of existence which is pre-thematically known, and has enabled him to shed a much needed light on such existential structures as the oriented space of *Dasein*, death, care, and what we may call *existential time*. His later studies of such specific topics as Nietzsche's saying, "God is dead," and Van Gogh's painting of the peasant's shoes, bear with them the very breath of the concrete and, at the same time, bring out meanings in depth that have not been noted before. His specula-tions concerning being, and his associated reading of the history of Western thought, culminating in the will to power of Nietzsche, may contain dubious features. But they are supported by historical studies, like those of Plato and Nietzsche, which are always sugges-tive and provocative. They make sense in our time, and I believe that they will constitute a lasting challenge to future thought.

Thus Heidegger has faced the three main questions confronting the concrete philosophy of our time, and worked out answers of unusual depth and cogency. Whether we agree with him or not, we must recognize him as a concrete thinker *par excellence*. Whether we decide to follow him or not in his special forest paths, he has shown us the general direction in which we must proceed, if phe-nomenological thinking is not to be abandoned, but is to advance and to grow.

Note on the Contributors

Zygmunt Adamczewski is Professor of Philosophy at Brock University. He is the author of *The Tragic Protest, Kant's Existential Thought,* and of numerous philosophical papers.

Edward G. Ballard is Professor of Philosophy at Tulane University and the author of *Art and Analysis, Socratic Ignorance,* and many papers in various areas of philosophical thought.

C. D. Keyes holds the Th.D. in Theology from Trinity College (Toronto) and the Ph.D. in philosophy from Duquesne University. He is Associate Professor of Philosophy at Duquesne.

Theodore Kisiel, Associate Professor of Philosophy at Northern Illinois University, received the Ph.D. from Duquesne University. In addition to several translations, he has published a number of papers dealing with phenomenology and philosophy of science.

Thomas Langan is Professor of Philosophy at the University of Toronto and is the author of serveral books and articles on contemporary philosophy including *The Meaning of Heidegger* and *Merleau-Ponty's Critique of Reason.* He is also co-author of *Recent Philosophy* and *Modern Philosophy* (with E. Gilson).

Ralph A. Powell, O.P. has studied at Louvain, Columbia, Georgetown, and the University of Chicago. He is the author of several publications including *Truth or Absolute Nothing.*

John Sallis is Associate Professor of Philosophy at Duquesne University and is the author of several papers dealing with modern and contemporary European philosophy.

André Schuwer, a native of The Netherlands, is currently Chairman of the Department of Philosophy at Duquesne University. He has studied at Louvain, Paris, and Freiburg and is the author of several papers on the philosophy of Heidegger.

Anna-Teresa Tymieniecka has taught at The Pennsylvania State University, Bryn Mawr College, and Duquesne University. Her many publications include *Phenomenology and Science in Contemporary European Thought, Essence et Existence, Leibniz' Cosmological Synthesis, Why is There Something rather than Nothing?,* and *Eros et Logos.*

John Wild has taught at Harvard, Northwestern, and Yale and is currently Professor of Philosophy at the University of Florida. He is the author of several books including *Existence and the World of Freedom* and *The Challenge of Existentialism*.